Actes du XIVème Congrès UISPP, Université de Liège, Belgique, 2-8 septembre 2001

Acts of the XIVth UISPP Congress, University of Liège, Belgium, 2-8 September 2001

ULg
UNIVERSITÉ de Liège

SECTION 13

ÉPOQUE ROMAINE
THE ROMAN AGE

Sessions générales et posters
General Sessions and Posters

Édité par / Edited by
Le Secrétariat du Congrès

Présidents de la Section 13 :
Xavier Deru, Raymond Brulet
Président de la Section :
Marc Groenen

BAR International Series 1312
2004

Published in 2016 by
BAR Publishing, Oxford

BAR International Series 1312

Acts of the XIVth UISPP Congress, University of Liège, Belgium, 2-8 September 2001
Section 13: Époque romaine / The Roman Age

ISBN 978 1 84171 661 9

Avec la collaboration du Ministère de la Région Wallonne. Direction générale de l'Aménagement
du territoire, du Logement et du Patrimoine. Subvention n°03/15718

Mise en page / Editing : Rebecca MILLER
Typesetting and layout: Darko Jerko

Marcel OTTE, Secrétaire général du XIVème Congrès de l'U.I.S.P.P.
Université de Liège, Service de Préhistoire
7, place du XX août, bât. A1, 4000 Liège Belgique
Tél. 0032/4/366.53.41   Fax 0032/4/366.55.51
Email: prehist@ulg.ac.be   Web: http://www.ulg.ac.be/prehist

BAR Publishing is the trading name of British Archaeological Reports (Oxford) Ltd.
British Archaeological Reports was first incorporated in 1974 to publish the BAR
Series, International and British. In 1992 Hadrian Books Ltd became part of the BAR
group. This volume was originally published by Archaeopress in conjunction with
British Archaeological Reports (Oxford) Ltd / Hadrian Books Ltd, the Series principal
publisher, in 2004. This present volume is published by BAR Publishing, 2016.

Printed in England

BAR
PUBLISHING

BAR titles are available from:

          BAR Publishing
          122 Banbury Rd, Oxford, OX2 7BP, UK
EMAIL   info@barpublishing.com
PHONE   +44 (0)1865 310431
  FAX   +44 (0)1865 316916
          www.barpublishing.com

TABLE DES MATIERES / TABLE OF CONTENTS

LOYALTY AND WEALTH:
THE NATIVE ARISTOCRACY OF ROMAN PANNONIA

Zsolt MRÁV

Endre Tóth sexagenario

THE ROMANIZATION OF THE NATIVE ARISTOCRACY

Whilst South Pannonia was subordinated with a tremendous effort, the North part of later Pannonia province got under Roman subordination and than into Roman authority peacefully in the first half of the 1st century AD. After the Roman conquest the communities of native tribes were organised into administrative units, *civitates peregrinae* which were kept under military control at the beginning. They were controlled by the commander of a nearby auxiliary troop or a centurion of a legion in the province. L. Volcatius Primus, the *praefectus* of *cohors I Noricorum*, stationed in Brigetio or Arrabona, was in charge of two bordering Pannonian tribes, the *Boii* and *Azali* (CIL IX 5363 = ILS 2737). L. Antonius Naso, as the centurion of *legio XIII gemina,* stationing in Poetovio (Ptuj, Slovenia), was the prefect of *civitas Colapianorum* (CIL III 14387 = ILS 9199). At the time of the military occupation the oppidums and mountain fortifications of the natives, which were still inhabited at the time, were evacuated for reasons of security, the defence-works were destroyed, while some Roman forts and garrison troops were moved into the place of previous Celtic mountain fortresses (Esztergom/Solva, Dunaszekcső/ Lugio, Slankamen/Acumincum?). The population of the hardly controllable communities far from the military garrisons on the river Danube were settled down closer to the forts. A number of earlier Celtic settlements definitely survived the Roman period and made an untroubled progress in the heart of the province.

After the security of the province was stabilised, military rule became more and more formal, surrendering government to the earlier leading circles of the native community, mostly to those native *nobiles* who belonged to high society, owned a considerable fortune and who proved to be the most faithful and loyal to Roman matters. These chosen aristocrats setting a stimulating example to their people with their loyalty, were allowed to retain their leading positions within the community, meanwhile owing to central support and their respected offices and landed property, they were able to increase their wealth. These *principes* could even be granted Roman citizenship out of the emperor's favour, certainly after an individual and rigorous judgement. The privileged and centrally subsidised wealthy native aristocracy discovered the comfort of Roman lifestyle and it soon borrowed Roman customs, clothing and the pretensions for luxury.

The life and lifestyle of the native aristocratic families as well as their positions in society are clearly demonstrated by the inscriptions and representations on their tombstones and graves.

The tribes beyond the Eastern Alps had no interest for the Romans for long (App. Illyr. 15). Altogether only a few commercial settlements were established mainly along the Amber Road (Nauportus/Vhrinika; Ljubljana-Grad). The able-bodied youth of the South Pannonian tribes who were subjugated by Augustus were recruited into auxiliary troops and were trained in the Roman way in order that they should fight against Maroboduus's Germans. Their commanders were chosen from among the Romanized aristocracy of the tribes. It was Velleius Paterculus who in relation to the Pannonian-Dalmatian revolt, which broke out in 6 AD, mentioned that these soldiers mastered the Latin and were familiar with Roman discipline (Vell. Pat. II. 110,5). After the revolt was put down, in order to withdraw those fit for military service-groups, a considerably large auxiliary troop was called into being, which served on the whole territory of the Empire. On returning home, veterans with Roman citizenship became the chief pillars of the Roman rule and they were to form the leading strata of the concerned tribes. This is well demonstrated by the cemetery of Verdun (Slovenia), where the richest tombs from the 1st century AD – containing bronze bowls, amphorae, samian plates and thin-walled bowls - yielded several weapons such as iron helmets, shield bosses, swords and spearheads, once used by auxiliary soldiers. In grave 1, the Roman helmet was damaged and the sword (*gladius*) was bent, ritually killed after the traditional Celtic custom. The rich grave of a Tauriscan noble, dated to the first half of the 1st century AD and found in Polhov Gradec, near Emona shows that the Romanization of the leading circle of the tribes beyond Southeastern Alps was of primary importance as far as the Romans' native policy is concerned. As municipalisation of South Pannonia was on, the military supervision managed by the *civitates* was gradually terminated by the Flavian emperors, and several notabilities of the South Pannonian tribes received Roman citizenship. Five of the seven witnesses of the military diploma issued on 5th April 71 AD (RMD 205) were *principes*; two of them belonged to the leading strata of the Boii and the others to the Iasi, the Breuci and the Andizetes tribes, one to each.

As witnesses, all of them authenticated the documents with a signet-ring, as was customary in Roman circles, and one of them, namely T. Fl. Serenus *pr(inceps) Iasio(rum) (!)*

owned Roman citizenship already in 71 AD. It was a Flavian emperor again who bestowed citizenship upon T. Flavius Proculus *pr(inceps) praef(ectus) Scor(discorum)*, a notability of the Southeast Pannonian Scordisci (AE 1958, 73).

The tribal territory of the Northwestern Pannonian Boii was along the strategically and commercially important Amber Road. Due to this fact tribal structures were soon to disintegrate and the tribal aristocracy had become highly Romanized by the 1st century AD. Most of their rich burials can be dated from this period. The name of a Boian *princeps* - M. Cocceius Caupianus, the first known owner of the villa in Bruckneudorf (Burgenland, Austria) and probably one of the richest native landowners in Pannonia - can be read in the inscription of his wife's tombstone (AE 1951, 64). Like the Boian arictocracy, he adopted the Roman way of farming, he owned slaves and he enjoyed all the privileges of Roman citizenship. Again, it was probably a family of Boian origin who owned the villa in Baláca, to the north of Lake Balaton, in the 2nd century AD.

One *princeps* of the neighbouring Azali, Iucundus, the son of Talalnus, had been known solely from his daughter's tombstone (RIU 790). She was called Solva after the earlier centre of the Azali, where the family lived (Solva/ Esztergom). Not long ago the tombstone of the Azalian *princeps*, Iucundus was also found carrying Latin inscription, dating from the end of the 1st century AD (AE

1997, 1261) (Fig. 1). His wife was represented in traditional Celtic costume while Iucundus, who had a Latin name, was wearing a Roman toga and hairstyle on his stele which was erected still in his lifetime by his son. The dedication *Dis Manibus sacrum* on the stele was not only a quite new Roman trend of the time but it also means that the images of the Other World connected to them were borrowed as well. In spite of all this, Iucundus was not a Roman citizen and also his son Asper was a simple cavalryman (*eques*) in an auxiliary troop. His *princeps* title was later erased from the inscription for an unknown reason. Perhaps he was dismissed from favour by emperor Domitian who was staying in Pannonia during his German wars?

Among the Celtic tribes living on Hungarian territory in the Roman period the *Eravisci* was the most important one. Their tribal territory was situated in Northeastern Pannonia. Compositional naming, characteristic of the Eravisci, shows the former clan organisation of the tribe which was less developed. The Celtic tribes of North Pannonia who surrendered peacefully were probably allied with the Roman Empire during the course of the Roman expansion. Eraviscan coinage, which was launched in the period of the Roman conquest and was performed according to the Roman money rates, the quite large number of Augustus coins found on the tribal territory of the Eravisci as well as the granting of Roman citizenship to some indigenous notabilities, like C. Iulius Magimarus (CIL III 3377) for instance, all stand as testimony to this relationship. Already during the reign of Claudius, Eravisci

Figure 1. The tombstone of Iucundus, the princeps of Azali from Solva/Esztergom.
Figure 2. Painted reconstruction of a native aristocratic couple from the 2nd century AD. (Painted by Zs. Mráv)

were recruited into the Roman army and mainly navy. Before the Danubian wars of Domitian the Eravisci were not a particularly privileged community, at first there were one, then two auxiliary cavalry troops stationed near their centre of *civitas* in Aquincum. At that time there were no rich burials connected to the leading strata of the tribe and all the few Eraviscan notabilities we know about were *peregrini* (RIU 1345, 1347). Living conditions changed radically at the end of the first century when the permanent legionary fortress was built in Aquincum (89 AD) and when the settlement became the governors' centre of the province Pannonia inferior (103-106 AD). From that time on the tribe and its aristocracy became more and more important and were getting more central support. Some of their noblemen like M. Cocceius Florus, the son of Matumarus were granted Roman citizenship (CIL III 3546) and Roman names and they became so rich that their lifestyles and burial rites could be described as lavishly luxurious in the 2nd century AD. As an evidence of their Romanization their tombs were made of stone and decorated in the Roman style; their inscriptions prove that they used Latin language in everyday life. At first the municipal élite of the *municipium Aelium Aquincensium* (Budapest-Óbuda) founded by Hadrian were mainly of Eraviscan origin. On the territory of a former Eraviscan oppidum, on Budapest-Gellért Hill (*mons Teutanus*), which was abandoned prior to the Roman conquest, - similarly to the Pfaffenberg near Carnuntum - a Roman place of worship dedicated to Iuppiter was founded as early as the 2nd century AD. The personality of the supreme deity of the Eravisci and the related ideas – owing to the slow but at the same time deep Romanization - has merged into the figure of the Roman Iuppiter almost completely and unrecognisably. This process is properly documented by the large number of altars which were dedicated to *I. O. M.* and which were erected in the first half of the 2nd century AD by the members of the tribal aristocracy of the Eravisci. This worship of the deity named on the altars was interspersed with local, indigenous traditions, or to be more precise, *I. O. M.* was like the own supreme deity of Eravisci in the eyes of the local *nobiles*. Behind the altars of the native aristocracy, however, we should rather regard the respect for the Roman supreme deity as the primary motive. The rich tribal aristocracy, who were granted Roman citizenship by Nerva, Trajan and Hadrian, by their inscriptions dedicated to *I. O. M.*, expressed their loyalty to the Roman state. The official nature of their cult, which is based on the worship of *I. O. M.*, is demonstrated by the close intertwining of the cult of the deity and that of the emperor. Their tribal identity remained quite strong for a long period due to their privileged role. The community of Eraviscan citizens (*cives Eravisci*), proud of their origins was held together by the official cult of the god Iuppiter – with a by-name after its cultic place (*mons Teutanus*) later Teutanus attached - until the end of the 3rd century AD.

THE BURIAL CUSTOMS OF THE ROMANIZED TRIBAL ARISTOCRACY

Traditions and wealth – these two words describe perfectly the burial rites of the native aristocracy in Pannonia.

The earliest known aristocratic burial place revealed is that on the territory of Polhov Gradec near Emona, on the Tauriscan land. Formerly thought to be a rich Italicus grave, the tomb with its extremely rich finds (samian cups, bronze and terracotta lamp, a range of bronze vessels, shallow and laced mosaic bowls) and with the weapons placed in the grave (shield boss, spearheads) is in all probability the burial place of a notability of Tauriscan origin from the 3rd-4th decades of the 1st century AD.

There were several expensive bronze vessels from Italy and Gaul found in the graves of the noblemen from the tribe of Boii who were buried after a cremation ceremony. These vessels however were always found in fragments or out of shape, because they were either put on the pyre or they were deliberately broken. This habit of destroying grave goods reflects the intentions to offer them for the infernal gods.

The richest burial sites are those of the leaders of autochtonous tribes as far as the grave goods of the quite usual Pannonian *tumuli* are concerned. These *tumuli* raised to the memory of noble families are usually built alone or in small groups and they are the largest of all. Probably the villa where the family lived stood nearby. The remains of a noble young man were buried in barrow 1. in Inota surrounded by a wall, with the inhumated saddle-horse and its silver threaded harnesses put into a separate pit. Next to the burial case and the glass urn in which the ashes were put there were bowls of samian ware, ceramic and glass vessels and weapons unearthed in the grave, which was covered with a shield. The planished funeral pyre and the remains of the objects placed over it turned up from the grave filling and its surroundings. There were probably wealthy native families (from the tribe of Boii) buried under the two groups of *tumuli* at Kemenesszentpéter along the Savaria-Arrabona road. One of them (Kemenesszentpéter-Dombi dűlő, barrow 1) was surrounded by a wall and it contained a dromos and a vaulted crypt decorated with floral painting, in which originally there was a wooden backed chair (*cathedra*) as well. In a nearby grave under a *tumulus* in Kemenesszent-péter-Pagony not only the cinerary urn but also weapons and bronze vessels burned at the funeral pyre were discovered. Supposedly the rich Romanized family who had the biggest known tumulus in Pannonia built, near the centre of their great estate at Baláca, was also of Boian origin. Beneath the tumulus, the graves of a dog and a saddle-horse cremated on pyre were excavated. The inscriptions of the tomb altars on pedestals along the sides of the tumulus – which have been reconstructed recently by Géza Alföldy - refer to a family that was granted citizenship by Claudius and held municipal offices in the towns of Savaria and Carnuntum. The tumulus built in the first half of the 2nd century AD was 10-11 m high, surrounded by a 3-m high wall and sepulchral altars, it included a dromos and a crypt. In this case the tumulus definitely reflects Italian prototype.

The skeleton of a man about 50-60 years old, suffering from spinal complaints was found in a grave at Szölösgyörök. The buried nobleman comes from the *Hercuniates* tribe living to the south of Lake Balaton (*lacus Pelso*). Thus, some aristocratic families cremated, but some of them inhumated like in Szölösgyörök or Káloz. In the grave from Szölösgyörök there were a glass vessel, a pair of bronze scissors, 10 pieces of bronze vessels (bowls, pails, straining and dipping sets, casseroles of different size, a hand-washing set with a towel) buried together with the dead body (Fig. 3). Noble Eraviscan families placed the everyday objects intact into the grave during the burial ceremonies. The complete and intact grave goods buried with the dead indicate a different tradition and different images of post-existence from those of the Boii. According to their belief the deceased continued their lives in their own bodies after death, so they needed their everyday objects not only in this world but also in the other one. This was the way the aristocrats of Eastern Pannonian tribes preserved their accustomed Roman lifestyles and luxury for eternity.

A pair of silver winged fibulas, which was worn by a native lady, and which is the most exquisite of those known, came up from an Eraviscan *tumulus* grave in Pátka (Fig. 4.). The pin-case of the fibula is decorated with open-work geometrical patterns and filigree golden sheets, with a carnelian pearl set in a square golden sheet in the middle. The social position and wealth of the noble families were expressed in their clothing as well. Men were depicted on the richest tombstones wearing togas following current Roman trends of hairstyle and costumes to irradiate dignity, while the women of the family appeared in their traditional Celtic dresses (Fig. 1-2.). On the evidences of the graves (Pátka) and hoards (Ászár, Tata, Nagyberki-Szalacskapuszta) aristocratic women's jewellery (pierced fibulas with filigree-work, neck-laces, torques, bracelets, belt studs) of local fashion were made of precious metals, mostly silver.

However it is not typical of all the Pannonian tribes to put expensive bronze vessels into the grave of an aristocrat. The leaders of the tribes which lived farther from the provincial centres and principal roads and played less important roles, were Romanized later and probably even then only on the surface. The financial position of their leaders was inferior to that of the Boii or Eravisci, which were centrally subsidised and were in the commercial circulation.

WITH CHARIOT TO THE OTHER WORLD

In spite of the fact that native aristocrats became Romanized in their appearances and lifestyles quickly, they strictly preserved their traditions and they stuck to their ancient ideas about the Other World. The Celts believed that it is somewhere in a remote corner of the earth (in the case of the Irish, for instance, on a remote island) which can be reached after a very long journey and from where there is no return. Thus according to their beliefs the deceased are not really dead but they set out on a long journey at the end of which they were welcome with all the eternal happiness of post-existence.

Reliefs which referred to the journey to the Other World has been found on several native tombstones dating from the end of the 1st century AD on the territory of the Boii on the river Leitha and the Eravisci in Northeastern Pannonia. Most of these were discovered on steles but some of them

3

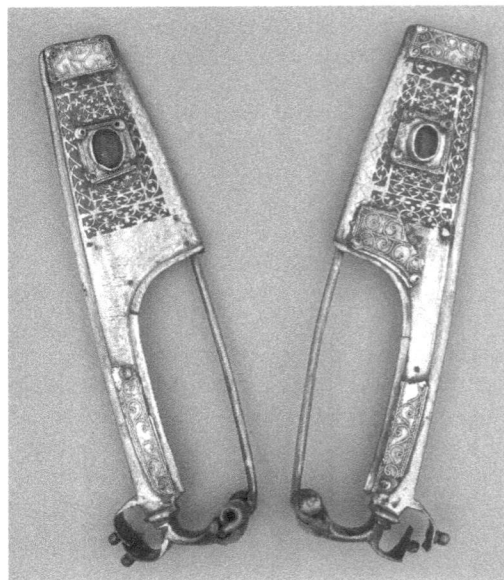

4

Figure 3. Bronze vessels from the Szölösgyörök grave.
Figure 4. Silver fibulas from Pátka.

turned up on large stone slabs belonging to funerary *aediculae*. On those reliefs numbering more than 70 that have been found so far where the deceased were represented as travellers sitting on 2-wheeled, or more often on 4-wheeled wagons, in many cases together with their servants, relatives and saddle-horses led in front of the carriage, and their favourite hunting-dogs. These reliefs, however, do not expressly depict the journey to the Other World, but an every-day journey of the deceased and his/her family. This scene taken from everyday life referred to the journey of the deceased to the Other World in a figurative sense. The mentioned reliefs showed the social position of the family as well since the type and decoration of the chariot, the number of servants and attendants on a journey was of representative importance in the imperial period. Another group of reliefs depicts chariots without passengers, only showing the necessary vehicles of the journey to the Other World. These representations could substitute for the carriage in the grave. Chest-like objects can be seen in the chariots in some reliefs, which as opposed to the former suggestions cannot be identified with an ossuarium but with the seat of the chariot without arm- and back rest.

The richest families however were not content with the simple representation of everyday journey or a carriage, which referred to the Other World, but from the beginning of the 2nd century AD they placed a real 2- or 4-wheeled carriage into the grave for the Next World journey together with harnessed horses to pull it. The graves give evidence of great luxury. The Roman chariots were decorated with bronze statuettes and fittings; expensive objects imported from Italy, the western provinces and the Orient were found among the grave goods, which were considered luxurious at that time. There are nearly thirty sites (27) in Pannonia where Roman chariot graves have been found. Most of them were discovered on the territory of the Eravisci and their neighbourhood in Northeastern Pannonia where native tombstones with the representations of the travelling on chariot were also widespread. The 4 exceptions from Southern Pannonia are from Kozármisleny, Petrovina, Poljanec and an unknown provenance. That is, burials involving a chariot were popular in Southeastern Pannonia. The remarkably rich chariot graves were probably marked with Latin tomb inscriptions – like the Romans did – as even the less wealthy, but still well-off native families considered it important to commemorate the dead in an epitaph (*titulus memoriae*). Most of the grave goods from chariot graves from Hungarian territories came up during earthworks at the end of the 19th century or at the beginning of the 20th century and then they were given or sold, sometimes incompletely, to different collections. Usually no archaeological studies or verifying excavations were carried out, so for a long period there was very little known about burial rites and the connections among the finds. Only in the past few decades presented the opportunity itself to unearth eight native graves from the Roman period with chariot using archaeological methods (Kozármisleny: 1969; Inota tumulus 2: 1973-75; Budakeszi: 1999; Budaörs grave 124, 125, 126 and 162: 2002; Budapest, Bécsi út 96/b grave 162: 2003). These burial traditions so typical of the Eraviscan native aristocracy in Pannonia can be

discovered more accurately on the evidences of the graves which were examined archaeologically.

Dating from the first decades of the 2nd century AD, the earliest known chariot graves turn up in Pannonia without any direct antecedents. The majority of the chariot graves are dated to the middle and second half of the 2nd century; we only know about a few such graves from the period of the Severan dynasty. Local notabilities – we can conclude - put an end to the fashion of this most extravagant burial custom in the first half of the 3rd century AD. This is definitely not explicable with the economic situation and with the impoverishment of noble families since the rite had already gone out of fashion before the economic crisis of the 3rd century. The disappearance of the chariot graves, however, coincides with the general abandonment of local traditions, the motives of which are in all likelihood the provincial elite's total adaptation to Roman externals.

The earliest known grave has been unearthed in Inota under *tumulus* 2 surrounded by wall. The peculiarity of the tumulus holding the remains of a cremated middle aged man is that – unlike in the case of chariot graves from later periods – the grave goods, and a 4-wheeled wagon are placed on the cremation pyre. The burned, out-of-shape iron pieces of the chariot were collected and forced into a separate grave pit. After the excavations of the Inota barrow it became evident that there were chariots buried under the *tumuli*, so there must be a relationship between the two types of burial. There must have been *tumuli* over the graves in Vajta, Nagylók, possibly in Érd, Káloz, Kozármisleny, and on the evidence of the filling of the grave pit which was transported from somewhere else, the Budakeszi grave. Like in Inota, the dead body, the horses and the chariot were put into separate pits under the *tumulus*. In the case of the Káloz grave, dated to the first half of the 2nd century, which turned up in several fragments in the first half of the 20th century the two dead men with weapons and the horse were probably put into separate gravepits as well as the grave goods with traces of burning and the wagon with two horses under a tumulus. In Kozármisleny and Budakeszi the Roman chariot which was found and the dead body, which has not been discovered yet, were put into separate pits. Both chariot graves were covered. The grave in Kozármisleny collapsed when the wooden pieces of the carriage putrefied completely and the irons fell onto each other, while when the Budakeszi grave collapsed, the irons were still held together by the wooden elements. The two known pits of the grave in Érd were found lying a few metres away from each other. One of the pits contained the saddle-horse and one part of the grave-goods, whilst the other the 2-wheeled chariot, the two harnessed horses and the rest of the grave-goods. The remains of the deceased were again not revealed.

The pits found in the cemetery of the *vicus Teuto* at Budaörs, and containing four carriages offers another explanation for interpreting the phenomena of chariot-graves without dead bodies. In the neighbourhood of the three pits, which constitute a group, and which contained the chariots, and horse grave number 117 only a single inhumed dead body was found accompanied with ceramic goods. Meanwhile, the pit of grave 162 containing the chariot was dug separately from the others despite the fact that they are dating nearly from the same period. Today, with our present knowledge we cannot be certain whether the grave of the deceased was destroyed and there no traces remained or – like the Thracian tumuli - they were buried far away from the grave containing the body. We cannot leave some further ideas unconsidered, according to which no dead body belonged to the chariots concerned. Should the idea be confirmed, we will have to interpret these pits dug out in cemeteries as chtonic sacrifices, just like the two pits from Gaul dating from the imperial period, which contained chariots and other grave-goods but no dead body (Saintes, La Bussiére-Etable).

The carriages were placed in the graves in a variety of ways. The size of the dug-out pits not rarely determined the way of burying the carriages. In Inota, for instance, the components deformed on the pyre were forced into the small-size pit. In the case of the pits from Káloz and Budaörs, both dated to the first half of the 2nd century AD, first the horses, numbering two or three, which drew the carriage, were placed and the dismantled carriage – sometimes upside down - was placed above (Fig. 5-6.). The carriages in Budaörs had been disassembled to the very base and in most of the cases placed incompletely in the pits. Wheels were often taken off the axle. The carriage in the cemetery of the *canabae* in Aquincum was literally taken to pieces, was sawn up and a part of these pieces was poured into the pit without any order. One reason offered for this phenomenon is that because of the small parcel and the rocky subsoil they could not dig a pit of adequate size and depth, therefore, they were compelled to dismantle the carriage. The pit in Budakeszi, however, with its parallelogram shape and 2,4 x 3,8 m size, was big enough to place a two-wheeler diagonally together with the draught-pole and the fixed-up wheels.

The short, harnessed horses (only 130-140cm high at the withers) which pulled the chariot were stabbed to death during the burial rite. In some cases the bronze studs of the yoke and the iron head of lances which were used to kill the horses were also found. The richly harnessed saddle-horses and hunting dogs of the dead were thrown into the grave as well (tumulus 1. in Inota: saddle-horse, Érd: saddle-horse, Káloz: saddle-horse and dog, Vajta: saddle-

horse and dog, and Zsámbék, where also the bronze fittings of the dog-collar were found). In the case of the Budakeszi chariot grave the harnessed horses which were killed during the burial ceremony were laid down around the chariot. The bones of two horses came to light but there are three reins which belong to the find. Two curb-bits were made with bronze rings and the one which was found in the mouth of an old stallion was made with iron rings. Presumably it means that the 2-wheeled Budakeszi chariot was a three-in-hand vehicle (with tandem hitch), like the chariots from Zsámbék and Budaörs grave 126. An iron spear with which the horses must have been killed was discovered at the feet of one of the horses.

The grave goods excel with their luxury, the everyday objects which turned up, all satisfied Roman tastes and they were indispensable requisites for Roman lifestyles. (The grave goods are made up of the same objects as those found in Thracian tumuli and chariot graves.) The grave goods were usually put into the pit of the chariot (except for Káloz and Inota), in Budakeszi evidently on the seat of the chariot. There were no grave goods except wagons found in Budaörs, in graves 124, 125 and 162, and in the case of all the graves in south Pannonia (Kozármisleny, Petrovina, Poljanec).

The most typical and most frequent grave goods are bronze vessels and different everyday bronze objects which were discovered in large numbers in good condition unlike the melted bronze vessels burned at the burial pyre in Inota. The set of a bronze ewer (*urceus*) and a handled dish (*trulleum*) was found in most chariot graves. They were used for ritual hand-washing before offering a sacrifice. In Érd two sets were uncovered in two adjacent pits belonging to the same grave in such a way that the pieces of the sets were confounded. The hand-washing set from the Szomor-Somodorpuszta find was made of bronze sheets by local craftsmen of the Danube region. The so-called Canterbury type set from the Budakeszi chariot grave was made in Italia in the 2nd century AD. On the handle of the ewer we can see Pegasus and probably Bellerophon depicted. There is a Hellenistic palmette running around the neck of the ewer, arranged in two lines and highlighted with silver marquetry. Although the set played an important role while offering the burial sacrifice, on the evidences of the sacrifice scenes so often seen on

Figures 5 and 6. Components of the 4-wheeled carriage and skeletons of horses under it in the pit 162 in Budaörs.

tombstones in Pannonia, the reasons why it was buried in the grave are rather profane. The dead needed the hand- and leg-washing set for maintaining personal hygiene in the everyday life of the Other World.

The other usual accessory of the Pannonian chariot graves, used for the same purposes was the *instrumenta balnei* consisting of vessels of different size to store oil in them (*aryballos*) and *strigiles*. There are more or less complete sets known from the graves in Nagylók, Érd, Zsámbék, Káloz, Inota, Vajta and Budakeszi. The simple strigilis and the large aryballos hanging on three lines of chains from Budakeszi do not belong to the same service. The globular aryballos with a separately turned lip which can be covered was made in the 1st-2nd centuries in West. The grave in Vajta yielded an iron aryballos and strigilis with Greek inscription on it. Among the profanely used buried objects we can find some iron folding chairs decorated with bronze or iron knobs (Nagylók, Érd [two pieces], Káloz, Zsámbék, Környe 1-2; 3) which were also found often in native Thracian graves. Earlier these chairs were thought to represent the high position of the dead, but in my opinion they are connected rather to baths and were used during the toilette, similarly to the other previously mentioned grave goods. Several mosaics are known from baths on which some figures appear wrapped in bath towels sitting on folding-chairs, or servants were carrying folding-chairs on their shoulders. The fact that in each case in the graves there were balsamaria and palestra sets, used in baths found with the iron chairs, reinforces this hypothesis.

The lampstands and oil lamps from the graves reflect the influence of Roman images of post-existence. There were an iron candelabrum, a large bronze lamp and a lamp- holder with a panther's head unearthed in Káloz, a bronze candelabrum and a bronze lamp in the shape of a man's foot in thin-thonged sandals from Budakeszi. There is another foot-shaped lamp from the same workshop held in the Dutoit collection in Paris but the shape of its handle is different and the foot is shaped without a *solea*. However there are three lamps found in Brač (Dalmatia), Tchirpan (Thracia) and in Solva/Esztergom which are identical in every detail to the one from Budakeszi. The latter one probably came with the same transport. The bronze lamp from Budakeszi made in an Italian workshop in the 1st-2nd century AD. Usually there were no lamps found in native graves, but all the more often did they turn up in Roman burial sites. The Romans believed that light protected and guarded the dead against any trouble on their long journey to the realm of post-existence. Lamps are indispensable in a dead man's house where besides food and drink they needed light as well. Ethereal existence is permeated by light, too. Possibly the fragments of a bronze *lanterna* from the grave in Káloz was devoted to the source of *lux perpetua* as well. R. Nenova-Merdjanova came up with another plausible possibility, too according to which "the lamps, lampstands, and laternae in the graves also belonged to objects used while the toilette was being made. This took place in the dark, very early in the morning or just before going to bed." Supposedly, both ideas can be accepted since the light given by the lamps was the safeguard of the deceased when making their way to the

Other World, whilst after the journey it served as an important object in the afterlife.

In two graves – one is from the Szomor-Somodorpuszta chariot grave, the other is from Környe - there were bronze folding-tables (*tripus*) decorated with the busts of Apollo and Mercurius. Several graves yielded chest mounts which were identified as furniture. On the basis of the carriage graves in Budaörs we might suppose that a few of these were travelling chests *(capsus)* attached to the carriage. The finds include bronze straining and dipping vessels (Káloz, Budakeszi), in the case of the former, supposedly as part of a wine-set. But the strainer and dipper which comes from the grave in Budakeszi, and dates from a later period should be seen as bronze kitchenware. The idea is supported by the later shape of the set and the eggshell found in the strainer. Rarely do the graves yield jugs hammered of thin bronze sheets (Érd, Káloz, Környe, Vajta), bronze kitchen utensils (Vajta, Környe) and also glass vessels, potteries and urns (Inota, Káloz, Budapest, Bécsi út 96/b).

Quite similarly to other tumulus graves there were weapons (sword, shield buckel, lance, hatchet) found in several chariot graves. One part of the weapons which came to light from aristocratic graves served the killing of the horses and dogs (lanceheads), whilst the other part – mainly those found in graves which date from the 1st century AD - belonged to the military equipment of the deceased who once served as auxiliary soldier. The majority, however, served the purpose of representing the high position of the owner and as hunting gear equipment. This is aptly verified by not only the will of a notability of Lingo origin (CIL XIII 5708) and the hunting dogs buried, but also by a bronze shield boss which was found in Budaörs and which represent Diana. The favourite pastime of local aristocracy must have been hunting as deceased noblemen were quite often depicted on their tombstones hunting, chasing hares, boars or deer galloping at full speed on their saddle-horses accompanied by their hunting- dogs in a Pannonian forest full of game. On a stone slab there is a noble hunter with his horse at a jump, grabbing his spear ready to stab while the two dogs are trying to bring down a boar. These hunting scenes bear a sepulchral meaning as well. The passion for hunting explains why some hunting weapons, spears, shields, daggers and swords were found in the graves of native aristocracy among the dead's personal objects, indispensable in the Other World. The dead's richly harnessed saddle-horse and the hunting-dog with a decorated collar, who were killed during the burial ceremony, were quite often laid into the grave together with weapons. An expensive saddle-horse and a well-trained hunting-dog were as valuable and representative for their owner as weapons.

The defects and the missing or used up parts of the grave goods from the chariot graves indicate that the objects had been in use for a long period. In the case of the Budakeszi grave for instance the lid of the oil-filling hole of the lamp in the shape of a man's foot is lost, just like the chains on which it was hung, the top of the bronze candelabrum and like the second *trulleum* from Érd, the handle of the bowl from the hand-washing set.

TRAVELLING CHARIOTS IN GRAVES

The most important finds from the graves are the Roman carriages themselves, richly decorated with bronze statuettes and fittings. From the first half of the 2nd century AD 2- and 4-wheeled wagons, which were used only for carrying people, were placed into the graves. The box of the wagons in the earlier period was fixed but later suspended by metal suspension strap or cord support and the chariots were decorated with bronze statuettes and/or bronze sheets and studs (two-wheelers from Nagylók, Érd, Környe, Zsámbék, Budakeszi, Petrovina; four-wheelers from Szomor-Somodorpuszta, Sárszentmiklós, Káloz 3., Poljanec, Inota, Kozármisleny).

The accurate reconstructions of the carriages became possible mainly on the evidences of those graves which were excavated with archaeological methods.

1. To the construction of 2-wheeled chariots: Due to the fact that the components remained in their original positions or were handed over to the museum, the chariot excavated from Budakeszi grave in 1999 can be reconstructed with a great certainty, although half of it was damaged and destroyed while a drain tank was dug out at the site. The chariot was a light 2-wheeled *essedum* with a suspended box to absorb bumping (Fig. 8). The same type is depicted in every detail on a funerary *aedicula* element from Csákvár and Tök (Fig. 7). During the excavations the positions and functions of several such pieces were defined of which there had been hardly any information before. In the present paper, for the sake of giving examples, I will only introduce a few component parts and structural accomplishments.

The comfortable seat of the carriage consisted of a lower wooden frame, in the corners of which wooden supporting elements arching upwards were mortised. Their ends – on either side of the seat - were joined with drop-off arm-rest irons which adjusted to the shape of the forearm. The fore ends ended in a ring, whilst the rear downward ends were pointed. The ring was pulled over the end of the fore arched wooden support and the vertical pointed end was driven into a looped bolt with staple ends which was reeved through the rear, taller curved wooden support. The top of all the three rear, arching back-rest supports were strut and connected with a long iron band, with the help of a ring at each junction point of the iron band and the curved supports of wood. The frame of the side and back of the seat consisted of the curved wooden supports and the connecting iron bands. This frame served to hold the leather sheets which were fastened to and stretched out on it, in this way giving shape to the sides and back of the seat. The 2-wheeled chariot which comes from grave 126 from Budaörs well illustrates this structure, since remains of leather were found above the frame of the seat. The iron bands which constituted the arm-rest and the back was covered with leather, and in order to achieve a more comfortable rest, they could make it softer by filling the place in between the iron and the leather with wool or something like that. The same kind of seat can be reconstructed in the case of the 2-wheeled chariots which were found in Érd and Zsámbék, and even the three 4-wheelers from the Budaörs cemetery which were made in the same workshop show similar structure. A bronze mount with a small-size hook was nailed to the end of the curved wooden supports of the seat, above the end of the armrest with rings, which beyond doubt served to hold the rein. The box of the 2-wheeled *essedum* from Budakeszi was suspended at the back with a metal suspension support which ended in a griffin's and swan's head; and at a third point the forefront of the chariot-platform was fastened and/or nailed to the draught-pole. In this way the box was not fixed in position, but was relatively free to move.

Figure 7. Representation of a 2-wheeled chariot on a funerary monument from Tök.
Figure 8. Reconstruction of the chariot from the grave unearthed in Budakeszi.

9   10

Figure 9. Representation of a 4-wheeled carriage on a funerary aedicula from Intercisa/Dunaújváros.
Figure 10. Reconstruction of the 4-wheeled carriage from the pit Budaörs 162.

2. To the construction of 4-wheeled wagons: The Inota chariot and the chariot-depictions on gravestones are usually identified with more simple wagons, which were used in agriculture. In generalising terms, this is definitely a false typological classification since – on the basis of the arm-rest and the back, just like in the case of the Inota chariot - seats are suitable for passenger transport. Founding our supposition on the graves in Budaörs, chariots with boxes fixed in position were decorated with bronze mounts, whilst the sidings of the boxes were covered with leather. Ornamentation rendered them unsuitable for agricultural use, although removable seats did not prevent them from being used as transport-wagons. The carriage box in the earlier period was usually fixed (Inota, Káloz, Budaörs grave 124, 125, 162) but later suspended by metal suspension strap or cord support and the chariots were decorated with bronze statuettes and/or bronze sheets and studs. A. Kiss reconstructed a 4-wheeler of a transitional type from his excavations in Kozármisleny. The back part of the wagon box above the axle of the chariot was suspended while the front rested on the pivoting front axle. The carriage from Szomor-Somodorpuszta is of a similar type. On the basis of the graves at Budaörs, the entire structural built-up of the front axle of travelling carriages can be reconstructed (Fig. 10): the severed draught-pole of Roman travelling carriages was connected to the front axle with the so-called "Zugarm" construction which came down to the Romans from the Iron Age. It primarily consisted of a draught-pole with severed end, which with the help of a large, massive spike run horizontally trough pulling arms, could move up and down like pole axles do.

On the basis of the survived representations, travelling carriages were divided into two different types, namely those with open and those with closed boxes. This classification, however, is misleading since depending on the weather light leather covers on wooden framework – which were easy to put on and take off - were used, instead

of heavy permanent wooden construction (see the reconstruction of the carriage from Wardartal by Ch. W. Röring, for instance). An open carriage, we can conclude, was converted into one with "closed box" if weather turned bad, but naturally without altering the type of the carriage. The bronze rings which were sewn on the siding of the carriage found in pit 162, Budaörs, served to fasten and bind the leather cover if needed.

3. The chariot bronzes. The exact position of the decorative bronzes on the carriage box was defined only in the case of the chariots from Budakeszi and Budaörs due to the damages done to the one from Kozármisleny by its finders. In the case of the chariot from Budakeszi, there was a metal-inlaid iron sheet running along under the back-rest of the seat decorated with the alternation of brass inlaid floral and geometrical patterns and the bronze busts on discs fastened on them, representing the company of Bacchus, two Silenos and a Maenad in the middle. Three discs next to each other placed on the wagon-box backing (Nagylók, Budakeszi, Budaörs grave nr. 162, and recently Mikri Doxipara) as well as the six cast discs – with or without busts - fitted onto the back surface of the rear bolster (Budaörs grave nr. 162; seven discs in the case of Kozármisleny) were often to appear as patterns on Roman carriages. At each end of the inlaid iron sheet of the Budakeszi chariot there are cases (in Germ.: Bronzen mit viereckiger Tülle) with animal figures resembling a panther leaning aside, fastened to the tips of the poles with nails at the socle. The species of the animal is quite difficult to define since her whiskers are of a tiger, her flagged tail is of a lion and her spots are of a leopard. The sculptor wanted to emphasise the fearfulness and exotic beauty of the animal instead of a realistic representation. On his triumphant march the chariot of Bacchus was pulled by wild beasts tamed by himself; that may be the reason why they are so often found on decorations. The panther-like figure hangs its paws over the bust of Pan. The case shaped bronze ornament rested on the back ends of the

wagon platform, which bent backwards. Besides its decorative role, originally it might have served as a buffer, which seems to be confirmed by a few mounts made in the shape of a rostrum.

Although differing from previous results, the arched sheets decorated with a panther figure or other statuettes were at the back of the chariot; they were arched from inwards and they covered the ends of the two arms of reach bracings which were bent backwards (in Germ.: Scherarm). Arched sheets appear on two-wheelers as well (Budakeszi, Nagylók), nevertheless, due to these 2-wheeled chariots' shorter structure, they were not decorated with statuettes, only with ornamental nails, which fastened the sheet cover.

The decorations of Roman chariots found in graves excel with their luxury as well, especially in the case of the ones found in Szomor-Somodorpuszta, Kozármisleny and Budakeszi. The back part of the carriages was lavishly decorated with bronze statuettes and studs, all with themes from the mythological cycle of Bacchus. The back part of the four-wheelers from Szomor-Somodorpuszta and Kozármisleny are decorated with a group of statuettes under a palmetto, with the figures of Bacchus and Pan with Satyros in his company. The bronze busts fastened on discs, depicting Silenoses who raised the young Bacchus, Satyros and Maenads, were found in the chariot's decorations. At the protruding ends of the reach bracings (in Germ.: Scherarm) there are statuettes of a female panther-like figure.

The buried Roman chariots had probably been used according to their functions for a long time. The bronze heads of the iron suspension cord support, which sustained the weight of the box were remarkably worn. The fact that some ornamental pieces were lost in the Roman period indicates that the carriages had been used intensively. One of the wheels of the Budakeszi chariot must have been repaired or replaced, in other words, the chariots were not made especially for the burial; they were put into the grave after they were used up. The grave goods from the chariot graves truly reflect the financial situation of noble families as they not only owned the previously enlisted objects but they could also do very well without them after the burial. Probably they used a lot of similar objects of the same quality in their households. There are hardly any chariot graves found among the richest burials within the Roman Empire. There was only *pars pro toto* finds in graves from Gallia Belgica (Long-Pont); complete chariots have been discovered only on Pannonian and Thracian territories.

Based on the finds of chariot graves, we might reconstruct the Eraviscan aristocrats' beliefs concerning afterlife in the imperial period as follows: We can take it for granted that Eraviscan aristocrats believed in life after death, according to which the deceased in his bodily reality lives further in the Other World. Therefore, he/she needs to have some objects there too, which are placed intact into the grave. In the Other World, not only the deceased, but the horses and dogs which were slaughtered during the funeral ceremony also come to life. The dismantled carriages and those lacking some parts will be ready for use again. Putting the carriages into the grave

refers to the fact that the belief in afterlife journey among the indigenous population survived in the Roman period as well. As long as we accept the suggested role of carriages in the afterlife journey (the deceased set off from the grave), than the scene of afterlife was probably not thought to be in the grave but, in accordance with Celtic beliefs, somewhere far away, but still on the earth. This provides an explanation for the fact why objects in connection with eating and drinking were only occasionally put into the chariot graves (except for the grave in Inota), which items are in close relation with the belief in the survival of a "living body" in the grave. Goods which bear relation with other earthly pleasures of everyday life, however, predominated in the grave, which reflect a definitely positive view of the Other World. The *balnearia* and the utensils of everyday washing are the prerequisites of bathing whilst the hunting weapons are those of hunting, both of which were thought to engage the deceased in the Other World. What was delineated above recalls one scene from the Celtic beliefs concerning afterlife, which scene depicts the country of the death as the Elysian Fields where all men and women live in unceasing happiness. According to Lucanus, this picture of the Other World is just the opposite of the classical Next World (Luc. Phars. I, 455-456). This is the point where one of the Celts' image of the Other World met with the Next World of the Bacchic mysteries which offered eternal happiness recalling the *aurea aetas*. This recognition by the indigenous population might explain why the Bacchic redemption-doctrines were so quickly and deeply absorbed by the local, native notability. It is undeniable that in Pannonia, already in the first half of the 2nd century AD carriages decorated intentionally with figures from the Bacchic cycle were placed into graves. This means that the deceased owned carriages with Bacchic decorations still in their lives, with which they wished to travel all way to the Other World after their death. And then, still with the same carriage they were to join the mythic thiasos of Bacchus, who ruled over all the fearful and mystic powers – like death – in this world and the other one.

The members of the native Pannonian aristocracy used the same objects for the conscious representation of their high status within society as the elite of other historic periods. They owned expensive horses and hunting-dogs with which they could pursue their favourite pastime, hunting. Men owned exquisite weapons, women wore ornate costumes, jewellery made of precious metals. When they left their residences equipped with all the commodities of Roman lifestyle, they used only 2- or 4 wheeled carriages which were decorated all over with bronze statuettes. Even their death and burial ceremonies were ostentatiously magnificent so that they would not be in need of their wealth to which they were used to in their lives.

Author's address

Zsolt MRÁV
Hungarian National Museum
Department of Archaeology
Múzeum krt. 14-16
1088 Budapest HUNGARY

Bibliography

ALFÖLDI A., 1939. Chars funéraires bacchiques. *Ant. Class.* 8, p. 347-359.

ALFÖLDY G., 1959-1960. Bronze Vessels in the Burial Rites of the native Population in North Pannonia. *Archeologia* (Warszawa) 11, p. 1-11.

ALFÖLDY G., 1994. La Pannonia e l'Impero romano. In.: *L. Pannonia e l'Impero Romano. Atti del convegno internazionale "La Pannonia e l'Impero romano".* (a cura di G. Hajnóczi) Roma, p.25-40.

ALFÖLDY G., 2004. Die Inschriften des Hügelgrabes von Baláca. *Balácai közlemények* 8, p. 23-122.

KISS A., 1989. Das römerzeitliche Wagengrab von Kozármisleny. *RégFüz* II, 25. Budapest.

MÁRTON A., 2002. Roman Burial with Weapon from the Bécsi Road Cemetery (Aquincum-Budapest). Communicationes Archaeologicae Hungaricae, p. 117-152.

MRÁV Zs., 2001. Kaiserzeitliche Wagenbestattungen in Pannonien. In: Sein & Sinn, *Burg & Mensch.* (Hg. F. Daim, Th. Kühtreiber) Wien, p. 122-129.

MRÁV Zs., 2001. L'aristocratie indigène à travers les rites funéraires. In.: *Romains de Hongrie.* Lyon, p. 30-41.

MRÁV Zs., 2003. Castellum contra Tautantum. Zur Identifizierung einer spätrömischen Festung. In: *Bölcske. Römische Inschriften und Funde.* Libelli Archaeologici Ser. Nov. No. II (Hg. E. Tóth – Á. Szabó). Budapest, p. 329-376.

MRÁV Zs., in press. *Dreichselmanschett. Zugarmkonstruktion bei römischen Wagen.* FolArch.

MRÁV Zs., in press. Polhov Gradec. Grave of a native Tauriscan aristocrat near Emona. *Communicationes Archaeologicae Hungaricae.*

MÓCSY A., 1957. Zur Geschichte der peregrinen Gemeinden in Pannonien. *Historia* 6, p. 488-498.

MÓCSY, A., 1959. *Die Bevölkerung von Pannonien bis zu den Markomannenkriegen.* Budapest.

NENOVA-MERDJANOVA R., 1999. Roman bronze vessels as part of *instrumentum balnei.* In: *Roman Baths and Bathing.* Proceedings of the First International Conference on Roman Baths held at Bath, England, 30 March – 4 April 1992. Part I.: Bathing and Society. (Eds. J. De Laine and E. E. Johnston) JRA Supp. Series 37. Portsmouth, p. 130-134.

NUBER H.U., 1972. Kanne und Griffschale. Ihr Gebrauch im täglichen Leben und die Beigabe in Gräbern der römischen Kaiserzeit. *BRGK* 53, p. 1-233.

PALÁGYI S.K., 1981. Die römischen Hügelgräber von Inota. *Alba Regia* 19, p. 7-93.

PALÁGYI S.K., 1997. Hügelgräber mit Dromos – Dromos-ähnlicher Vorkammer. *Balácai közlemények* 5, p. 11-26.

PALÁGYI S.K. & NAGY L., 2002. *Römerzeitliche Hügelgräber in Transdanubien (Ungarn).* Budapest.

RÖRING Ch. W., 1983. *Untersuchungen zu römischen Reisewagen.* Koblenz.

SCHERRER P., 2004. *Princeps civitatis* – Ein offizieller Titel lokaler Autoritäten? In: *Orbis antiquus. Studia in honorem Ioannis Pisonis.* (Ed. Ch. Roman, C. Gazdac) Cluj-Napoca, p. 132-142.

VISY Zs., 1997. *Die Wagendarstellungen der pannonischen Grabsteine.* Pécs.

ZABEHLICKY H., 1999. Fundus Cocceianus, oder „Wem gehörte die Villa von Bruckneudorf?" In: *Steine und Wege. Festschrift für D. Knibbe zum 65. Geburtstag.* (Hg. P. Scherrer, H. Taeuber, H. Thür) ÖAI Sonderschriften Bd. 32. Wien, p. 397-401.

DACIA, PANNONIA AND RAETIA IN THE TIME OF GALLIENUS: A COMPARATIVE APPROACH

Coriolan Horatiu OPREAN

Abstract: The author makes a comparative study of the three Danubian provinces: Raetia, Pannonia and Dacia during the reign of Gallienus based on the recent results of the archaeological epigraphic and numismatic research. Neither one of the three were definitively occupied by the barbarians after their plunder expeditions of AD 260-ties in the Roman Empire. While Raetia and Pannonia ceased to be under the authority of the central power of the Empire, represented by the emperor Gallienus, being parts of the Roman territories under the rule of usurpers of the imperial power, Dacia kept its loyalty for Gallienus. The emperor used the Dacian legions to protect Italy and his interest for the territory of the province of Dacia was lower and lower. Even he did not give up to Dacia, the process finished by Aurelianus with the official withdrawal from Dacia already began. The author analyzes all the available evidence trying to clarify this last decade of Dacia.

Résumé : L'auteur entreprend une étude comparative sur les trois provinces danubiennes: la Rétie, la Pannonie et la Dacie pendant le règne de Gallien, en base des résultats les plus récents de la recherche archéologique, épigraphique et numismatique. Aucune de ces trois provinces ne fut définitivement occupée par les Barbares après leurs dévastations de l'an 260 ap. J.C. dans l'Empire romain. Tandis que la Rétie et la Pannonie ont échappé au contrôle de l'autorité centrale de l'Empire, représentée par l'empereur Gallien, devenant des territoires placés sous l'autorité de certains usurpateurs de la pourpre, la Dacie est restée loyale à Gallien. L'empereur a utilisé les légions de Dacie afin de protéger l'Italie, et sa préoccupation pour la sort de la province de Dacie s'est diminué toujours. Même s'il n'a pas abandonné la Dacie, le processus qui toucha sa fin sous Aurélien avec l'abandon officiel de la province était déjà démarré. L'auteur fait l'analyse de toutes les sources disponibles, essayant de tirer au clair ce dernier décennie de la Dacie.

It is beyond any doubt that the political crisis that devastated the Roman Empire during the second half of the 3rd century A.D.[1] reached its peak in the time of Gallienus.

As written sources, archaeological and numismatic evidence are scarce for the province of Dacia (today Romania) during this period, it is necessary and useful a comparison among Dacia and other frontier provinces, as Raetia and Pannonia.

RAETIA

Based on written sources and certain archaeological contexts, modern historiography outlined the picture of the province of Raetia and of a large and important section of the Roman limes. Thus, a passage of the panegyric to Constantius Chlorus from March A.D. 297 says that "sub principe Gallieno...amissa Raetia"[2]. Adding the results of the intensive archaeological research carried out along the limes from Mainz to Regensburg, a catastrophic background was proposed, suggesting the destruction of this vital sector of the Roman northern frontier in the years A.D. 259-260[3]. New evidence, as well as new analysis of old archaeological and numismatic finds recently done undermined this interpretation. P. Kos[4] demonstrated that the coin hoards from the Raetian territory belonging generally to this period have not been buried in the catastrophic years A.D. 259-260 and do not support the idea of the collapse of the limes defence under barbarian attacks.

A new perspective on the history of Raetia under Gallienus rule was possible after the publication of a recent epigraphic discovery at Augsburg (Augusta Vindelicum)[5], Raetia's most important Roman town. The altar was dedicated to the victory of the province's governor against the Alamanni[6]. It was raised on 11 September 260 during the consulate of the usurper Postumus[7] and of Honoratianus, as it is written in the text. The using of a "Gallic' consulate by the governor himself suggests that Postumus area of domination and his "Gallic Empire" included Raetia also[8]. There is a good reason to believe that Gallienus lost control over the Raetian limes, due not only to the barbarian attacks, but mainly because the province of Raetia gathered to Postumus unofficial "Gallic Empire". That must be also the meaning of the phrase "amissa Raetia", where the Roman administration endured after A.D. 260, but Gallienus authority was no longer recognized[9].

PANNONIA

The events that have taken place on the Middle Danube frontier in the winter of A.D. 259-260 suggest that Lower Pannonia was devastated by the Quadi and the Sarmatians, probably inspired and encouraged by the successful expedition of the Alamanni in Northern Italy[10]. J. Fitz believed that the usurpation of Ingenuus, the governor of

---

[1] ALFÖLDI 1967; ALFÖLDI 1989.

[2] Pan. Lat. 4 (8), Paris, 1952 (ed. Galletier)

[3] SCHOENBERGER 1985, p. 126; NUBER 1990, p. 51-68.

[4] KOS 1995.

[5] BAKKER 1993; STROBEL 1998, p. 83.

[6] LORETO 1994.

[7] KÖNIG 1981; DRINKWATER 1987.

[8] STROBEL 1998, p. 88.

[9] STROBEL 1999, p. 14-16

[10] FITZ 1966, p. 7-9.

Lower Pannonia, was the first accident, followed then by the barbarian invasion. If Ingenuus was defeated easily by Gallienus, a next usurpation of Regalianus seems to have had more important consequences. Regalianus probably ruled over Upper Pannonia, Dacia and Lower Moesia. The army at Sirmium (Lower Pannonia, composed of vexillations of the legions from Britannia and the two Germanies, kept its loyalty to Gallienus[11]. As these regions were very important for the defence of Italy, Gallienus himself concentrated all efforts to keep his control over the Illyricum. He succeded to defeat Regalianus and after A. D. 260 he tried to rebuild and reorganize the two Pannonias, where towns like Gorsium and Aquincum were hard damaged by the barbarian attacks. Lower Pannonia was in a worse situation as Upper Pannonia[12]. The first stage of this policy of consolidation of Illyricum started with a special attention to the southern part of Pannonia, crossed by the direct route to Italy. At Poetovio, a main strategic town, were concentrated the four legions of the Pannonias, while at Sirmium was brought the 8th legion Augusta from Argentorate. Gallienus also set up a new mint at Siscia to pay the troops and to restore the economy of the provinces[13]. In a second stage, between A.D. 264-266, Gallienus rebuild several forts on the Danube frontier, so the Pannonian legions returned to their previous garrisons. They were replaced at Poetovio by the loyal Dacian vexillations[14].

DACIA

In the last 50 years Romanian historiography has generally focused on the moment when Dacia ceased to belong any more to the Empire, emphasis being laid on the analysis of the 4th century A.D. written sources[15]. The written evidence is very brief and contradictory, talking about Gallienus and Aurelianus, who both lost the province, or withdrew the provincials and the Roman army. Most contemporary authors explained this contradiction of the ancient texts as a first partial abandonment of certain territories by Gallienus, followed by a final and total retreat to the south of the Danube ordered by Aurelianus[16]. H. Daicoviciu[17] expressed a different point of view to this issue. His ingenious conclusion was that Gallienus did not lose Dacia for the Empire, but he only lost his control over the province in a period well known for the usurpation all around the Empire. The problem is that it is not so easy to choose the precise moment when Dacia was lost to the authority of Gallienus. At a first sight the inscription recently found at Augsburg seems to help the H.

Daicoviciu's idea. The two phrases known from the literary texts, "amissa Raetia" and "Dacia amissa" are identical, both referring to the same emperor. It would be logical to have also the same meaning. Due to the inscription at Augsburg we know now that Raetia has been lost by Gallienus to the authority of Postumus, the "Gaulish Emperor". We think that only the logic deduction is not enough to accept unreservedly the hypothesis of H. Daicoviciu for Dacia. For a final conclusion we must analyze the archaeological, epigraphic and numismatic evidence available for Dacia.

More extensive archaeological research has been made on the frontier of Dacia Porolissensis (i.e. Northern Dacia)[18]. Here, recent excavations revealed that the auxiliary fort at Ilisua end in a general fire[19]. As the last coin comes from Philippus Arabs[20], the final destruction layer does not necessary belong to Gallienus time, nor this situation can be take into consideration for the whole defence sector of the province, as some authors suggested[21]. A similar final fire has been found under the tile debris only in the fort at Buciumi[22], quite far to Ilisua. That means we do not have at the moment serious archaeological evidence to accept that some parts of Dacia were lost to the barbarians by Gallienus.

In this frontier sector we have instead well attested two general operations carried out during the last decades of existence of the province. First, there are identified many works of fixing the defensive elements of the forts. In the important fort at Porolissum-Pomet an inscription raised by the neighbour town of Porolissum in honor of the emperor Philippus Arabs was found reused in the walls of a tower of the decumana gate[23]. Another inscription dedicated in A.D. 251 to Herennia Etruscilla, Decius' wife, was found built in a wall[24]. It represents a terminus post quem for the repair activity at Porolissum. In the curtain tower no. 2, which has traces of fixing too, a coin of Salonina from A.D. 260 has been found[25]. There are good reasons to believe that the reconstruction of the walls of the fort at Porolissum took place, very probable, in Gallienus time, as N. Gudea suggested[26]. As we have seen before, the same happened in Lower Pannonia. That means the forts of Dacia Porolissensis were seriously damaged, but not abandoned sometime after A.D. 250. That means Gallienus' time seems to be the most probable chronology for such an action. Similar works were also identified at the auxiliary forts at Buciumi[27], Romita[28], Tihau[29] and

[11] FITZ 1966, p. 11-16.

[12] FITZ 1976, p.35-36.

[13] FITZ 1976, p. 76.

[14] FITZ 1976, p. 79.

[15] ILIESCU 1971; ARICESCU 1973; PETOLESCU 1984; RUSCU 1998.

[16] MACREA 1960, p. 465 (eastern part of Transylvania); TUDOR 1978, p. 39-40 (Olt River defence line in Little Walachia-Oltenia); PROTASE 1980, p. 260 (north and east Transylvania); BENEA 1996, p. 11 (south-east Transylvania).

[17] DAICOVICIU 1979.

[18] See the last results of the excavations at ISAC 1999.

[19] PROTASE, GAIU 1999, p. 419.

[20] ARDEVAN 1997, p. 69, no. 238-262.

[21] PROTASE, GAIU 1999, p. 420.

[22] GUDEA 1997a, p. 61.

[23] GUDEA 1997b, p. 40.

[24] GUDEA 1989, p. 765, no. 20.

[25] GUDEA 1997b, p. 42.

[26] GUDEA 1997b, p. 49.

[27] GUDEA 1997a.

[28] MATEI, BAIUSZ 1997, p. 40; 43-44; 55; 137.

[29] PROTASE 1994, p. 93-95.

Gilau[30]. All around there were used all categories of monuments, honorary, funerary and votive. The same situation was identified at the auxiliary fort at Brincovenesti[31] on the eastern frontier of Dacia Apulensis.

The second important operation made to the forts in a later period consists of the raising of some "special" buildings, which do not belong usually to the inner structure of a Roman fort. The first type of these buildings was erected on the inside slope of the turf-wall and over via sagularis, which ceased to exist in that sector. In the fort at Porolissum[32] large, rectangular shape buildings were raised in this position near porta principalis dextra, porta principalis sinistra and porta praetoria. The same situation was found at Buciumi[33], where they are placed on both sides of the praetoria gate, at Bologa[34] near porta principalis dextra, and at Tihau[35] near porta praetoria. The second type of buildings consists of extensions of the commanders' houses, built also over via sagularis. Extended praetoria are known at Porolissum, Buciumi, Bologa and Casei[36]. We think it was a plan carried out by the provincial headquarters. Concerning the chronology of the buildings we do not have too many elements. At Buciumi inside the building C4 (which was only trenched) were found only coins from the second half of the 3rd century A.D[37]. At Porolissum inside the building B6 (trenched) were discovered only tiles with the stamps of the legions III Gallica and VII Gemina Felix, both units from other provinces[38]. Legio VII Gemina Felix is also mentioned in an inscription at Potaissa[39] together with legio V Macedonica, but it cannot be precisely dated. Our hypothesis is that all these buildings were nothing but extra lodgings for supplement troops brought from other provinces to strengthen the defence line along this sector of the limes.

Little is known concerning the situation of Roman towns during the last decades of the province. New information was recently provided by the excavations in ancient Napoca[40] (today Cluj-Napoca). In the sector researched in V. Deleu street, were uncovered several stone buildings. The second and last period of building C2 had two layers. On the clay floor corresponding to first layer were found different objects and traces of fire. Inside a pit dug in antiquity in this floor was found a hoard of 1268 silver coins, the latest being issued by Severus Alexander in A.D. 235. The last layer is a reconstruction dated by two coins

from the time of Philippus Arabs found on the floor. This last reconstruction does not seem to suffer a violent destruction. The conclusion is that sometime between A.D. 235 and the time of Gallienus Napoca may have been attacked from the exterior. Then, at the end of this interval the buildings were rebuild and life went on for a while.

The monetary circulation during Dacia's last decades of existence is not very well studied. A recent approach[41] to this issue tried to study Dacia also comparative with the neighbour provinces. The conclusion was that after A.D. 253 the quantity of coins diminished in Dacia, as well as in the two Pannonias, reaching a dramatic collapse towards A.D. 260. Dacia's precarious financial situation seems very similar to that of Lower Pannonia. Another dramatic decrease in the monetary circulation in Dacia can be identified after A.D. 268, the coins issued by Claudius II being much fewer in comparison with south of the Danube, in Moesia, where they are very numerous[42].

The situation of the coin hoards known in Dacia is partially different. In Dacia there are 32 coin hoards buried certainly during the rule of Philippus and 14 more whose latest coins were issued by Gordianus III, but hidden, very probable, also in the time of Philippus, most of them in A.D. 247[43]. It was a consequence of the war against the Carpi who invaded Dacia. Few hoards whose most recent coins are from A.D. 247-248 were buried in Decius' time, or later. An identical situation was reported for Moesia. Also few hoards end with coins of Trebonianus Gallus, being buried, probably, under Gallus, or later[44]. There are also 5 hoards ending with coins of Gallienus. The first of these is the hoard at Olteni[45] (Little Walachia-Oltenia) ending with two coins of Valerianus A.D. 257. Another one is in Banat at Golet[46] (today lost) had the last coin from Gallienus. Three hoards were found in Transylvania, three in the main military and political center of Dacia, Apulum[47] (Alba Iulia), and another not very far, in the neighbourhood of the little town of Aiud[48]. The hoard Apulum II, today lost, was composed of 115 silver coins. Among the latest coins were identified 23 pieces from Valerianus, 12 from Gallienus, 8 from Cornelia Salonina, 5 from Valerianus II, 2 from Saloninus, that means almost half of the accumulation was made in Gallienus time! Very similar seems the hoard Apulum III (lost), even its latest coin is from Aurelianus. From 235 silver pieces, 25 are from Valerianus, 16 from Gallienus, 8 from Cornelia Salonina, 5 from Claudius II and 2 from Aurelianus. There are 49 coins accumulated under Gallienus. Hoard Apulum IV of 1213 coins had only 1 from Valerianus, 1 from Mariniana, 1 from Gallienus, 1 from Salonina, 24 from Valerianus II, 1 from Saloninus, the latest coin being from A.D. 268. The

---

[30] ISAC 1997, p.56; 58; 62; 64.

[31] PROTASE , ZRINYI 1992.

[32] GUDEA 1997b, p. 41.

[33] GUDEA 1997a, p. 56.

[34] GUDEA 1997c, p. 45.

[35] OPREANU 1998, p. 79-81, fig. 99.

[36] ISAC, HÜGEL, ANDREICA 1994, fig 7; 8; 25; 27.

[37] GUDEA 1997a, p. 61.

[38] GUDEA 1997b, p. 41.

[39] BARBULESCU 1987, p. 26-27.

[40] COCIS, VOISIAN, PAKI, ROTEA 1995.

[41] GAZDAC 1998.

[42] GEROV 1977, p. 142.

[43] CHITESCU, POPESCU 1975, p. 226.

[44] WINKLER 1974.

[45] SUCIU 2000, p. 48, no. 92.

[46] SUCIU 2000, p. 40, no. 64.

[47] SUCIU 2000, p. 19-21, nos. 3, 5.

[48] SUCIU 2000, p. 19, no. 1.

hoard from Aiud (lost) had around 300 pieces, 44 from Valerianus and 7 from Gallienus. The antoninians issued by Gallienus exists also in a little hoard from outside the Roman frontier, in western Romania, at Diosig[49] (Bihor County). Here out of 65 coins, 8 belong to Gallienus.

We can say that there is a contradiction between the image of the Dacian economy under Gallienus as resulted from the analysis of the monetary circulation and the coin hoards where the accumulation of the coins of Gallienus seems to be substantial. We must stress that the main part of the hoards were discovered at Apulum, among them Apulum II and Apulum III inside a building considered in the past as the baths, but recent reconsideration proved it was the headquarters of the governor of the three Dacias[50]. Taking into consideration all the elements, our explanation to the contradiction mentioned above is that the accumulation of the coins from Valerianus-Gallienus period has been done, probably, outside the province of Dacia. The most suitable social category able to do this outside during this time and then to come back to Dacia was the army. Dacian vexillations have been taken to Oriental expedition by Valerianus. If the emperor never came back, dying in Parthian captivity, little is known about the fate of the Dacian troops[51]. In the light of the composition of coin hoards II and III from Apulum and Aiud it seems that at least some of the legionaries from the unit at Apulum, 13th Gemina, succeeded to return to their home-garrison sometime later, if our hypothesis is correct. What happened to the auxiliary units taken from Dacia to the Parthian expedition is little known.

Epigraphically point of view the Decius-Gallienus period is represented in Dacia by only 11 inscriptions[52]. Out of these, those raised by the Dacian legions are of major importance to the present discussion. The latest inscription attested the 5th legion Macedonica in its garrison at Potaissa under Donatus praefectus legionis can be dated between the end of A.D. 257 and beginning of A.D. 258[53], probably before the death of Valerianus II at the beginning of A.D. 258[54]. We do not have any inscription coming from Apulum raised by the other legion, 13th Gemina, at the same time, but it is considered generally that it still kept its garrison in central Transylvania. But after a few years something happened, very probable. The altar of M. Aurelius Veteranus, praefectus legionis XIII Geminae was found at Mehadia[55] (Ad Mediam in antiquity) and dates after A.D. 260 when Gallienus ruled alone. This inscription was considered generally as discovered at Herculane Spa, where the praefectus went for the water[56] (which was considered the indirect proof that the legion was still at

Apulum). We appreciated that this idea is at least naïve and there is no any reason to reject the information that the inscription comes from Mehadia[57]. We also made for the first time[58] the connection between this information and a brick stamp having the inscription vexillatio Daciarum at Mehadia. We considered also another brick stamp found at Mehadia with the name of the two Dacian legions (previously[59] dated without any serious reason after the creation of the new Dacia of Aurelian to the south of the Danube) as evidence which emphasizes J. Fitz's[60] conclusion. He showed that Ad Mediam was a fort of great strategic importance in that period where troops were concentrated after A.D. 260 to keep the contact between Dacia and Moesia. It is obviously that the legions of Dacia participated to this new war thinking to Gallienus. In conclusion, while we do not have inscriptions of the two legions after A.D. 258-260 in their traditional garrisons Apulum and Potaissa they left epigraphic traces in south-west Dacia, at Ad Mediam.

After A.D. 264 Dacian vexillations are also epigraphically attested in Pannonia, at Poetovio[61], another very important strategic point, replacing the Pannonian legions which had to return to their previous forts on the Danube frontier. The Dacian troops at Poetovio were under the command of a praepositus, T. Flavius Aper[62]. The loyalty of the Dacian legions to Gallienus is also proved by the antoninians with their names minted by the emperor in A.D. 260-261, to commemorate the victories over the barbarians and the usurpers[63].

Other inscriptions attesting officers of the Dacian legions are known from Northern Italy. Three funerary inscriptions raised for military and their families were discovered at Dertona[64], one of them Aurelius Veteranus, beneficiarius laticlavi legionis, being dead in battle. Another inscription comes between Tergeste and Aquileia[65] attesting Antonius Valentinus, princeps legionis XIII Geminae, killed by latrones in the Julian Alps. Latrones were usually named in the inscriptions barbarian groups infiltrated across the border with the purpose of looting. Recently a new inscription mentioning a soldier from the 13th legion has been found at Tortona[66]. E. Ritterling[67] considered that the presence of these troops in northern Italy was an echo of the battles against the Alamanni of Claudius II and Aurelianus. Although the date of the inscriptions cannot be established we believe it is quite likely that they belong to the time of Gallienus, when Dacian vexillations are

[49] SASIANU 1980, p. 122, no. 47.

[50] DIACONESCU, PISO 1993.

[51] This problem was for the first time mentioned in the Romanian literature by OPREANU 1999.

[52] A last approach to the subject HÜGEL 1999.

[53] BARBULESCU 1996

[54] KIENAST 1990, p. 221.

[55] CIL III 1560=IDR III/1, p. 54

[56] MOGA 1985, p. 29; 71.

[57] The conclusion belong to OPREANU 1999.

[58] OPREANU 1999.

[59] MACREA, GUDEA, MOTU 1993, p. 52.

[60] FITZ 1966, p. 40.

[61] FITZ 1976, p. 79.

[62] HOFFILER, SARIA 1938, p. 314-317.

[63] FITZ 1966a, p. 365.

[64] CIL V 7366=IDRE I, p. 138.

[65] IDRE I, p. 146.

[66] MENELLA 2000, p. 646-647.

[67] RITTERLING 1925, col. 1722.

attested in Poetovio, whence they could rapidly intervene in northern Italy. On the other hand an inscription from Ticinum[68] attests Caecilius Valentinus, optio spei legionis XIII Geminae. But a military concentration is known to have existed in Ticinum in AD 268[69]. The inscriptions reveal that the soldiers who died in northern Italy were there together with their families, which means they were in the area for unlimited time. That is why we think there is a connection with the same military concentration created by Gallienus at Poetovio. The main mission of this group consisting of Dacian vexillations was to protect Italy[70]. We should remember that Raetia, a province having an essential position in safeguarding Italy was no longer under the authority of Gallienus after AD 260, but under that of Postumus.

The first evidence attesting Dacian vexillations as loyal to a usurper, are the aurei issued at Trier by Postumus' successor, Victorinus[71]. The coins were issued at the end of AD 269, after Gallienus death. It is possible that the issue could reflect a slightly previous situation, although Victorinus became Augustus only in the fall of AD 269[72].

Taking into consideration all the available evidence it is difficult to find a period when Dacia's army ceased to be loyal to Gallienus. As J. Fitz[73] suggested such a situation was maybe possible when Regalianus usurpation has taken place. H. Daicoviciu's hypothesis is hard to be accepted. On the contrary, most indication demonstrates that Dacia was still under the authority of Gallienus even in the second part of his reign. The more important question is if the Dacian vexillations moved by Gallienus to Poetovio and to northern Italy ever returned to Dacia? It is hard to believe they were sent back to Dacia by Claudius II the military situation being not improved. At the same time we must remember that other Dacian vexillations were taken to the Oriental expedition by Valerianus, but there is no evidence they arrived back to their previous garrisons after AD 260. The picture suggested by these informations is that after AD 260 a part of the Dacian army was scattered in other parts of the Empire due to the political and military situation. If finally Aurelianus decided to abandon the Carpathian area and Little Wallachia (Oltenia) the reasons must have been very serious. Recently it was suggested that Aurelianus action have been designated to save the provincial elite, the so-called honestiores, for keeping the Empire's honor[74]. L. Mrozewicz[75] expressed the opinion that after Decius death at Abrittus, in Dacia, as in Upper Germany, the Romans were controlling only the

fortified towns and the forts. The upper class of the province tried to remind to the careless emperors that Dacia is an important and loyal province, asking for their support.

The only possible conclusion after this analysis is that Gallienus-Aurelianus period was a time of slow agony for the province created by Trajan north of the Danube. The Roman withdrawal seems to be a long-term process, started by Gallienus, but without an obvious intention. Aurelianus finished this process consciously and intentionally. As a matter of fact, the written sources do not contradict[76] this picture based on the archaeological, epigraphic and numismatic evidence.

Author's address

Coriolan Horatiu OPREAN
Romanian Academy
Institute of Archaeology and History of Art
Str. C. Daicoviciu 2
3400 Cluj-Napoca, ROMANIA
E-mail: oprean@personal.ro

Bibliography

ALFÖLDI, A.,1967, Studien zur Geschichte der Welt-Krise des 3 Jahrhunderts n. Ch., Darmstadt.

ALFÖLDI, G,1989, Die Krise des Römischen Reiches, Stuttgart.

ARDEVAN, R,1997, Monedele descoperite in castru si vicus (1978-1995). In: D. Protase,C.Gaiu,G.Marinescu, Castrul roman si asezarea civila de la Ilisua. *Revista Bistritei*, X-XI, p. 79-94.

ARICESCU, A.,1973, Despre o recenta interpretare a izvoarelor literare privind parasirea Daciei. *SCIV* 24/3, p. 485-491.

BAKKER, A., 1993, Raetien unter Postumus-Das Siegesdenkmal einer Juthungenschlacht im Jahre 260 n. Chr. aus Augsburg.*Germania* 71, p. 369-386.

BARBULESCU, M, 1987, Din istoria militara a Daciei romane. Legiunea V Macedonica, Cluj-Napoca

BARBULESCU, M., 1996, Païens et chrétiens en Dacie au milieu du IIIe siècle. *Transylvanian Review* 5/3, p. 32-37.

BENEA, D., 1996, Dacia sud-vestica in secolele III-IV, Timisoara.

CHITESCU, M., POPESCU, E., 1975, Tezaurul monetar de la Simburesti (jud. Olt). *SCN* 6.

COCIS, S., VOISIAN, V., PAKI, A., ROTEA, M., Raport preliminar privind cercetarile arheologice din strada V. Deleu in Cluj-Napoca. I Campaniile 1992-1994. *ActaMusei Napocensis* 32/I, p. 635-652.

DAICOVICIU, H., 1979, Gallieno e la Dacia. In: *Filias harin. Miscellanea in onore di Eugenio Manni*, Roma, p. 651-666.

DIACONESCU, A., PISO, I., 1993, Apulum. In: *La politique édilitaire dans les provinces de l'Empire romain*, Cluj-Napoca, p. 67-82.

DOMASZEWSKI, v. A., 1918, Die Legionsmünzen des Victorinus. *Germania* 2/2.

DRINKWATER, J., F., 1987, *The Gallic Empire*, Stuttgart.

---

[68] CIL V 6423=IDRE I 165

[69] Aurelius Victor, De Caes 33, 35.

[70] On the attack of AD 260 against Italy and the Alamanni's raid direction, see LORETO 1994.

[71] ELMER 1941, p. 71, no. 715; 718; DOMASZEWSKI 1918, p. 113 dated the coins too late (AD 271) and reached to the wrong conclusion that the Dacian legions were already in their new south Danubian garrisons at Oescus and Ratiaria.

[72] KIENAST 1990, P. 243.

[73] FITZ 1966, p. 15.

[74] OKAMURA 1996, p. 19.

[75] MROZEWICZ 1998.

---

[76] RUSCU 1998, p. 253-254.

ELMER, G., 1941, Die Münzprägung der gallischen Kaiser in Köln, Trier und Mainland. *BJ* 146, p. 1-105.

FITZ, J., 1966, *Ingenuus et Regalien*, Bruxelles.

FITZ, J., 1966a, Les antoniniani des légion de Gallien. In: *Mélanges d'archéologie, d'épigraphie et d'histoire offerts à Jérôme Carcopino*, Verdôme, p. 359-360.

FITZ, J., 1976, *La Pannonie sous Gallien*, Bruxelles.

GAZDAC, C., 1998, The Monetary Circulation and the Abandonment of Dacia. A Comparative Study. *ActaMusei Napocensis* 35/1, p. 229-234.

GEROV, B., 1977, Die Einfälle der Nordvölker in den Ostbalkanraum im Lichte der Münzschatzfunde I. Das I und III Jahrhundert (101-284). *ANRW* II/6.

GUDEA, N., 1989, Porolissum. Un complex la marginea de nord a Imperiului Roman, Zalau.

GUDEA, N., 1997a, Castrul roman de la Buciumi, Zalau.

GUDEA, N., 1997b, Castrul roman de la Porolissum, Zalau.

GUDEA, N., 1997c, Castrul roman de la Bologa-Resculum, Zalau.

HOFFILER, V., SARIA, B., 1938, *Antike Inschriften Jugoslawien*, Zagreb.

HÜGEL, P., Inscriptiile si sfarsitul stapanirii romane in Dacia. In: *Napoca. 1880 de ani de la inceputul vietii urbane*, Cluj-Napoca.

ILIESCU, V., 1971, Parasirea Daciei in lumina izvoarelor literare. *SCIV* 22/3, p. 425-442.

ISAC, D., HÜGEL, P., ANDREICA, D., 1994, Praetoria in dakischen Militäranlagen. *SJ* 47.

ISAC, D., 1997, Castrele de cohorta si ala de la Gilau, Zalau.

ISAC, D. 1999, Die Entwicklung der Erforschung des Limes nach 1983 im nördlichen Dakien (Porolissensis). In: *Roman Frontier Studies XVII/1997*, ed. N. Gudea, Zalau, p. 151-170.

KIENAST, D., 1990, Römische Kaisertabelle. Grundzüge einer römischen Kaiserchronologie, Darmstadt.

KOS, P., 1995, Sub principe Gallieno...amissa Raetia? Numismatische Quellen zum Datum 259/260 n. Chr. in Raetien. *Germania* 75/1, p. 369-386.

KÖNIG, I., 1981, Die gallischen Usurpatoren von Postumus bis Tetricus, München.

LORETO L., 1994, La prima penetrazione alamanna in Italia (260 d. Ch.) come ipotesi alternativa per la storia dei conflitti romano-germanici. In: *Germani in Italia*, ed B. and P. Scardigli, Roma, p. 209-237.

MACREA, M., 1960, Sfirsitul stapinirii romane in Dacia. In: *Istoria Romaniei* I, Bucuresti.

MACREA, M., GUDEA, N., MOTU, I., 1993, Praetorium. Castrul si asezarea romana de la Mehadia, Bucuresti.

MATEI, A., BAIUSZ, I., 1997, *Castrul roman de la Romita*, Zalau.

MENELLA, G., 2000, Legionari del Donau a Dertona e Ticinum: una nuova testimonianza. In: *Les légions de Rome sous le Haut-Empire* II, ed. Y.Le Bohec, Lyon, p. 645-653.

MOGA , V., 1985, Din istoria militara a Daciei romane. Legiunea XIII Gemina, Cluj-Napoca.

MROZEWICZ, L., 1998, Les villes de Dacie et de Germanie Supérieure face à la chute du limes vers le milieu du IIIème siècle. In: *Les empereaurs illyriens* VIII, ED. E. Frézouls, H. Jouffroy, Strasbourg, p. 35-41.

NUBER, H., U., 1990, Das Ende des obergermanische-raetischen Limes- Eine Forschungsbericht. In: *Archäolgie und Geschichte des ersten Jahrtausends in Südwestdeutschland*, ed. H. U. Nuber, Sigmaringen, p. 51-68.

OKAMURA, L., 1996, Roman Withdrawal from Three Transfluvial Frontiers. In: *Shifting Frontiers in Late Antiquity*, ed. I. Mathison, H. Siran, London, p. 11-19.

OPREANU, C., 1998, Tihau. In: *Cronica cercetarilor arheologice. Campania 1997*, Bucuresti, p. 79-81.

OPREANU, C., 1999, Raetia, Pannonia si Dacia in vremea lui Gallienus. *Analele Banatului* VII-VIII, p. 393-406.

PETOLESCU, C., C., 1984, Varia daco-romana VIII. Izvoarele privind parasirea Daciei. *Thraco-Dacica* 5/1-2, p. 187-193.

PROTASE, D., 1980, *Autohtonii in Dacia* I, Bucuresti.

PROTASE, D., ZRINYI, A., 1992, Inscriptii si monumente sculpturale din castrul roman de la Brancovenesti (jud. Mures). *Ephemeris Napocensis* 2, p. 95-110

PROTASE, D., 1994, Castrul roman de la Tihau. *Ephemeris Napocensis* 4

PROTASE, D., GAIU, C., 1999, Le camp romain et l'établissement civil d'Ilisua. Les résultats des fouilles arcéologiques effectuées dans le courant des années 1978-1995. In: *Frontier Studies Roman* XVII/1997, ed. N. Gudea, Zalau.

RITTERLING, E., 1925, Legio.*RE* XII.

RUSCU, D., 1998, L'abandon de la Dacie romaine dans les sources littéraires. *Acta Musei Napocensis* 35/1, p. 233-254.

SASIANU A., 1980, Moneda antica in vestul si nord-vestul Romaniei, Oradea.

SCHOENBERGER, H., 1985, Die römischer Truppenlager der frühen und mittleren Kaiserzeit zwischen Nordsee und Inn. *BerRGK* 66, p. 319-497.

STROBEL, K., 1998, Raetia amissa? Raetien unter Gallienus: Provinz und Heer in Licht der neuen Augsburger Siegesinschrift. In: Spätrömische Belfestigungsanlagen in den Rhein-und Donauprovinzen. Beiträge der Arbeitsgemeinschaft "Römische Archäologie" bei der Tagung des West- und Süddeutschen Verbandes der Altertumsforschung in Kempten 1995. BAR Internat Ser 704, ed, C. Bridger, K-J Gilles, Oxford.

STROBEL, K., 1999, Pseudophänomene der römischen militär- und provinzialgeschichte am Beispiel des "Falles" des obergermanisch-raetischen Limes. Neue Ansätze zu einer Geschichte der Jahrzente nach 253 n. Chr. an Rhein und oberer Donau. In: *Roman Frontier Studies XVII/1997*, ed. N. Gudea, Zalau, p. 14-16.

SUCIU, V., 2000, Tezaure monetare in Dacia romana si postromana, Cluj-Napoca.

TUDOR, D., 1978, *Oltenia romana*, Bucuresti.

WINKLER, J., 1974, Despre compozitia tezaurului monetar descoperit la Apoldul de Jos. In: *In memoriam Constantini Daicoviciu*, Cluj, p. 421-428.

LE CAMP ROMAIN DE MALDEGEM (FLANDRE ORIENTALE, BELGIQUE)

Wouter DHAEZE & Hugo THOEN avec la collaboration de Frédéric HANUT

Résumé : Le camp romain de Maldegem-Vake (Flandre orientale, Belgique) a été découvert au cours de prospections aériennes vers la fin des années 1970. Entre 1984 et 1992, le département d'Archéologie de l'Université de Gand a fouillé environ un tiers de la superficie du site. Les recherches archéologiques et l'examen des sciences naturelles ont démontré que le camp fut érigé suite à des invasions des Chauques dans les années 172-174 de notre ère. La fortification, construite en terre et en bois, a connu deux périodes de très courte durée et fut un des premiers sites fortifiés de la défense côtière en Belgique. Le camp a été occupé par une troupe auxiliaire d'infanterie et de cavalerie, provenant probablement de la Germanie. Le site de Maldegem-Vake est d'une importance exceptionnelle pour la connaissance de l'architecture militaire de la période des Antonins. En plus le matériel archéologique nous livre, à cause de la courte durée de l'occupation du site, une référence unique pour l'archéologie romaine provinciale. Dans cette contribution sont présentés les résultats des fouilles et de l'examen du matériel archéologique trouvé dans le système défensif (fossae et titulum) fouillé dans le secteur Est. Ces trouvailles nous donnent une première idée de l'approvisionnement de l'unité occupant cette forteresse temporelle.

Abstract: The Roman fort at Maldegem-Vake has been discovered at the close of the seventies through aerial photography. Between 1984 and 1992, the Department of Archaeology of the Ghent University excavated one third of the total occupation area. Archaeological research and studies of natural sciences have shown that the site was built as a reaction against the incursions of the Chauci in the years 172-174 A.D. The fortification, made in earth and wood, was occupied for two short periods and was one of the first fortified sites of the coastal defence system in Gallia Begica. The military unit was a part-mounted cohort, probably originating from Germania. The site of Maldegem-Vake is very important for the knowledge of the military architecture in the Antonine period. Because of the short occupation, the site is an unique reference for Provincial-Roman archaeology. In this contribution will be discussed the excavation results and the material found in the defence system (fossae and titulum) in the eastern sector. These finds give a first idea of the supply of this temporary fortification.

1. LA FORTIFICATION

Le plan du camp est celui d'un carré parfait mesurant 157,50 m de côté extérieur (500 pieds romains). La superficie totale comprend 2,5 ha et l'espace construit à l'intérieur est d'une superficie de 1,3 ha (Thoen 1991: 187). (fig. 1 et 2) La fortification fut érigée en terre et en bois; il s'agit donc d'un camp du type *Holz-Erde-Kastell* (Johnson 1987: 70-71).

1.1 Le système défensif

Le système défensif du *castellum* est du type classique, ce qui veut dire qu'il comprend deux fossés (*fossae*) et un *vallum* qui était formé par une levée de terre (*agger*) et couronnée d'une palissade en bois (Thoen 1991: 187) (fig. 3).

Les deux fossés, d'une largeur d'environ 4 m et d'une profondeur de 2 m, sont pourvus d'un *ankle breaker*, typique pour des *fossae fastigatae*. Le talus qui sépare les fossés est large d'1 m (Thoen 1991: 187).

Jouxte au fossé interne, il y a un espace de quelque 12 m, réservé pour le *vallum* et l'*intervallum*. La levée de terre du *vallum*, couverte de mottes de terre, mesure 6,40 m à la base. Si nous supposons que la partie supérieure avait une largeur de 2 m et compte tenu d'une pente de 65° pour la partie externe et de 45° pour la partie interne (Johnson 1987: 72), nous pouvons estimer la hauteur du rempart à 3 m. Couronné d'une palissade de 2 m, la hauteur totale du *vallum* était de 5 m (Thoen 1991: 187).

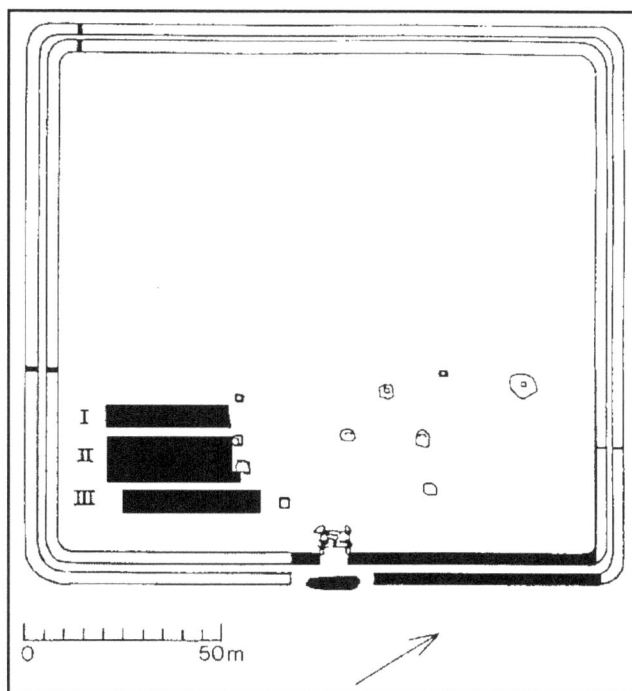

Figure 1. Le contexte topographique de Maldegem-Vake (Thoen 1991: Figure 1).

L'*agger* était couvert de mottes, une méthode de construction très fréquent pendant la période flavienne jusqu'au règne de Trajan et même encore utilisée sous Antonin le Pieux (par exemple dans la plupart des *castella* le long du *Vallum Pii*) (Johnson 1987: 74). Le *castellum* de

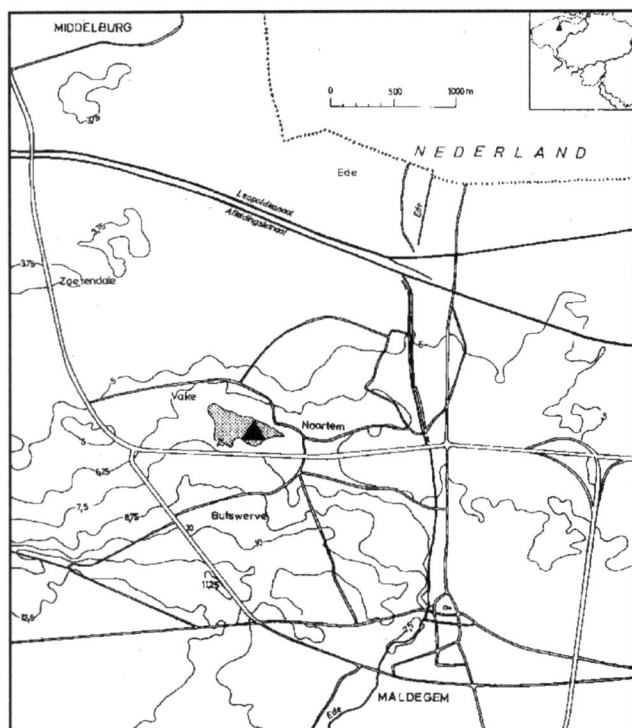

Figure 2. Plan du castellum de Maldegem-Vake
(Thoen 1998: Figure 4).

Maldegem-Vake nous prouve que ce type de construction était encore en usage pendant le gouvernement de Marc-Aurèle (161-180 ap. J.C.).

Aux quatre angles du fortin était construit une tour en bois, incorporée dans le rempart. Cette supposition est due aux trouvailles de nombreux clous et fragments de fer recueillis dans les terriers de blaireaux dans l'angle nord-est (Thoen 1996: 262).

Aux quatre côtés, le système défensif (*fossae* et *vallum*) était interrompu au centre pour la construction des portes d'entrée. Une de ces portes, la *porta decumana*, a pu être examinée en détail. Le solide bâtiment en bois montre un plan carré de 9 m de côté. La porte même a 3 m de largeur et est flanquée de deux tours de défense (Thoen 1996: 262). Un *titulum* d'une longueur de 13,80 m, d'une largeur de 4,40 m et d'une profondeur de 2 m, bloquait d'une manière très efficace la voie d'accès (Thoen 1996: 258). Les *titula*, typiques pour les camps d'occupation limitée dans le temps (camps d'exercice et camps de marche), ont rarement été employées dans les camps d'occupation prolongée, car la construction d'une solide porte d'entrée les rendait inutile. Quant à Maldegem-Vake on y trouve la construction de *titula* en même temps que l'utilisation de portes d'entrée solides.

L'*intervallum*, avec lequel est désigné l'espace entre le *vallum* et les baraquements, comprenait la *via sagularis*. Ce chemin, bordé de petits fossés d'écoulement, avait une largeur de 3 m et était pavé de grès panisélien (Thoen 1996: 266).

1.2. L'intérieur du camp

Environ un tiers de l'espace intérieur a été fouillé. L'état actuel des fouilles montre que les bâtiments ont tous été érigés en bois. Il faut cependant tenir compte du fait que la partie centrale, là où se situait le quartier général (*principia*), n'a pas encore été examinée. Dans la zone Est ont été retrouvées les traces de trois baraques, d'un atelier (*fabrica*), d'un bâtiment officiel dont la fonction exacte n'est pas encore connue, d'une dizaine de puits d'eau et d'une latrine (*latrina*) (Thoen 1996: 264).

Les trois baraques montrent une implantation systématique. Elles sont disposées parallèlement avec un espacement de 2,50 m; elles sont alignées, excepté le bâtiment III décalé d'environ 2 m. Les bâtiments mesurent

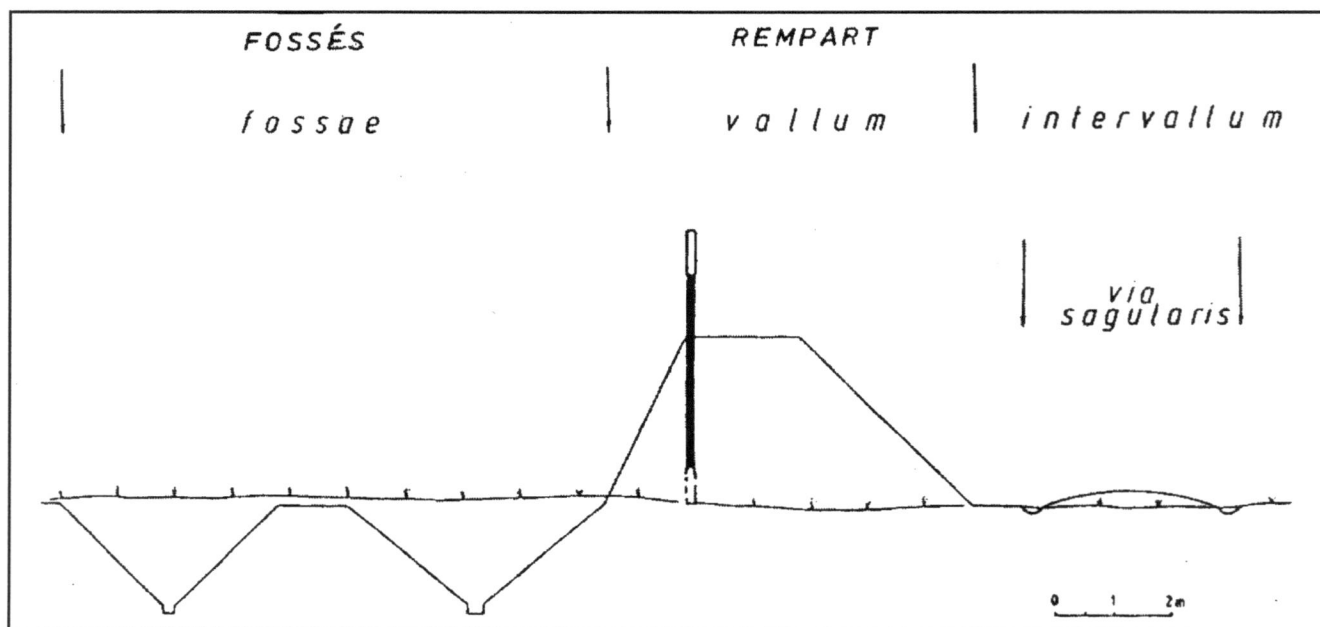

Figure 3. Reconstruction du système défensif (Thoen 1998: Figure 3).

33 m sur 6,50 m (le double baraquement II étant évidemment deux fois plus large). Dans la partie méridionale du bâtiment III, l'on a pu discerner la partie réservée pour le centurion/décurion. Une autre annexe est accolée au bâtiment IIB. Les baraquements simples (I et II) sont construits suivant un module à une nef et un toit à doubles pans. Le bâtiment II présente une construction plus complexe: dans la partie ouest, il est construit suivant le même module; dans la partie est, une rangée de lourds poteaux porteurs nous fait supposer que cette aile était une écurie. (fig. 4)

Il est important de constater que la méthode de construction des baraques du *castellum* de Maldegem-Vake ressemble à celle des *castella* du *Vallum Pii* (Robertson, Scott & Keppie 1975: 16-17). Dans les deux cas, des trous individuels ont été employés pour la fixation des poteaux. Pas seulement la profondeur et la largeur des trous, mais aussi l'intervalle entre deux poteaux sont identiques. Cela nous montre que cette méthode de construction, typique pour la période antonine (Davison 1989: 77-78), était encore en usage sous Marc-Aurèle.

Le grand soin apporté à l'approvisionnement en eau potable démontre une présence quasi certaine d'animaux dans le camp. Chaque baraque disposait de son propre puits. Pour la zone fouillée, dix puits ont été localisés, dont quatre furent examinés. Ils sont tous du même type, c'est-à-dire de plan carré, à quatre piliers d'angles et avec cuvelage en bois d'aulne (Thoen 1991: 190-192).

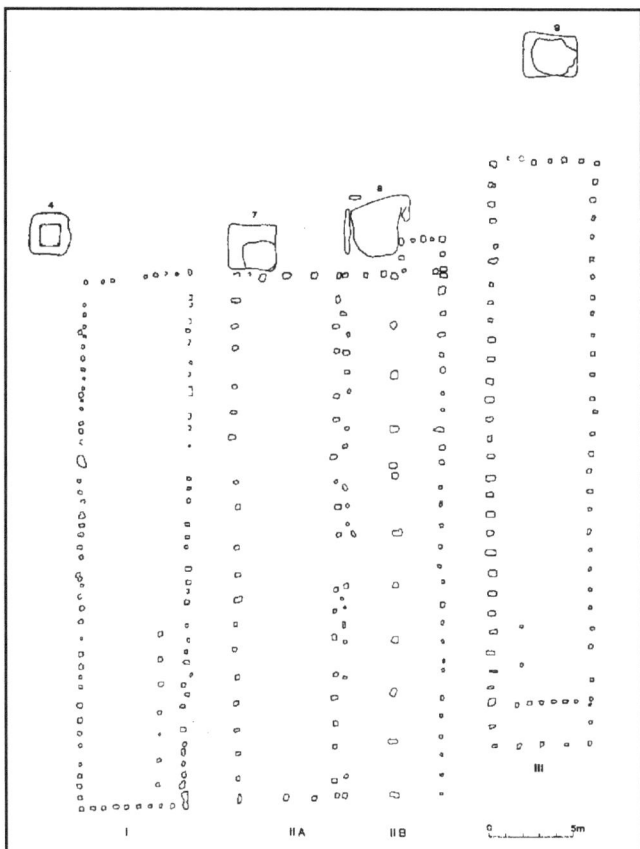

Figure 4. Les trois baraquements et leurs puits respectifs dans le secteur sud-est du camp (Thoen 1991: Figure 6).

Le caractère des constructions dans la partie centrale ainsi qu'au nord-est n'est pas tout à fait claire. Certains éléments plaident néanmoins pour la présence d'un bâtiment central administratif et d'un atelier situé dans le secteur nord-est du camp (Thoen 1991: 192).

2. LA DATATION

Deux monnaies sont d'une grande importance pour la datation du camp. Un sesterce de Marc-Aurèle frappé à Rome en 170/171 ap. J.C., nous fournit un *terminus post quem* pour la construction du camp. Cette monnaie fut retrouvée dans les sillons laissés par le passage de charrettes sur un chemin de terre aménagé pendant la construction du camp (Thoen 1988: 24). La monnaie la plus récente, également un sesterce de Marc-Aurèle, mais frappé en 171/172 ap. J.C., a été retrouvée dans le comblement d'un fossé défensif. Cette monnaie donne un *terminus post quem* pour l'abandon du camp.

Les données archéologiques et pédologiques révèlent d'ailleurs très manifestement le caractère temporaire du camp. L'examen des fossés défensifs (*fossae*) et du *titulum* démontre que le camp a connu deux périodes d'occupation de très courte durée (quelques saisons, quelques années au maximum). Pendant la période 1, les fossés ont été creusés lors d'un niveau étiage (automne); ce même hiver, les parois se sont ébréchées et les fossés se sont envasés. L'année suivante les fossés ont été recreusés. Pour éviter l'érosion, les parois ont été recouvertes de pierres et de mottes. Le fond des deux nouveaux fossés était moins profond que pendant la première période (Thoen 1996: 258). Lors du démantèlement du camp, les mottes couvrant le *vallum* ont été jetées dans les fossés. Les archéologues ont pu constater que les mottes n'étaient pas encore soudées, ce qui démontre que le camp n'a connu qu'une occupation de courte durée.

3. CONTEXTE HISTORIQUE ET IMPLANTATION STRATEGIQUE

Sur base de données historiques, la fortification peut être mise en corrélation avec les invasions des Chauques, mentionnées dans la *Vita* de Didius Julianus[1]. Les Chauques, une tribu germanique de marins habitant près de l'embouchure de l'Elbe, envahissaient la Gaule Belgique pendant les années 172-174 de notre ère. Avec leurs bateaux ils descendaient la Mer du Nord et la Manche et envahissaient le continent en pénétrant par des chenaux marins et des grandes rivières. De nombreuses traces d'incendie et de destruction attestent que les Chauques opéraient surtout dans une zone située entre la côte et la Somme. La Gaule Belgique devait se défendre au plus vite. Didius Iulianus, à ce moment gouverneur, prit l'opération en charge. Le long du littoral, il fit

---

[1]   "Après quoi il administra la Belgique, impeccablement et pendant assez longtemps. C'est là qu'il résista avec des troupes auxiliaires recrutées en hâte parmi les habitants de la province, aux Chauques, peuple de la Germanie qui habitait dans les environs de l'Elbe et qui fit des incursions inattendues et brutales. Pour cette raison le consulat lui fut attribué par autorité de l'empereur" (*Vita Didii Iuliani* I, 6-9).

construire des fortifications de défense (Thoen 1991: 193-198).

Maldegem-Vake était une de ces fortifications. Sa position démontre une implantation stratégique. Le camp se situe sur une des dernières buttes sablonneuses bordant la plaine maritime, à environ 1 km du ruiseau Ede (Thoen & Vandermoere 1985: 13). Ce ruisseau jaillit dans les collines tertiaires au sud de Maldegem, passe non loin du *castellum* de Maldegem et se dirige vers Aardenburg pour aller rejoindre un chenal de mer. Avec les *castella* d'Oudenburg et d'Aardenburg, également construits à la suite des invasions des Chauques, Maldegem-Vake faisait partie d'un système stratégique de blocage des chenaux maritimes, routes d'accès pour les incurseurs (Thoen 1991: 196-197; 1996: 268).

Les fortifications de Maldegem, Oudenburg et Aardenburg et d'autres fortins situés entre Aardenburg et Katwijk-Brittenburg (Hessing 1995: 97-99) constituent en faite une première ligne de défense côtière, précurseur du *Litus Saxonicum* du Bas-Empire.

4. LE CONTINGENT

En nous basant sur le plan, la superficie du camp et le plan des bâtiments, nous pouvons supposer que le camp était équipé par une unité mixte de soldats d'infanterie et de cavalerie (*cohors equitata*). En effet, la grande quantité de puits et la présence du double baraquement/écurie nous indiquent la présence de cavalerie. Pour en déterminer la force numérique et la proportion soldats/cavaliers, le camp devrait être examiné dans sa totalité. Dans l'état actuel des fouilles, nous ne pouvons savoir si le *castellum* abritait une *cohors quingenaria equitata* (608/488 individus) ou une *cohors milliaria equitata* (1056 individus) (Thoen 1991: 192-193).

Il est fort probable que l'unité stationnée à Maldegem était originaire de la Germanie. Pour cela nous nous basons sur l'origine de la munition, c'est-à-dire des cailloux destinés au lancement. L'examen pétrographique (R. Nijs, Institut Géologique de l'Université de Gand) prouve que ces projectiles proviennent d'un terrassement de la Meuse situé entre Maastricht et Liège. Il est très probable que l'unité venant de la Germanie ou de la *Civitas Tungrorum*, se ravitaillait en munition dans le bassin de la Meuse (Thoen 1996: 270).

5. L'APPROVISIONNEMENT

Vu la courte durée de l'occupation du site (172-174 ap. J.-C.), le matériel archéologique nous livre une référence unique pour l'archéologie romaine provinciale. Ici nous traitons du matériel retrouvé dans les fossés défensifs (*fossae*) et le *titulum* du secteur est[2]. Les trouvailles nous livrent une information importante concernant les

matériaux de construction, l'approvisionnement de la fortification et même le régime alimentaire du soldat. Pour compléter l'image, nous présentons quelques objets remarquables et le résultat des analyses scientifiques.

5.1. Les matériaux de construction

5.1.1. Le bois

Des morceaux de bois ont seulement été retrouvés dans l'*ankle breaker* du *titulum* de la première période. Notons des fragments de branches, mais aussi des fragments de poutres et de planches, des piquets et des éléments de toiture. La plupart de ces fragments sont en chêne et montrent des traces d'utilisation de la scie et de l'herminette.

Des analyses palynologiques nous révèlent que le paysage était presque totalement déboisé et mis en culture avant l'arrivée de l'armée romaine; les quelques arbres ont été abattus lors de la construction du camp. Le chêne et le bouleau ont été abattus dans la région sablonneuse avoisinante, tandis que l'aulne a été recherchée dans les terrains humides au nord du camp (De Ceunynck 1988: 31-36). Le chêne était utilisé pour la construction des baraques, des portes d'entrée et du système défensif, le bouleau et l'aulne pour des puits (Thoen 1996: 255).

5.1.2. Les tuiles

Quelques 193 fragments de tuiles (*tegulae* et *imbrices*) ont été comptés. Deux techniques différentes ont été observées et révèlent donc au moins deux ateliers. Selon toute probabilité, elles sont fabriquées en argile bartonienne. Cette argile tertiaire affleure sur la cuesta Oedelem-Zomergem, qui se situe à 5 kilomètres au sud du camp. Des analyses nous montrent que les constructions en torchis étaient bâties avec la même argile, probablement extraite à Kleit, hameau de Maldegem, à quelque 4 km vers le sud (Thoen 1991: 192).

5.1.3. La pierre

Nous avons reconnu du tuf volcanique de l'Eifel, du grès panisélien provenant de la région Aalter - Tielt, du grès micacé, quartzite et ferrugineux, de la pierre calcaire du Tournaisis et de l'ardoise des Ardennes. Le grès panisélien forme, avec 407 fragments, le groupe le plus important. Ce grès fut exploité pour l'aménagement routier à l'intérieur du camp. Des trois autres sortes de grès seulement 5 fragments ont été retrouvés; certains d'entre eux ont une surface polie et proviennent donc d'objets en pierre. Les fragments de pierre calcaire Tournaisienne (26 fragments) et de tuf volcanique de l'Eifel (12 fragments) proviennent probablement des substructions des bâtiments principaux. Enfin, il est probable que les ardoises, dont on a récupéré 67 fragments, ont été utilisées comme élément de toiture.

Notons que la grande masse de ces matériaux est d'origine locale. Les bâtisseurs ont d'ailleurs pu profiter du caractère morphologique diversifié de l'arrière-pays: sols sablonneux, affleurements tertiaires et plaine littorale. Les

---

[2] L'étude de ce matériel fut l'objet d'un mémoire de licence à l'Université de Gand, sous la direction du professeur H. Thoen (Dhaeze 2000).

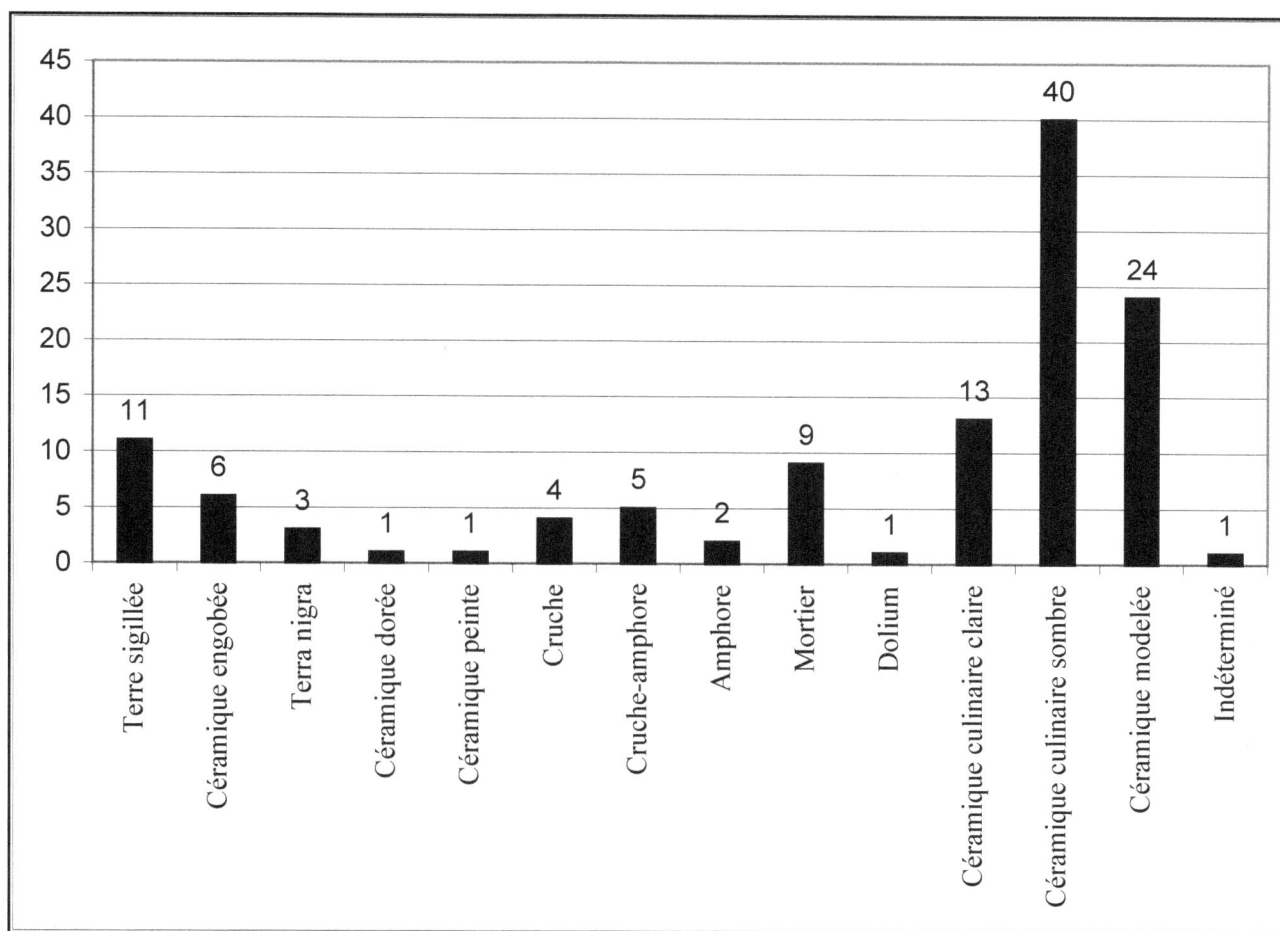

Figure 5. Histogramme des catégories céramiques au départ de leur valeur en NMI.

matériaux importés furent transportés en bateaux par les grandes axes 'internationaux'. Il est fort probable que les cargaisons de pierres étaient accompagnées d'autres produits comme des aliments, de la poterie, de la verrerie, etc.

5.2. Les objets

5.2.1. La poterie[3]

Sur un total de 1312 tessons, 121 exemplaires en NMI[4] ont été comptés. La céramique de luxe (sigillée, engobée, dorée et *terra nigra*) représente 22 individus. Les cruches, cruches-amphores et amphores sont assez mal représentées par 11 individus. On compte 9 mortiers. La rareté relative de *dolia* (1 individu) surprend. Il est d'ailleurs possible que d'autres types de jarre de stockage ont pris la place des *dolia* de type classique. Les catégories les plus abondantes sont la céramique culinaire sombre avec 40 individus et la céramique de tradition indigène avec 24 individus. Ces deux catégories dépassent 50 % du total et représentent des poteries à fonction culinaire, à savoir plats, jattes,

bouteilles, marmites, couvercles et jarres. Les céramiques communes sombres sont presque quatre fois plus nombreuses que les céramiques communes claires (13 individus). (fig. 5, 6 et 7)

La présence élevée de céramique de tradition indigène - faite à la main ou réalisée au tour lent - est remarquable. On compte 24 individus. Pour un site militaire ce chiffre paraît haut, mais ce pourcentage élevé s'explique facilement par le fait que les établissements ruraux régionaux fabriquaient cette céramique en masse pendant toute la période romaine (Vermeulen 1992a: 103-112, Vermeulen 1992b, Thoen & Hanut 2001).

Une forme en céramique modelée retient notre attention: il s'agit d'un type de bouteille modelée, caractérisée par une panse globulaire, un col court et large, un ressaut à la transition du col vers la panse, une lèvre simple évasée et une perforation circulaire d'environ 2 cm à hauteur de l'épaule. Sur la lèvre de la bouteille, exactement au prolongement de la perforation, se trouve une petite anse. Ces bouteilles ont un décor linéaire au peigne. Comme elles sont trop grandes pour être utilisées comme gourde, elles seraient plutôt utilisées comme jarre pour conserver l'un où l'autre liquide (fig. 7, n°s 1-2). Ce type de bouteille, mais dans une forme plus petite, nous est seulement connue à Douvres, dans le fortin de la *Classis Britannica* (Philp 1981: 243 et fig. 70).

---

[3]   Pour sa thèse de doctorat, F. Hanut a revu la poterie de cet assemblage (HANUT, F. & THOEN, H., avec la collaboration de DHAEZE, W., 2001).

[4]   Nombre Minimum d'Individus.

Les céramiques se caractérisent par leur origine diversifiée. Une grande quantité de céramique est de production locale (19,8 %) ou régionale (25,6 %). Cette dernière catégorie est surtout représentée par les vases tournés fabriqués probablement en argile rupélienne et provenant du Pays de Waes. Cette technique fut employée pour la fabrication de vases culinaires, de cruches, de cruches-amphores, de *dolia* et même de la *terra nigra*. Plus loin ont été recherchées des produits en pâte septentrionale (22,3 %). Elles sont originaires de la zone sablo-limoneuse (Nord de la France et Hainaut belge). Ces productions en pâte septentrionale sont surtout représentées par des céramiques à fonction

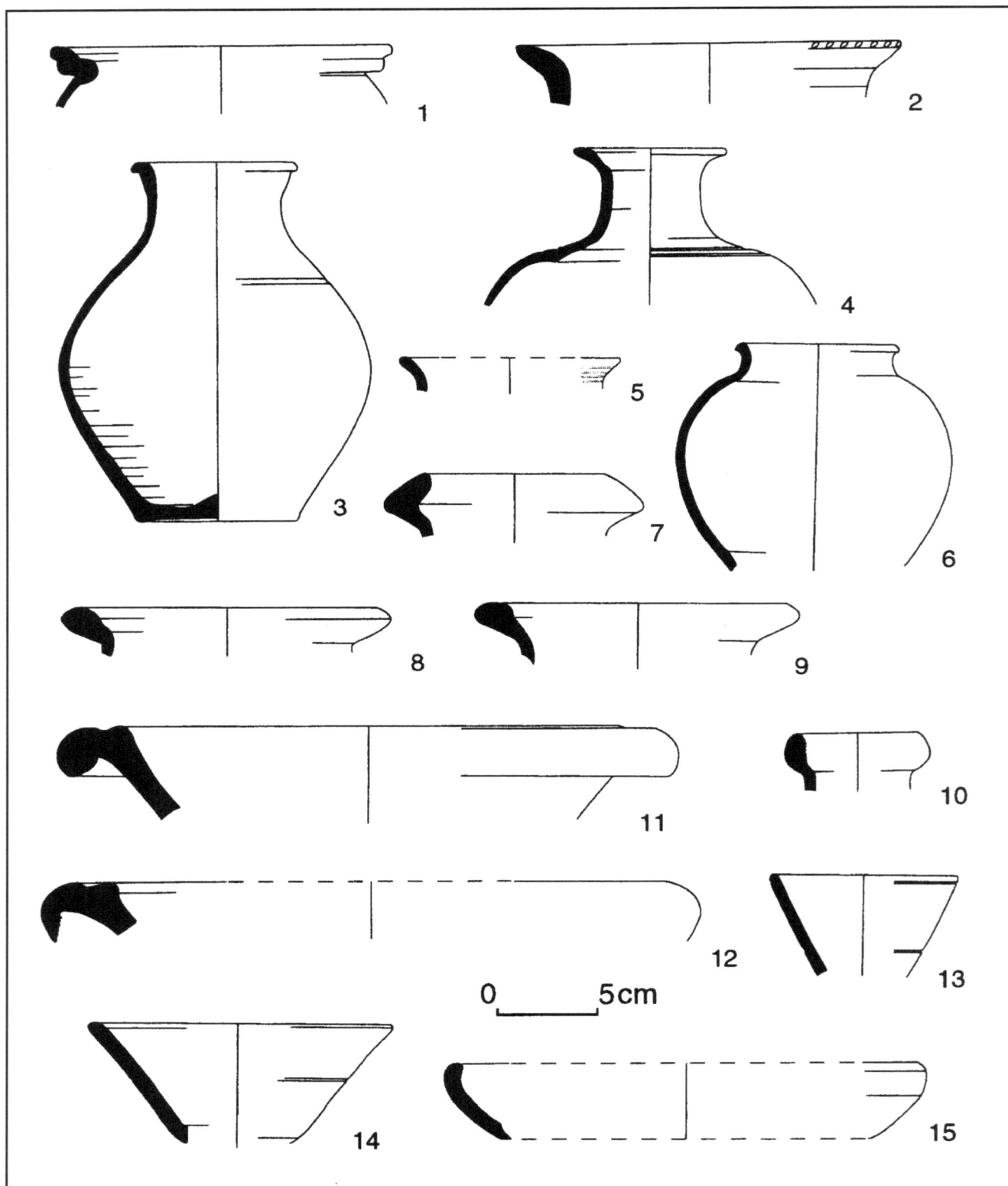

Figure 6. Sélection de céramique tournée provenant du système défensif (HANUT & THOEN 2001: Figure 9).

culinaire. Egalement de la région sablo-limoneuse proviennent les productions en pâte savonneuse, dont nous avons compté un gobelet en *terra nigra*, une cruche dorée, une cruche fine et un mortier.

Les importations provenant de régions plus éloignées sont assez nombreuses. De la région de la Meuse viennent des mortiers, des cruches et des cruches-amphores en pâte mosane. De Bavay ou ses environs proviennent des mortiers

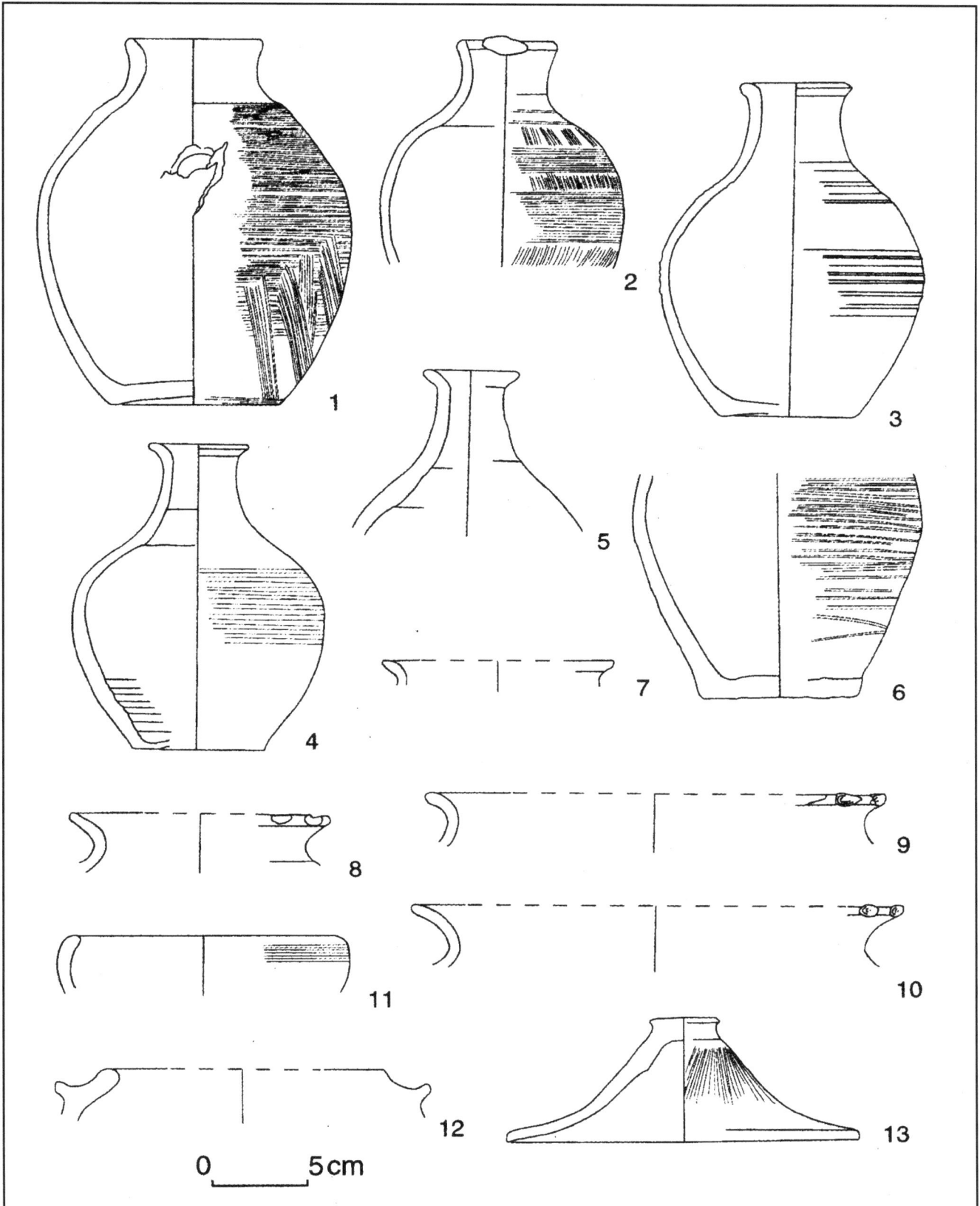

Figure 7. Sélection de céramique modelée provenant du système défensif (HANUT & THOEN 2001: Figure 8).

et des cruches, de la cité des Tongres des marmites et des couvercles en pâte riche en grosses inclusions blanc laiteux de quartz. La terre sigillée se partage entre productions du Centre de la Gaule et productions des ateliers de l'Est (Trèves et Rheinzabern). De Cologne et de la Rhénanie Inférieure viennent non seulement des céramiques engobées, mais aussi des cruches, des mortiers et des *dolia*. Des fragments d'amphores à vin Narbonnaise de type Gauloise 4 et d'amphores à huile Bétique de type Dressel 20 ont également été retrouvés. Toutes ces céramiques ont été importées par les grands axes commerciaux, fluviaux et marins, bien connus.

5.2.2. La verrerie

A l'exception d'une perle, tous les fragments peuvent être attribués aux bouteilles de types Isings 50 et 51. Ces deux types ont été utilisés pour le transport et le stockage de liquides.

5.2.3. Les métaux

On a compté 116 objets en fer et 1 en cuivre. Parmis les objets en fer nous avons déterminé un crochet, une petite lame, un chaînon, des clous de construction et des petits clous de sandales. Le seul objet en cuivre est une monnaie d'Hadrien; il s'agit d'un *as* frappé à Rome dans les années 132-138 ap. J.-C. Des scories de fer ont été dégagés dans le secteur nord-est du camp, là où l'on suppose l'existence d'une forge (Thoen 1991: 192).

5.2.4. Les objets en bois

Mentionnons également les quatre objets en bois trouvés dans les puits: une petite bêche en chêne, un marteau en chêne et deux objets assez remarquables, l'un des deux en chêne, l'autre en aulne; ils ont la forme d'une bobine (Vynckier 1993). Leur fonction n'est pas vraiment connue, mais il n'est pas exclu qu'ils ont servi à tendre des cordes.

5.2.5. La munition

Un grand nombre de cailloux destinés au lancement à la main (12 exemplaires complets et 5 fragmentaires) ont été retrouvé. Ces projectiles sont des cailloux de rivière, originaires d'un terrassement de la Meuse entre Maastricht et Liège (voir 4.) Les dimensions et les poids sont relativement uniformes. La plupart des cailloux ont une longueur entre 7,8 et 9,3 cm. Les cailloux, à l'exception d'un exemplaire de 0,810 kg, pèsent entre 0,10 et 0,49 kg, avec une prépondérance pour la catégorie 0,20-0,29 kg.

5.3. L'alimentation

Grâce aux analyses macrobotaniques (Bastiaens & Verbruggen 1995) nous avons obtenu quelques informations sur les produits végétaux faisant partie de la diète des soldats: du blé, de l'épeautre, *Triticum dicoccum*, de l'orge, des lentilles, des concombres, des noisettes, des noix, des mûres et des baies de sureau. L'avoine servait de fourrage pour les chevaux. Beaucoup de ces produits ont été livrés par les établissements ruraux de la région

sablonneuse. Par contre, le blé et l'épeautre venaient des sols limoneuses. Une autre étude mentionne encore la présence du seigle et du sarrasin (Groenman-van Waateringe 1993).

Bien que des restes d'animaux n'ont pas été retrouvés, on peut supposer que les soldats consommaient de la viande et des produits laitier du cheptel local. Le *garum* et probablement aussi du poisson faisaient également partie de la diète.

Les jarres nous fournissent des informations supplémentaires concernant la nourriture des soldats. Ils buvaient de la bière, transporté dans des cruches-amphores rouges (théorie de Van der Werff, Van Dierendonck & Thoen 1997), et du vin importé dans des amphores Gauloise 4. Des gobelets en céramique engobée et une cruche avec des traces de poissage, confirment la consommation de vin. L'huile d'olive d'Espagne méridionale (Dressel 20) n'était pas seulement utilisée dans la cuisine, mais servait également aux soins corporels et sans doute aussi comme combustible pour les lampes à huile. L'usage de mortiers montre entre autre la préparation de fromage blanc. La consommation de sel a été démontrée par la présence de fragments de containers fabriqués pour le transport de sel marin.

Authors' addresses

Wouter DHAEZE
Aspirant du Bijzonder Onderzoeksfonds (B.O.F.)
Département d'Archéologie, Université de Gand.
Blandijnberg 2, B-9000 Gent BELGIQUE

Hugo THOEN
Professeur en archéologie romaine provinciale
Département d'Archéologie, Université de Gand.
Blandijnberg 2, B-9000 Gent BELGIQUE

Frédéric HANUT
Aspirant du Fonds National de la Recherche Scientifique (F.N.R.S.).
Centre de Recherches d'Archéologie Nationale (UCL)
Avenue du Marathon 3
B-1348 Louvain-la-Neuve BELGIQUE

Bibliographie

BASTIAENS, J. & VERBRUGGEN, C., 1995, Archeobotanisch onderzoek van het Romeinse kamp van Maldegem-Vake (Oost-Vlaanderen, België). Macroresten van de opgravings-campagnes 1986 en 1987. *Handelingen der Maatschappij voor Geschiedenis en Oudheidkunde te Gent, Nieuwe reeks* - XLIX, p. 33-45.

DAVISON, D.P., 1989, *The barracks of the Roman army from the 1st to 3rd centuries AD. A comparative study of the barracks from fortresses, forts and fortlets with an analysis of building types and construction, stabling and garrisons*, Part i, (= BAR International Series 472(i)). Oxford.

DE CEUYNYNCK, R., 1988, Palynological investigation at the Roman fortified site of Maldegem (East-Flanders, Belgium). Dans THOEN, H., 1988, p. 31-36.

DHAEZE, W., 2000, *Het castellum van Maldegem-Vake. Studie van het verdedigingssyteem en de bevoorrading*. Universiteit Gent (mémoire de licence).

GROENMAN-VAN WAATERINGE, W., 1993, Palynological investigation of a Ditch fill at the Roman site of Maldegem. Dans *Archeologisch Jaarboek Gent 1992*. Gent, p. 163-167.

HANUT, F. & THOEN, H., avec la collaboration de DHAEZE, W., 2001, La céramique de tradition indigène dans le facies ménapien du Haut-Empire'. Dans *Sociéte Française d'Etudes de la Céramique Antique en Gaule, Actes du Congrès de Lille-Bavay*. Sous presse.

HESSING, W.A.M, 1995, Het Nederlandse kustgebied. Dans *De Romeinse Rijksgrens tussen Moezel en Noordzeekust*, édité par T. Bechert & W.J.H. Willems. Utrecht, p. 97-99.

JOHNSON, A., 1987 (übersetzt von SCHULTE-HOLTEY, G., bearbeitet von BAATZ, D.). *Römische Kastelle des 1. und 2. Jahrhunderts n. Chr. in Britannien und in den germanischen Provinzen des Römerreiches*, (= Kulturgeschichte der Antiken Welt 37), Mainz am Rhein.

PHILP, B., 1981, *The excavation of the Roman forts of the Classis Britannica at Dover 1970-1977*. Kent.

ROBERTSON, A., SCOTT, M. & KEPPIE, L., 1975, *Bar Hill: a Roman fort and its finds*, (= BAR British Series 16), Oxford.

THOEN, H., 1988, *The roman fortified site at Maldegem (East Flanders). 1986 Excavation Report*, (= Scholae Archaeologicae 9), Gent.

THOEN, H., 1991. Le camp romain de Maldegem (Flandre Orientale, Belgique) et les invasions des Chauques en 172-174 de notre ère. Dans *Studia Archaeologica. Liber Amicorum Jacques A.E. Nenquin*, édité par H. Thoen, J. Bourgeois, F. Vermeulen & P. Crombé. Gent, p. 185-200.

THOEN, H., 1996, Nieuw licht op onze Romeinse geschiedenis. Het Romeinse kamp van Maldegem-Vake. *Heemkundige Kring 'Het Ambacht Maldegem'. Jaarboek 1996*, p. 253-274.

THOEN, H., 1998, Le camp romain de Maldegem (Flandre orientale, Belgique) et son contexte régional'. Dans *Archéologie du Littoral Manche – Mer du Nord. I. Des origines à l'époque gallo-romaine*, (= Bulletin historique et artistique du Calaisis. Les Amis du Vieux Calais, 160-161-162), édité par S. Curveiller & C. Seillier. Calais, p. 519-530.

THOEN, H. & HANUT, F., 2001. Un lot de céramiques modelées dans une fosse-dépotoir d'époque Trajane à Destelbergen (Belgique, Flandre orientale). Dans *Belgian Archaeology in a European setting II*, (= Acta Archaeologia Lovaniensia Monographiae 13), edited by M. Lodewijckx. Leuven, p. 185-195.

THOEN, H. & VANDERMOERE, N., 1985, *The Roman fortified Site at Maldegem (East Flanders). 1984 Excavation Report*, (= Scholae Archaeologicae 2), Gent.

VAN DER WERFF, J.H., THOEN, H. & VAN DIERENDONCK R.M., 1997, Amphora Production in the Lower Scheldt Valley (Belgium)?. *Rei Cretariae Romanae Fautorum Acta*, 35, p. 63-71.

VERMEULEN, F., 1992a, Céramique non tournée du haut et du bas-empire en Flandre sablonneuse (Belgique). Dans *Sociéte Française d'Etudes de la Céramique Antique en Gaule. Actes du Congrès de Tournai 28-31 mai*, édité par L. Rivet, p. 279-289.

VERMEULEN F., 1992b. *Tussen Leie en Schelde. Archeologische inventaris en studie van de Romeinse bewoning in het zuiden van de Vlaamse Zandstreek*, (= Archeologische Inventaris Vlaanderen, Buitengewone reeks 1), Gent.

VYNCKIER, J., 1993. Note on the treatment of some waterlogged wooden objects from the Roman camp excavation at Maldegem. In *Archeologisch Jaarboek Gent 1992*. Gent, p. 181-185.

LA FRONTIERE LINGUISTIQUE : NOUVELLES PROPOSITIONS (REGION NORD-PAS-DE-CALAIS)

Pierre LEMAN

Résumé : Grâce à des découvertes archéologiques nombreuses et précises, il est possible de reconsidérer la question de la frontière linguistique. Celle-ci correspondrait, au plus tard au premier siècle à une ligne Boulogne-Bavay. Cette limite est celle aussi de deux zones différentes de romanisation, plus dense au Sud qu'au Nord. Ces différences ont été amplifiées par les implantations militaires du IVè s. puis par les grandes invasions postérieures au Vè s. La position de cette limite s'expliquerait par l'extrême ligne d'avancée des peuples germaniques, tout à fait parallèle au Rhin.

Abstract: Thanks to many and precise archaeological discoveries, it is possible to think differently about linguistic frontier. At the beginning of the 1st century, at the latest, this frontier corresponded to a line Boulogne-Bavay. In the north, romanisation is more important than in the south. These differences have been amplified by the military establishments of the fourth century and by large invasions coming after the fifth century. This frontier could be due to the position of the Germanic People, parallel to the Rhine.

La parution récente de quelques articles et ouvrages à propos de la frontière linguistique en Belgique et dans l'est de la France, l'accroissement considérable des découvertes archéologiques relatives au Bas Empire et au Haut Moyen-Age nous ont incité à aborder quelques aspects de cet épineux problème dans un secteur limité, la région Nord-Pas-de-Calais.

Depuis l'étude de J. Stengers (Stengers 1959), nous devons à A. Joris (Joris, 1967) une présentation particulièrement claire de l'historiographie de la question linguistique. Mais, outre cette qualité, l'auteur a le mérite de proposer une esquisse d'explication particulièrement intéressante à propos de laquelle nous reviendrons. Paul A. Piemont (Piemont 1981) y fait allusion dans son livre *L'origine des frontières linguistiques en Occident*. Enfin, dernier paru, l'ouvrage de nos collègues Danny Lamarcq et Marc Rogge (Lamarcq & Rogge, 1996), fait état de nouvelles propositions à la fois archéologiques et linguistiques. Ces deux auteurs ont bénéficié de la contribution importante de Luc Van Durme. Très récemment, J. Devleeschouwer (Devleeschouwer, 2000), de son côté, étudie la frontière linguistique par une approche qu'il a mise au point depuis une vingtaine d'années, celle des doublets toponymiques. Plus éloignée du champ géographique de notre enquête, l'ouvrage de Patrick Galliou et Michael Jones (Galliou & Jones, 1993), nous semble devoir être cité pour ses arguments proches des nôtres, de même que celui d'Alain Simmer (1998). Pour ces chercheurs, à la fois archéologues et linguistes, il semble impossible d'attribuer aux seules invasions des V et VIè s., les causes des phénomènes linguistiques dans la Gaule de l'est et de l'ouest.

Du côté des textes, on a tiré tout ce qu'on a pu à la fois à propos des implantations de peuples nouveaux que sur les destructions des villes romaines. Il faut donc se tourner vers les archéologues afin qu'ils nous disent quels sont les « marqueurs » matériels du peuplement germanique, et refaire la même démarche vers les toponymistes pour nous dresser la cartographie avec datation, des parlers germaniques dans les *civitates* des Morins, Ménapiens et Nerviens.

Au début de sa campagne, César rapporte les propos de deux chefs du peuple rème, selon lesquels les Belges sont, pour la plupart, d'origine germanique (*Plerosque Belgas esse ortos ab Germanis*) (B.G. II, 4, 1). Nous sommes en 57, après la victoire des Romains contre les guerriers d'Arioviste. César entre alors dans un pays inconnu, du moins à propos duquel les géographes antiques et Posidonios n'ont pas laissé de description. Le renseignement livré au général romain a donc une connotation militaire : les combats seront rudes car les Germains sont des guerriers redoutables. De plus, leurs mœurs sont différentes des Celtes et chez eux, il n'y a pas d'*oppidum* et on y sacrifie peu.

S'il est difficile de trouver les preuves archéologiques des spécificités qui relèvent des habitudes de vie (par exemple les arts de la table, les traditions culinaires, les rituels de la naissance, du mariage et de la mort), il est maintenant possible de trouver dans le sol des traces d'une certaine « germanité » : absence d'*oppida* édifiés avant la conquête, rareté des sanctuaires avec sacrifices humains.

La prise en compte géographique de ces éléments aboutit à une frontière grossièrement établie d'est en ouest de Bavay à Thérouanne-Boulogne. Au nord, pas d'oppida laténiens, ni de sanctuaires avec traces de sacrifices humains. Avec toute la prudence rendue nécessaire par les dangers de l'argumentation *a silentio*, il convient de remarquer cependant que cette frontière est celle aussi d'une autre réalité archéologique. Depuis la multiplication des fouilles de sauvetage effectuées sur de vastes surfaces et surtout le long de structures linéaires comme le T.G.V. ou les tracés d'autoroute, il apparaît que cette limite est aussi une frontière délimitant deux zones : au nord, les découvertes de céramique non tournée, de tradition indigène, repérée dans des gisements d'époque romaine, sont plus fréquentes qu'au sud de cette ligne Bavay-Thérouanne. Ainsi, à

Pitgam la fouille de 350 structures à l'emplacement d'une station de compression de gaz a mis au jour un lot considérable de céramiques dont 85 % non tournées (Lemaire 1977). Par ailleurs, semblable constat peut être dressé en ce qui concerne la densité des découvertes d'éléments épigraphiés, de vestiges de mosaïques qui, à des titres divers, sont des éléments marqueurs de la civilisation romaine : densité faible au Nord, plus importante au sud. L'archéologue belge, R. De Mayer (1937) avait déjà amorcé ce débat mais en se fondant sur la répartition des *villae*. Nous avons donc la conviction qu'existaient dans le nord des populations aux mœurs et aux pratiques spécifiques, précisément là où apparaissent des traces évidentes de toponymie germanique et ce, dès le début de notre ère. On peut alors se demander si la remarque relevée par César selon laquelle une partie des Belges était d'origine germanique ne fait pas allusion au fait que ces Belges différents par leur origine, leur mode de vie étaient aussi différents par leur langue. L'implantation de groupes de Lètes pour la défense des points fortifiés, de fédérés pour la mise en culture des terres abandonnées au IVè s. n'aurait fait que renforcer cette germanisation. Mais reste le problème toujours intrigant de l'emplacement de la frontière linguistique proprement dite.

LE PROBLÈME DE LA FRONTIÈRE LINGUISTIQUE

Cette limite suit un tracé d'est en ouest puis vers la Suisse, qui ne tient aucun compte ni du relief ni du réseau hydrographique. Plusieurs explications ont été proposées : route fortifiée de Bavay à Cologne, Forêt charbonnière, et la dernière en date, la route romaine Cassel-Tongres. De ces deux villes, partent en effet des éléments de voie bien attestés qui passent par l'important *vicus* de Velzeke. Mais depuis cette agglomération jusqu'aux environs de Cassel, la réalité de cette voie n'a pas été prouvée (peut-être s'agit-il d'une route non terminée, dont il ne resterait que les secteurs de départs, l'un à l'est, l'autre à l'oust, la partie médiane jamais réalisée). Peut-être faut-il se rallier tout simplement à la proposition de bon sens de Lucien Musset (Musset 1994) selon laquelle la limite linguistique serait la ligne extrême d'une certaine poussée germanique depuis le Rhin, telle l'ultime avancée de la marée haute sur la plage (avec une exception cependant pour la zone Boulogne-Montreuil où la colonisation saxonne venue de la mer a compliqué les choses). En reprenant cette image, mais pour le début de notre ère, ce mouvement de peuple depuis le Rhin dont César a donné quelques échos, s'inscrirait dans l'histoire d'une série de vastes migrations, avec un renforcement avec les implantations du IVè s. puis les invasions du Vè s. Mais de celles-ci, quel est l'impact réel ?

LE CAS DES INVASIONS FRANQUES

Nous savons que l'hiver 406-407 a vu le déferlement de vagues germaniques et que vers 446, des bandes germaniques sont établies dans le nord de la France comme l'atteste le récit de l'affaire du *vicus Helena*. Deux siècles plus tard encore, dans le jeune diocèse de Thérouanne,

l'évêque Omer est capable de prêcher en langue germanique à ses ouailles qui n'entendent pas le roman. Depuis une vingtaine d'années, l'archéologie mérovingienne a fait des progrès considérables, et il est possible maintenant de repérer les éléments marqueurs de l'avancée franque, tant au niveau des modes de sépultures (incinérations, tumulus), des armes (angons) et des bijoux. Or, la densité des sépultures repérées avec ces marqueurs, leur répartition est indépendante de la frontière linguistique. Leur report sur la carte coïncide surtout avec les données des textes à propos de l'avancée des Francs au Vè s. depuis Tournai, comme l'a montré Patrick Perrin (Perrin, 1998).

CONCLUSION

Nous sommes conscients que ce discours pêche par excès de généralisation et de simplification mais le traitement d'un détail de notre enquête aurait à lui seul demandé tout l'espace qui nous fut accordé. Nous avons simplement donné un état rapide de la question, étayé par d'indispensables références bibliographiques, tout en insistant sur le traitement le plus en amont possible de la question linguistique, en sollicitant à la fois les données archéologiques pour la période du Ier siècle, sous-tendues par le recours obligatoire au texte de César.

A l'époque de celui-ci, existait déjà, selon nous, une frontière linguistique bien en deçà du Rhin, mais selon une limite parallèle au fleuve, extrême avancée d'une immigration germanique, et perceptible par le relevé de certains indices archéologiques. D'autres documents de cette nature ont permis également aux chercheurs de bien repérer la progression des armées franques du Vè et VIè s., tout à fait conforme aux textes, mais indépendante de la frontière linguistique. Par ailleurs, au nord de celle-ci, les implantations germaniques pour raisons militaires au IVè s. ont renforcé encore les différences linguistiques, en préambule aux mouvements du Haut Moyen Age pour lesquels nous ne savons pas grand chose. De toute façon, et dès le début de notre ère, cette question n'a guère troublé les dirigeants de ces pays où le bilinguisme était naturellement acquis, élément qu'il ne faut pas également perdre de vue.

Adresse de l'auteur

Pierre LEMAN
3, rue du Marais
F 59152 Tressin France

Bibliographie

CESAR, *Guerre des Gaules*, trad. L. A. CONSTANS, 1929

DEVLEESCHOUWER, J., 2000, Les doublets toponymiques en Belgique romane et dans la région française du Nord, *Bulletin de la Commission royale de toponymie et de dialectologie*, 72, p. 103-116.

GALLIOU, P. & JONES, M., 1993, *Les anciens Bretons. Des origines au XVè s.*, Paris

JORIS, A., 1967, *Du Vè au milieu du VIIIè siècle*, Bruxelles

LAMARCQ, D. & ROGGE, M., 1996, *De taalgrens van de oude tot de nieuwe Belgen*, Leuven

PIEMONT, P. –A., 1981, *L'origine des frontières linguistiques en Occident*, Strasbourg

LEMAIRE, F., 1997, Pitgam, *Bilan scientifique, Service régional de l'archéologie Nord-Pas-de-Calais*, p. 55-56

MAEYER, R. DE, 1937, *De romeinsche villa's in Belgie*, Gand

MUSSET, L., 1994, *Les invasions: les vagues germaniques*, Paris

PERRIN, P., 1998, La progression des Francs en Gaule du Nord, *Cahiers archéologiques*, p. 5-16

SIMMER, A., 1998, *L'origine de la frontière linguistique en Lorraine. La fin des mythes ?* Knutange

STENGERS, J., 1959, *La formation de la frontière linguistique en Belgique ou de la légitimité de l'hypothèse historique*, Wetteren

VAN DURME, L., 1983, De vroege Germaans-Romanse taalgrens in België en Noord-Frankrijk, *Handelingen van de Koninklijke Commissie voor Toponymie en Dialectologie*, 57, p. 189-247

THREE ETRUSCAN TREPHINNED SKULLS BELONGING TO THE VII-IV CENTURY B.C. FROM SOUTHERN ETRURIA

G. BAGGIERI & M. DI GIACOMO

Abstract: There are three cases coming from the area of Southern Etruria. We present two cases of probable cranial trephination, and a third case which is still in research. They are the only trephinned Etruscan skulls coming from this area. They represent excellent evidence of the neurosurgical practice, and are in direct continuity with the cranial trephinations belonging to the Neolithic Age and the Last Bronze Age, in this area. The interest for these trephinations leads us to the medical context that begins to appear between the VII and the VI century B.C. In fact two of the skulls belong to the VII century, and the third to the VI century. The skulls were found in Vulci, Tarquinia, and in the necropolis of Ferrone. The skulls belong to adult subjects of two males and a female; they show cranial lesions that present a survival between six months and less than one month. The techniques used for the trephinations probably are the incision, the chisel, and the curette techniques.

PREFACE

Les professeurs Germana et Fornaciari, mes illustres collègues et grands spécialistes d'anatomie pathologique, dans la première page de leur ouvrage « Trépanations, craniotomies et traumatismes crâniens en Italie » précisent : « Chaque perte de substance osseuse provoquée, intentionnellement, sur le neurocrâne soit des vivants soit des morts, est communément appelée trépanation indépendamment de l'instrument et du but pour la quel a été fait ».

Cet utile précision doit être pris en considération chaque fois on analyse lésions de tel gendre.

Les crânes objet de cet étude présentent tous les deux des altérations sur le plateau osseux du calvaire avec perte de substance osseuse, portantes les traces d'un traitement manuel *intra vitam* que font supposer à des techniques de trépanation et de pansement. Les crânes appartenant à des personnes de sexe masculin, proviennent de l'ancienne Etrurie Méridionale, un emplacement à environs 100 Km au nord de Rome. Ces pièces, avec un troisième crâne trépané de sexe féminin qui est actuellement encore en phase d'étude, représentent les plus originaux et anciens témoignages de la chirurgie neurocranienne qui se remmènent à des lieux vécus par le peuple étrusque en appartenant à un' époque datable entre le VII et IV siècle avant Christ.

LE CRÂNE DE OSTERIA-VULCI

INTRODUCTION

La première pièce anthropologique qu'on analysera ici vient d' un tombeau à dé déterré en 1986 dans la nécropole de Osteria , village dans les environs de Vulci, sous la direction de Madame A. M. Moretti pour le Bureau Archéologique de l ' Etrurie Méridionale. Le tombeau, que lors du percement présentait signes évidents de viols, est datable à la deuxième moitié du VIéme siècle avant Christ. La trousse funéraire présentait seulement un calice en bucchero, fragments d'un kantharos et d'un oinochoe en bucchero, morceaux d'une lance en fer. Etendu sur un des lits de la deuxième chambre du tombeau se trouvait le squelette d'un homme adulte dont son crâne, qui représente l'objecte ce travail de recherche, montrait signes de perte d'os.

LA PIECE ANTROPOLOGIQUE

Le crâne, constitué par la calotte crânienne et par la mandibule est presque complet. Il manque la squame de l ' occipital, dont il reste seulement un parti derrière la suture pariétale et temporale de droite, les processus zygomatiques des deux régions temporaux, le condyle mandibulaire gauche.

La mandibule est complète des dents, alors que l'os maxillaire met en évidence l'absence du troisième molaire gauche dû probablement à perte *intra vitam* (l'alvéole correspondent, même si ouvert, présente signes évidents de réorganisation vers la clôture, pendant que le canine a été perdu post mortem).

Dans l'ensemble, l'état de la denture apparaît bon, sauf 5 dents sur 30 que présentait légères stries d'hypoplasie sur l'émail.

L'état de conservation de la pièce est excellent sauf que tant la calotte crânienne que la mandibule ont la cortical assez abrasées.

Le crâne appartient à un homme probablement mort à un âge datable depuis le niveau d'usure dentaire entre 25 et 35 ans. Pourtant selon le niveau d'oblitération des sutures crâniennes l'âge est estimable à 39 ans depuis le système de la voûte et à 41 depuis le système latéral.

Dans la suture pariéto-occipitale droite il y a un osselet wormien (astérion) situé à environ 1cm de distance de la suture pariéto-occipito-temporale. La présence éventuelle sur le côté gauche d'un osselet homologue n'est pas vérifiable à cause de la perte de la portion d'os pariétal coïncident avec la suture pariéto-occipitale.

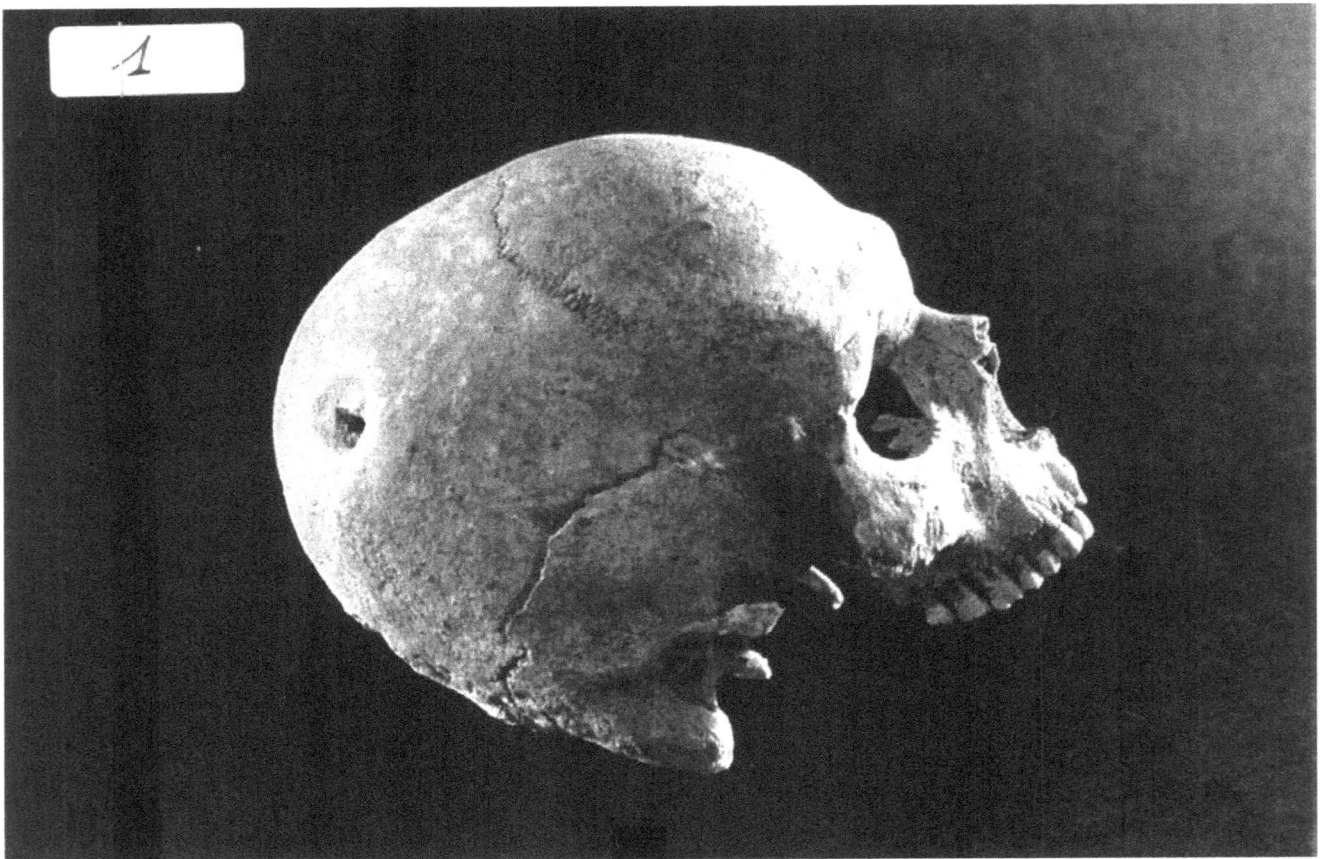

Figure 1. Vulci cranium, lateral profile.

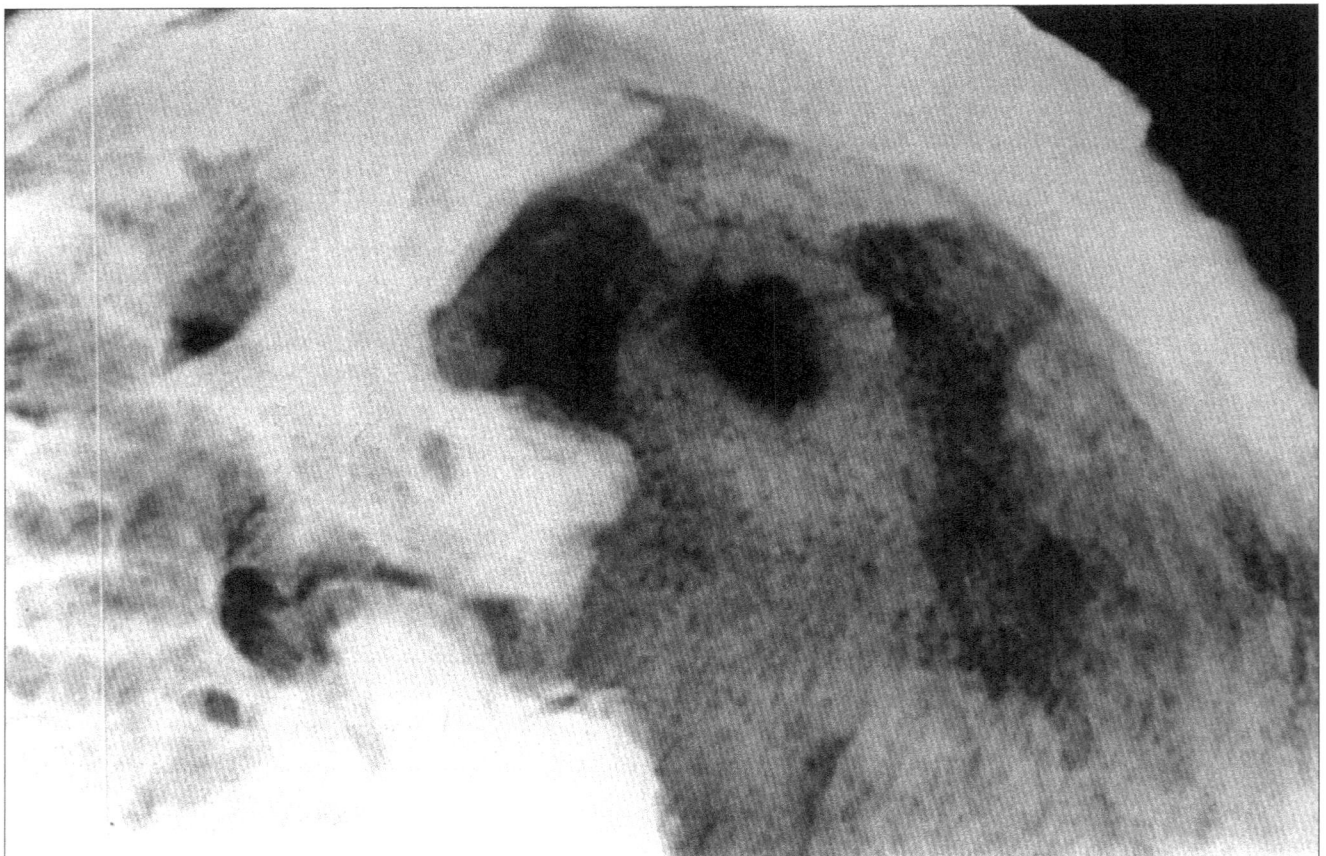

Figure 2. Vulci cranium, X-ray. Detail of the cranial trephination, significant thickening of the bone.

LA LESION

Sur le pariétal droit, juste au-dessus de la bosse, il y a une lésion continue de forme grosso modo elliptique dont son axe le plus long est légèrement oblique dans le sens du derrière gauche vers l'antérieur droit.

La lésion continue mesure 10 x 8 mm et présente une zone enfoncée de 23 x 21 mm.

Les marges du trou sont obliques, non escarpées, et présentent des petits spicules osseux de réparation. La diploe est oblitéré par cicatrisation et la conformation de la lésion est rendue irrégulière par la présence d'un éclat d'os renforcé qui ferme partiellement l'ouverture.

Á l'examen radiographique la lésion est apparue encerclé d'une bordure sclérosée.

INTERPRETATION

Rebus sic stantibus la lésion doit être considérée une trépanation effectuée sur le vivant avec une technique dite de raclage. La partie à racler venait abrasée jusqu'à la perforation totale avec mouvements giratoires ou directionnels en utilisant un instrument doué d'une superficie plate abrasive. Ce fait explique tant la forme ellipsoïdale de la trépanation que la présence de la zone enfoncée autour du trou.

Il faut souligner la présence sur la pièce d'une partie d'os que ferme partiellement la lésion et représente probablement le résultat de la réparation d'un éclat produit pendant la trépanation.

Pour l'instant on a préfère laisser prudemment cette partie d'os à sa place vu que il appaire recollée parfaitement. Á la trépanation fit suite une survivance plutôt prolongée (au moins un an).

LE CRÂNE TRÉPANÉ ÉTRUSQUE DE LA DONATION « BARUCCI » DE TARQUINIA

INTRODUCTION

On peut comparer le crâne trépané de Osteria à celui dit « Barucci » que représente l'objet de cet deuxième cas de trépanation.

LA PIECE ANTROPOLOGIQUE

Il s'agit d'un crâne avec mandibule et du sarcophage qui le contenait donné par la famille Barucci lors d'une donation de pièces archéologiques exceptionnelles.

Cette pièce, probablement moins importante du sarcophage en péperin, est restée pour quelques dizaines d'années au Musée National Etrusque de Tarquinia. Le crâne avec la mandibule présente des traits que nous font supposer une origine remontant grosso modo au IV siècle avant Christ. On ne connaît pas exactement le lieu original de cette sépulture mais on peut croire qu'il

s'agit d'un enterrement de l'ancienne nécropole étrusque de Monterozzi, dans les environs de Tarquinia. La petite ville de Tarquinia se trouve au centre de l'Italie sur le versant de la mer Tyrrhénien et a été déjà depuis l'époque orientalisant une ville étrusque important au point de vue commercial. Tarquinia et les autres villages à l'intérieur de la côte représentent avec ses sites archéologiques un des lieux les plus importants pour l'histoire étrusque.

La mâchoire présente cinq molaires (16-17-26-27-28) avec respectivement niveau d'usure dentaire (4+), (4), (5+), (5), (3) selon Brotwell ; sur la mandibule restent quatre dents (45-46-36-38) avec niveau d'usure en moyenne (5+). Les alvéoles libres ne présentent lésions dues à lésions ou inflammations. D'après ces observations on peut supposer un décès compris entre 35-45 ans.

LA LESION

La suture sagittale montre un fluage que si observée par derrière coïncide avec le côté droit de la trépanation qu'a forme quasi parfaitement pentagonale.

La cavité s'étende sur l'os pariétal d'une longueur de 2,7 cm sur le diamètre majeure et d'une longueur de 2,3 cm et 2,4 cm sur les plus petits.

Les marges de la trépanation sont légèrement arrondies et repliées à l'intérieur de l'ouverture.

La pièce, vu avec une microscopie optique de 28 lentilles grossissantes, montre réactions osteofitiques semblables aux dents d'une scie. Toujours à la microscopie on observe une obliquité de 2 mm entre la superficie esocrânienne et la superficie endocrânienne que nous autorise à estimer que il y a été un réaction précédente de l'os. La bordure et les angles intérieurs du crâne sont tous arrondis. Aux rayons X on observe une réaction osseuse compacte et limitée.

INTERPRETATION

La zone de l'ouverture derrière la suture, la forme géométrique, la réactivité aux marges de l'os et l'analyse aux rayons X nous poussent à retenir qu'on est en présence d'une trépanation crânienne avec une survie du patient assez modeste : pas plus d'un mois.

La forme géométrique de la lésion indique qu'il a été probablement une trépanation avec la technique du prélèvement à cheville : localisées des points à perforer ils ont été unis avec des incisions déchaussant la cheville. (Campillo *).Toutefois on doit souligner qu'on reste ici dans le champ des hypothèses parce que dans toutes les trépanations antiques il reste fondamental montrer l'intervention de la main humaine. Même si on fuisse en présence seulement d'un intervention de médication pour un trauma il reste selon moi la définition de trépanation crânienne des professeurs Germana et Fornaciari.

CONSIDERATIONS ET HYPOTHESES D'ETUDE

Sur les motivations de ces trépanations provoquées soit par des pathologies intracrâniennes ou extracrâniennes, soit par

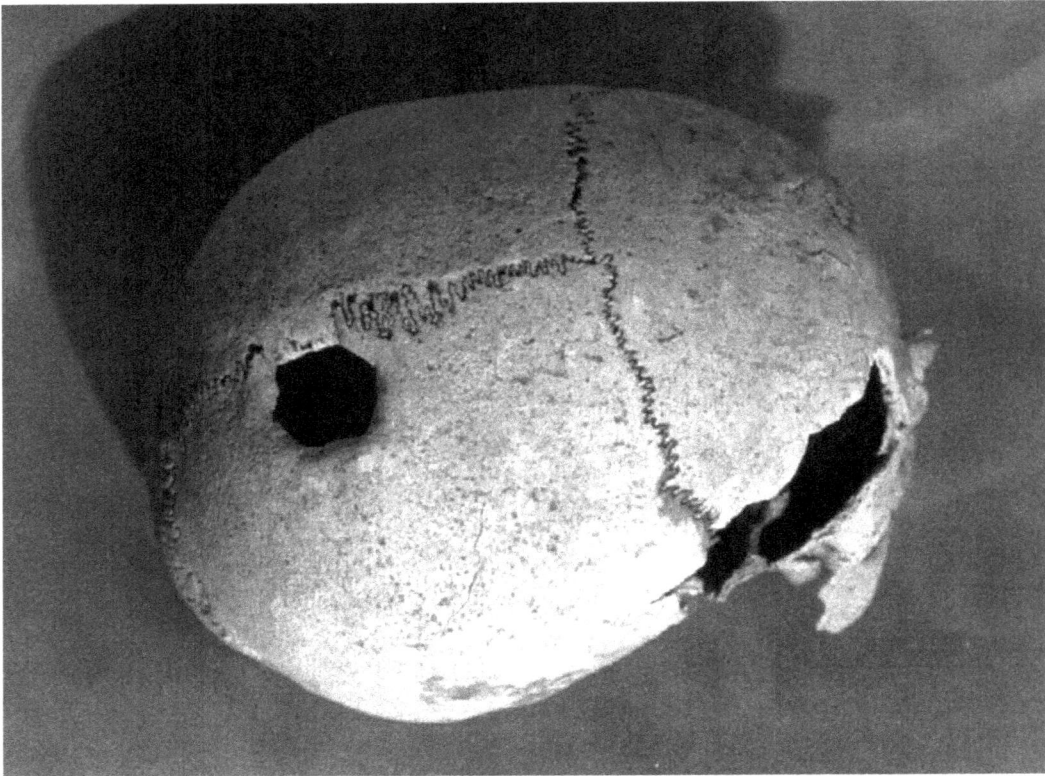

Figure 3. Barucci cranium, superior profile.

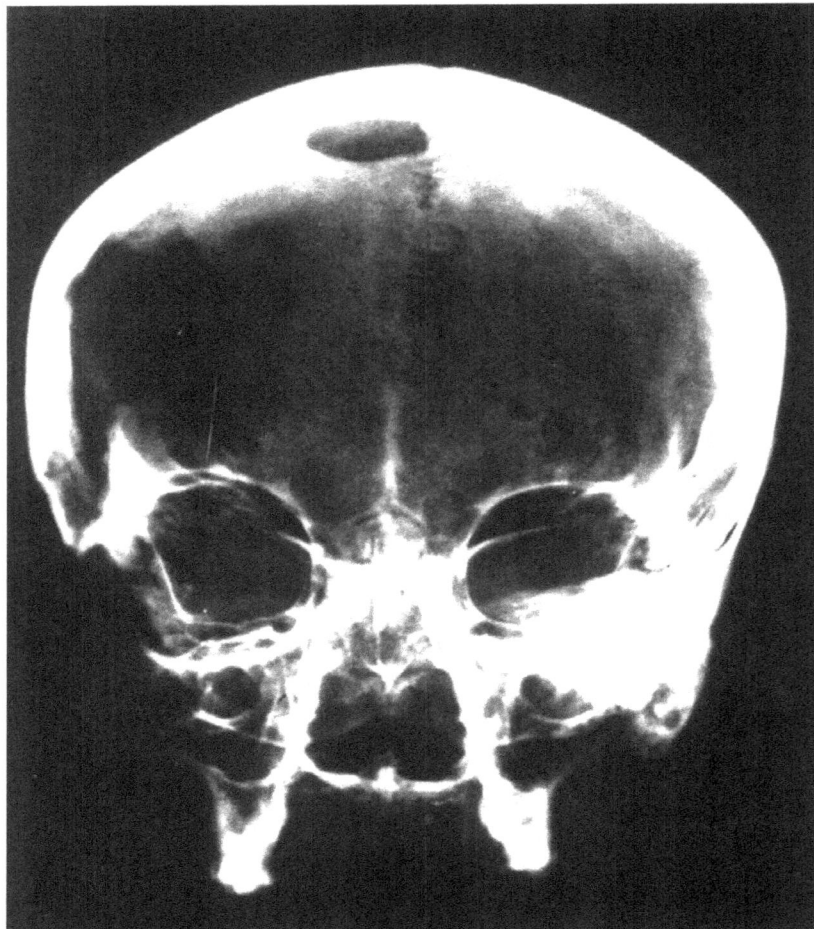

Figure 4. Barucci cranium, X-ray. Detail of the foramen of the cranial trephination.

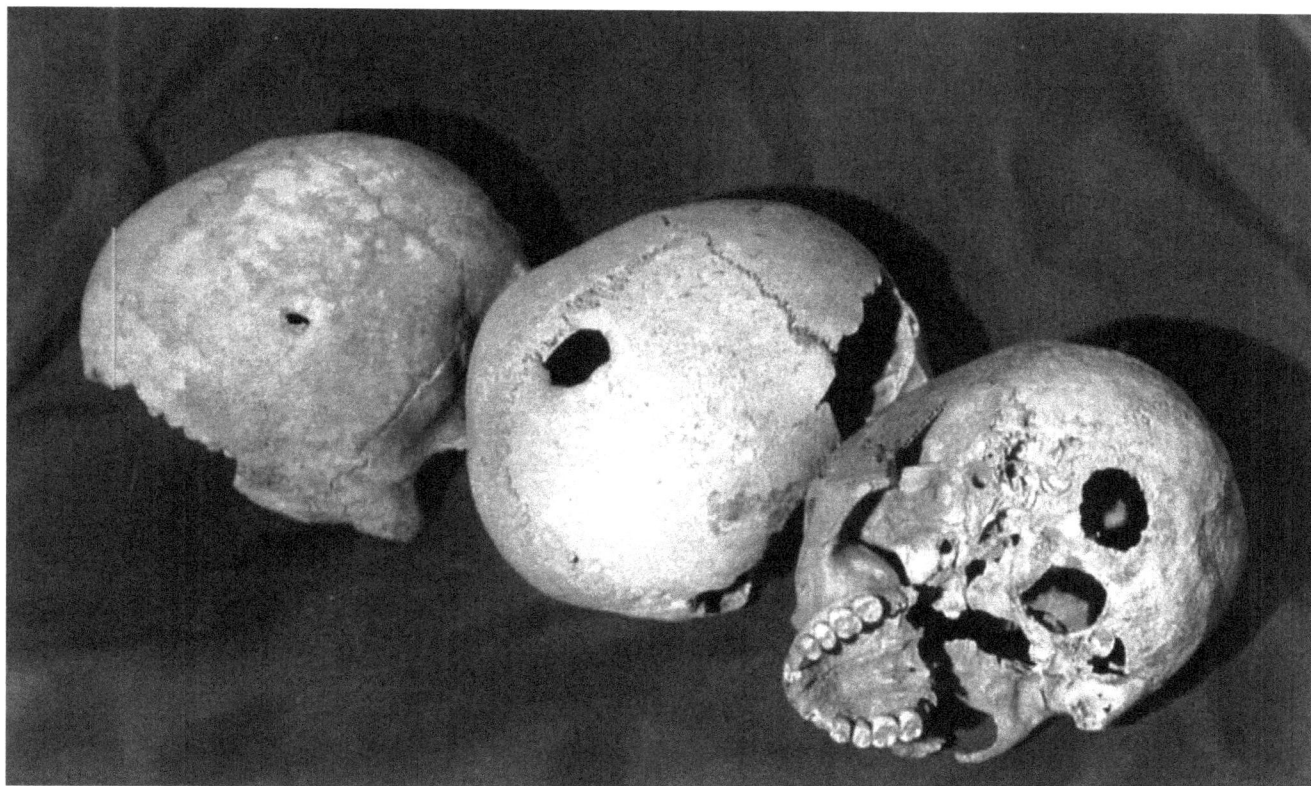

Figure 5. The three Etruscan crania, with the Ferrone cranium whose foramen is close to the formane occipitalis.

des traumas, ce que est important de vérifier est si l'intervention de l'homme a été justifié par soin physique médicale ou par rites théurgiques sacrés.

Dans les trépanations qu'on a analysé ici on doit estimer d'être en présence d'évidentes soins médicales : une hypothèse validé par plusieurs témoignages d'une école médicale étrusque que semble-t-il avoir eu un intense activité dans les environs de la découverte de la pièce anthropologique. En effet ont été trouvé importantes traces de thérapies dentaires et une jolie collection de pièces archéologiques que représentent parfaitement : des organes internes du corps, des instruments de chirurgie et de cosmétologie.

LE CRÂNE DE « FERRONE » (TOLFA)

Récemment ont été découverts des ultérieurs crânes que sont encore à l'étude. Par exemple dans la nécropole de Ferrone, site archéologique dans les environs de Tolfa, un outre crâne étrusque montre probables témoignages de trépanation crânienne. Cet troisième crâne a été trouvé, avec sis outres individus, dans un tombeau à chambre du VIIéme siècle avant Christ. Le crâne appartiens à une femme de sexe féminin mort probablement à l'age de 20/ 30 ans et présente une lésion circulaire sur l'os occipitale derrière et a gauche du *foramen magnum* de 3,1 centimètres dans le diamètre transversale et 2,6 centimètres dans le diamètre longitudinale.

Pour l'instant on ne est pas en mesure d'établir si on est en présence d'une trépanation effectuée intra vitam ou post mortem. L'observation à la microscopie optique du bord du trou ne permette pas de confirmer avec certitude l'éventuelle réaction de l'os. On peut supposer que si il y a eu une trépanation intra vitam l'individu n'a pas survécu plus de quelques jours.

On pourrait même estimer cette ouverture circulaire liée simplement à une pratique religieuse, par exemple l'ablation de la rondelle dans un but purement apotropaique.

En considération du fait que tous les sépultures trouvées dans l'Etrurie présentent caractéristiques communes et typiques d'un classe sociale élevée on est autorisée à croire que cet interventions chirurgicales fuissent réservées à des individus aristocratiques ou d'un particulière classe sociale.

AUTRES TRÉPANATIONS EN ITALIE

Les crânes de qui on parle douent être ajouté aux outres environs trente avec traces de trépanation dont l'existence est connue actuellement en Italie. Chronologiquement on doit considérer les pièces remontantes à l'époque de l'age historique du période italique.

Ces crânes sont les seuls de l'époque étrusque découverts dans l'Etrurie Méridionale ; dans le reste du Lazio outres découvertes de crânes avec lésions de trépanations viennent de Cerveteri (époque néolithique) et de Casamari (époque éneolithique).

CONSIDERATIONS ET HYPOTHESES D'ETUDE

En analysant la distribution géographique des crânes connus trépanes en Italie il est intéressant de souligner que Sardegna et Toscana présentent tous les deux un importante concentration de ces pièces archéologiques, surtout datables à l'âge du bronze. Il est possible de supposer des liaisons culturelles entre ces deux régions, comment d'ailleurs témoigne la découverte, il y a des années, de quelques petits bronzes nuragiques dans des tombes d'évident culture étrusque.

En outre les crânes en question se trouvaient à quelques dizaine de kilomètres de la *Grotta dello Scoglietto* dont viennent plusieurs crânes trépanes qui remontent à l'âge du Bronze Antique ; la circonstance évoque l'hypothèse d'une continuité de cette tradition culturelle depuis la préhistoire jusqu'à l'époque étrusque dans le même territoire.

Adresse des auteurs

G. BAGGIERI & M. DI GIACOMO
Ministero per I Beni e Le Attività Culturali- Servizio Tecnico per Le ricerche Antropologiche e Paleopatologiche- Sez. S. Michele Roma ITALIE

Bibliographie

ALCIATI, G., FEDELI, M., PESCE DELFINO, V. (1987), *La malattia dalla Preistoria all'Età antica,* Laterza, Bari.

BAGGIERI, G, ALLEGREZZA, L., CAPASSO, L. (1995), *Un nuovo caso di trapanazione cranica,* Atti del XIX Convegno di Studi Etruschi ed Italici, Volterra.

BAGGIERI, G. (1997*), Antichi pazienti...in neurochirurgia* in Archeologia Viva anno 1997 -XVI n.63:pp.76-79.

BAGGIERI, G. (1999), Les objets votifs des Etruscques, Dossier Pour La Science (Scientific American), octobre 1999.

BERRY, A.C., Berry, R.J. (1967), *Epigenetic variation in the human cranium,* Journal of Anatomy.

BROTWELL, D.R., SANDISON, A.T., (1967) *Disease in Antiquity,* Thomas, Springfield, Illinois.

BROTWELL, D.R. (1981), *Digging up bones,* British Museum Natural History, Oxford Univ. Press, Oxford.

GENNA, G. (1930-32), *La trapanazione del cranio nei primitivi. Contributo alla sua conoscenza alla preistoria italiana,* Rivista di antropologia, 29: 139-159, Roma.

GERMANÀ, F., FORNACIARI, G. (1992), *Trapanazioni, craniotomie e traumi cranici in Italia,* Collana di Studi Paletnologici dell'Università di Pisa, Giardini Editori e Stampatori in Pisa.

LO SCHIAVO, F. (1994), *Bronzi Nuragici della I Età del Ferro a Pontecagnano,* in La Presenza Etrusca nella Campania meridionale, Olschky, Firenze.

MESSERI, P. (1962), *Aspetti abnormi e patologici nel materiale scheletrico umano dello Scoglietto,* Arch. Antrop. Etnol., Firenze, 92: 129-159.

OLIVIER, G.(1960), *Pratique Antropologique,* Vigot, Paris.

PATRIZI, S., RADMILLI, A.M., MANGILI, G. (1950), *Sepoltura ad inumazione con cranio trapanato nella grotta Patrizi, Sasso-Furbara,* in Rivista di Antropologia, Roma, 41: 3-68.

PALLOTTINO, P. (1968), *Etruscologia,* Milano.

TORELLI, M. (1990), *Storia degli Etruschi,* Laterza.

TORELLI, M., STEINBOCK, R.T. (1976), *Paleopathological osis d Interpretation,* Thomas, Sprigfield, Illinois.

UBELAKER, D.H. (1984), *Human Skeletal Remains,* Smithsonian Institution, Taraxacum Washington.

A DIGITAL PHOTOGRAPHIC RECONSTRUCTION
OF THE GAULISH COLIGNY CALENDAR

Garrett OLMSTED

Abstract: Since only 40% of the original Coligny calendar survives as a fragmentary mosaic, the reconstruction of the original whole depends upon recognizing repetitive patterns and filling in the missing sequences of these patterns. A determination of the missing sequences was the subject of a previous study (Olmsted 1988: JIES, XVI, pp. 267-339; and Olmsted 1992: The Gaulish Calendar). My new digital photographic reconstruction verifies the results of this previous study. Indeed the original fragmentary mosaic is embedded in a digitally-reconstructed Coligny calendar (Olmsted 2001: JIES Monograph no. 39). Thus the fragmentary calendar was brought to photographic completion utilizing the original wording and engraving found on the surviving fragments. Since the photographic reproduction actually preserves the original fragments of the calendar, the typescript reconstruction presented in my 1992 study is shown to be one which fits within the parameters of the original calendar and lines up with the surviving notation. One interesting aspect emerging from this study is that the day numbers as well as some of the other notation were actually ruled off with a measure (2.76 .02 cm) based upon one twelfth of a pes Drusianus (33.0 cm), the standard of measure in Roman Gaul and Germany during the later part of the Augustan period.

Résumé : Puisqu'il n'existe plus que 40 pour cent du calendrier original de Coligny, et cela en mosaïque fragmentaire, sa reconstruction en entier n'est possible que par déterminer des patterns répétitifs et les en utilisent pour la reconstitution des séquences disparues de ces patterns. Des études précédentes se sont donné pour but d'identifier ces patterns répétitifs (Olmsted 1988: JIES, XVI, pp. 267-339; et Olmsted 1992: The Gaulish Calendar). Les résultats de ces études précédentes ont été vérifiés grâce a ma nouvelle reconstitution phonographique digitalisée. Ainsi le calendrier fragmentaire a pu être restituer en entier a partir du texte et des gravures des fragments du calendrier original. Effectivement, la mosaïque fragmentaire de l'original se retrouve dans un calendrier de Coligny digitalement reconstitué a l'aide de la photographie digitale utilisant les mots originels et les gravures trouvés déjà sur les fragments survivant (Olmsted 2001: JIES monograph no. 39). Etant donné que la reproduction digitalisée conserve les fragments du calendrier permettant le calque utilisant les mots originels et les gravures trouvés déjà sur les fragments survivant, la présentation par texte dactylographie de mon étude de 1992 se révélé fidèle aux paramètres du calendrier original et s'aligne avec ses notations survivant. Un aspect intéressant de cette étude est le fait que la numérotation des jours aussi bien que quelques-unes des autres notations ont gravé a l'aide d'une règle basée sur la douzième fraction d'un pes Drusianus (33.0 cm), la norme des mesures dans la Gaule Romaine et en Allemagne pendant les dernières années de l'époque Augustinienne.

INTRODUCTION

The fragmentary calendar plate from Coligny (near Lyons) apparently dates to the second-century AD, although the Gaulish calendar engraved on this plate is plainly the result of a long transmission process. The 25-year-cycle calendar, the final system of this transmission process, probably originated early in the first-century BC, before Caesar's conquest. It is within this late pre-Roman period that the calendar took on its final form and notation to enter a two-century long transmission process during which many copying errors were introduced (Olmsted 1992: tab. 58).

Embedded within the notation of the 25-year-cycle Coligny calendar is a 30-year-cycle calendar. The notation on the Coligny plate indicates that the original constant-lunar 30-year-cycle calendar system (from which the later shifting lunar calendar developed) had each month begin on the first day of the new moon. In contrast Plinius states (*Naturalis Historia*, XVI: 250 ; perhaps taken from observations of Poseidonius) that the months and years of the 30-year-cycle Gaulish calendar began on the sixth day of the moon.

> Est autem id rarum admodum inventu et repertum magna religione petitur et ante omnia sexta luna, quae principia mensum annorumque his facit, et saeculi post tricesimum annum, quia iam virium abunde habeat nec sit sui dimidia (Zwicker 1934: 55).

Plinius's statement implies that the earliest Gaulish calendar originated some 1000 years before the period of the observation he recorded. The earliest of the surviving Gaulish calendrical systems had its origins clearly in the late Bronze Age. This 1000-year span of the 30-year calendar is an inevitable conclusion of Plinius's statement. The 30-year-cycle constant lunar calendar runs ahead of the moon by 1 day every 199 years (Olmsted 1992: 70-71, 132-133). Though the months originally began on the first day of the moon, after 1000 years of operation of the calendar the months would have shifted to beginning on the sixth day of the moon.

Because of its long evolutionary development with earlier stages still embedded within the later calendar, the Coligny calendar gives a unique window into the astronomical capabilities of a supposedly barbarian people, the Celts of pre-Roman Gaul. The calendar also contains a large number of abbreviated terms describing the day-to-day operation of the calendar, much of it in a seemingly archaic dialect of Celtic. Most of these terms have a clear functional context so that their meaning is not only discernable but verifiable. Because of its significant astronomical and linguistic implications, the Coligny

```
          : LOVDIN    : LAGET     :                 : LOVDIN    : LAGET    :
 MONTH    : TII ITI IIT: TII ITI IIT:    MONTH      : TII ITI IIT: TII ITI IIT:
 ...........:...........:...........:    ...........:...........:...........:
 INT(1) M:            :           :     INT(2) M:            :          :
          :            :           :             :            :          :
          :            :           :             :            :          :
          :            :           :             :            :          :
          :            :           :             :            :          :
 ...........:...........:...........:    ...........:...........:...........:
 SAM 1  M:            :           :     GIA 7  A:            :          :
        : PL1   2   3 :           :             :            : PL1   2   3:
        : PL7   8   9 :           :             :            : PL7   8   9:
        :  13  14  15 :           :             :            :  13  14  15:
        :  19  20  21 :           :             :            :  19  20  21:
        :  25  26  27 :           :             :            :  25  26  27:
 ...........:...........:...........:    ...........:...........:...........:
 DVM 2  A:            :           :     SEM 8  M:            :          :
        :            : PL5   6   7:             : PL5   6  T7:          :
        :            :  11  12  13:             :  11  12  13:          :
        :            :  17  18  19:             :  17  18  19:          :
        :            :  23  24  25:             :  23  24  25:          :
        :            : N29 N7A    :             : N29 N30  T7:          :
 ...........:...........:...........:    ...........:...........:...........:
 RIV 3  M:            :           :     EQV 9  A:            :          :
        : PL2   3   4 :           :             :            : PL2   3   4:
        : PL8   9  10 :           :             :            : PL8   9  10:
        : N14 N15  16 :           :             :            : N14 N15 N16:
        :  20  21  22 :           :             :            :  20  21  22:
        :  26  27  28 :           :             :            :  26  27  28:
 ...........:...........:...........:    ...........:...........:...........:
 ANA 4  A:            :           :     ELE 10 A:            :          :
        :            : PL6  N7   8:             :            : PL3   4   5:
        :            :  12  13  14:             :            :   9  10  11:
        :            :  18  19  20:             :            : N15 N16 N17:
        :            :  24 N25  26:             :            :  21  22  23:
        :            : N25 N17G   :             :            :  27  28  29:
 ...........:...........:...........:    ...........:...........:...........:
 OGR 5  M:            :           :     EDR 11 M:            :          :
        : PL3   4   5 :           :             : PL6  T7  T8:          :
        :   9  10  11 :           :             :  12  13  14:          :
        : N15  16  17 :           :             :  18  19  20:          :
        :  21  22  23 :           :             :  24  25  26:          :
        :  27  28  29 :           :             : N30  T7  T8:          :
 ...........:...........:...........:    ...........:...........:...........:
 QVT 6  M:            :           :     CAN 12 A:            :          :
        : PL4   5   6 :           :             :            : PL4   5   6:
        :  10  11  12 :           :             :            :  10  11  12:
        :  16  17  18 :           :             :            :  16  17  18:
        :  22  23  24 :           :             :            :  22  23  24:
        :  28  29  30 :           :             :            :  28  29 T15:
 ...........:...........:...........:    ...........:...........:...........:
```

Plate 1 – Reconstructed series of TII marks (Neglecting yearly distribution and transferred days).

calendar is undoubtedly the most important inscription from Celtic Europe.

A total of 5 years are arrayed on the calendar plate from Coligny, comprised of 62 months made up of 5 repetitions of the 12 lunar months and 2 intercalary months (see plates 3-5). Except for the first 5-year phase of a 25-year or 30-year cycle, when the first intercalary month is not utilized, each 30-month period (2 1/2 years) is preceded by an intercalary month on the calendar. The intercalary months then immediately precede either the normal midwinter month SAMON (*samonios*) "summers end" or the normal midsummer month GIAMON (*giamonios)* "winters end". The intercalary months (Column-1 and Column-9 of the Coligny calendar) are utilized to achieve a realignment of the sun and the moon vis a vis the days counted out by the calendar, which are based upon, but during the stage of the calendar's final 25-year-cycle slightly longer than, the lunar cycle.

Since only 40% of the original five-year Coligny calendar survives as a fragmentary mosaic, the reconstruction of the original whole must depend upon recognizing repetitive patterns in the daily notation and filling in the missing sequences in these patterns which can be projected onto the lacunae. The patterns apparent in the recurrent notation on the Coligny calendar already have been set forth in my earlier publications. The most significant of these patterns is that discerned in the schemes of the TII and the N lunar/solar counting marks and their associated notation. Unlike the N notation, the pattern in the TII marks (plate 1) only became clear after first determining the original positions of the shifted days, some of which are specified by ordinal numerals indicating their original day positions (see my article in JIES: XVI (1988), nos. 3-4, pp. 267-339; also see review by Claude Lamoureux in *Études celtiques*: 30, 1994, 313-315, who compared the importance of this article to that of the earlier article of MacNeill in *Eriu* X: 1928, 1-67).

Pinault, one of the coauthors along with Duval of RIG: III: *Les Calendriers,* has also accepted my reconstruction of the original pattern in the distribution of these TII marks and their associated terminology (in a review in *Gnomen* (1996), vol. 68: 706-710), although indicating reservations about some of the etymologies for rarely- or uniquely-occurring terminology indicated on the calendar (which I had suggested in a fuller study of the calendar (*The Gaulish Calendar*, Bonn 1992). His reservations are dealt with in full in *JIES Monograph no. 39*, which contains a complete etymological glossary. Moreover, Pinault accepted as well my suggestion that these marks functioned as a lunar/solar counting scheme.

Il est évident que P.-M. Duval était conscient que ... ces signes [trigrammes] avait bien une raison d'être don't il n'avait pu trouver la clé. L'idée de relier ces trigrammes (qu'il désigne commodément par TII comme sigle général) aux notations PRINNI LOVDIN et PRINNI LAGET et d'en faire des indicateurs en rapport avec les solstices est, sans aucun doute, l'idée la plus féconde de l'Auteur [Olmsted]... En raison de l'abondance relative des TII (de l'ordre de 200), il a été possible d'élaborer sur ordinateur différents schémas de distribution qui ont abouti à son tableaux 28 et aux 29-32 permettant de déterminer la date des solstices dans le cycle de 25 ans. C'est là semble-t-il un apport capital à la compréhension de la mesure du temps chez les Gaulois. Cela s'obtient au meilleur prix: dans DP [Duval et Pinault] 411-415, j'avais tendé de justifier l'hypothèse de Mac Neill sur un mois EQVOS, pourtant cave, de 30 d aux années I, III, V, mais 28 d aux années II et IV. Si cela apparaît certain en I, II, III et V, c'était moins évident en IV et comme l'hypothèse d'Olmsted d'un EQVOS IV de 29 d, scripturairement possible, permet d'expliquer l'ensemble de l'économie du calendrier, je crois qu'il convient de s'y rallier.

Thus the reconstructions of the counting scheme patterns and their functions toward keeping track of the lunar and solar pathways have been accepted by the scholars who have studied the calendar most closely. So why do I now return to a new study of the calendar? At the time of my earlier studies there was no readily-available means of verifying that the reconstruction of the notational patterns of the calendar in typescript (Olmsted 1992: 137-168) actually did fit into the space provided by the lacunae in the fragmentary calendar mosaic without cramping. Any convincing reconstruction must fill in the missing letters to the same size and spacing as the surrounding lettering, while still aligning with the surviving notation and partial

notation engraved on the calendar plates. By its very nature, working from a typed transcript, even with the photos of the fragmentary months in hand, is one step removed from the actual reconstruction process and thus potentially prone to error.

The foremost question in my mind at the time of my original study was whether or not in every instance there actually was room enough in the lacunae separating the surviving fragments of the calendar to contain the missing notation suggested by the patterns apparent in the surviving notation. The actual computer-generated photographic reconstruction of the calendar introduced here (plates 2-4) and presented in a full in *JIES Monograph no. 39* (Olmsted 2001) was developed to alleviate these concerns.

Using a photo-processing program (*Adobe Photoshop V*) segments duplicating the missing notation were copied from surviving fragments of the Coligny calendar and then were utilized to fill in the missing sequences on the calendar maintaining the original spatial integrity of the fragmentary mosaic (originally reproduced digitally at high resolution from the RIG: III originals to 3/4 scale and 1200 dpi halftone, but of necessity depicted in plate 4 at 300 dpi grayscale (in plates 2 and 3 at about 1/6 scale) and in *JIES Monograph no. 39* at much lower resolution in the month plates to 1/2 scale and 150 dpi grayscale to comply with the printer's specifications. Indeed, the original fragmentary mosaic is still embedded in the digitally-reconstructed whole calendar (plates 2-3). Thus the fragmentary calendar was brought to photographic completion utilizing the original wording and engraving to be found on the surviving fragments.

As the photographic reproduction introduced here actually preserves the original fragments of the calendar, the typescript reconstruction presented in my 1992 study is shown to be one which fits within the parameters of the original calendar and lines up with the surviving notation. The reconstruction of the calendar based upon the date patterns of the surviving notation presented in my previous studies do indeed fit convincingly within the lacunae. Furthermore, these reconstructions fit within the alignments for the nota-tion worked out by the original engravers of the calendar.

Except for a few insignificant changes in word order or in the wording of the abbreviations probably utilized in specific locations, in only a single instance was a correction in the nature of the notation developed in my 1992 study actually necessary. On day 5 of month 12 Cantlos in year 5 the IIT notation should not be indicated alongside of N, even though IIT is the correct mark for that date. It is also now clear that the fuller phrase DS MA NS cannot occur on day 15 of month 5 Ogronios in year 3 (as suggested in my 1992 study) simply because there is not enough room in the lacuna, and the shorter abbreviation NS DS for the same term must have been used here instead.

But for these minor corrections having no significance for the operation of the calendar, this computer-driven

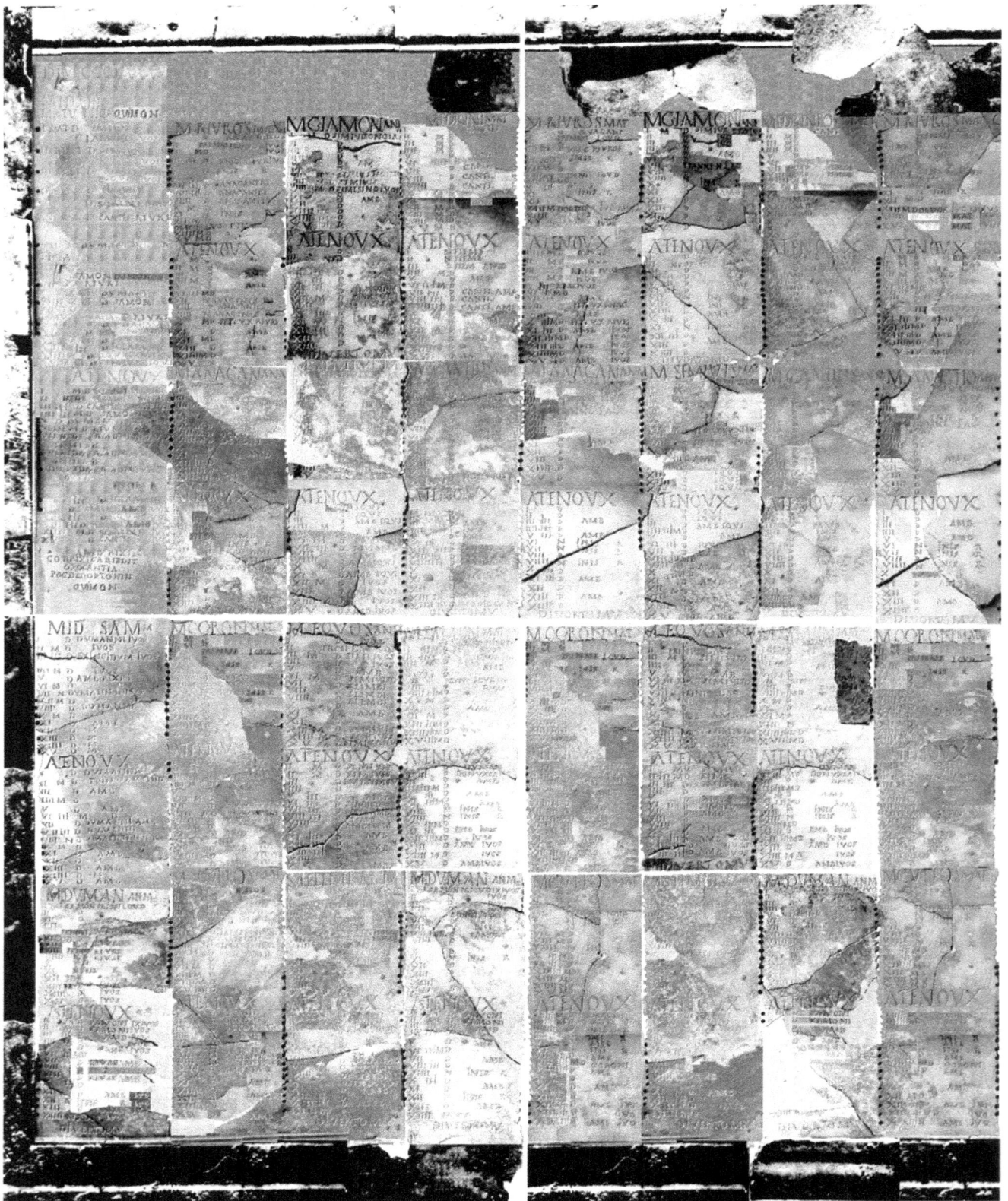

Plate 2 – Coligny Calendar. Left half.

photographic reconstruction of the Coligny calendar verifies that my 1992 reconstruction of the distribution of the notation on the calendar is one certainly capable of fitting within the surviving parameters of the calendar. To the extent that the 1992 reconstruction accurately discerns the repetitive patterns on the calendar, it is one that is likely to be correct. For anyone attempting to understand the nature and working of the Coligny calendar, the 1992 reconstruction is adequate.

Nonetheless the computer-driven transcription given in *JIES Monograph no. 39* does more accurately reflect the

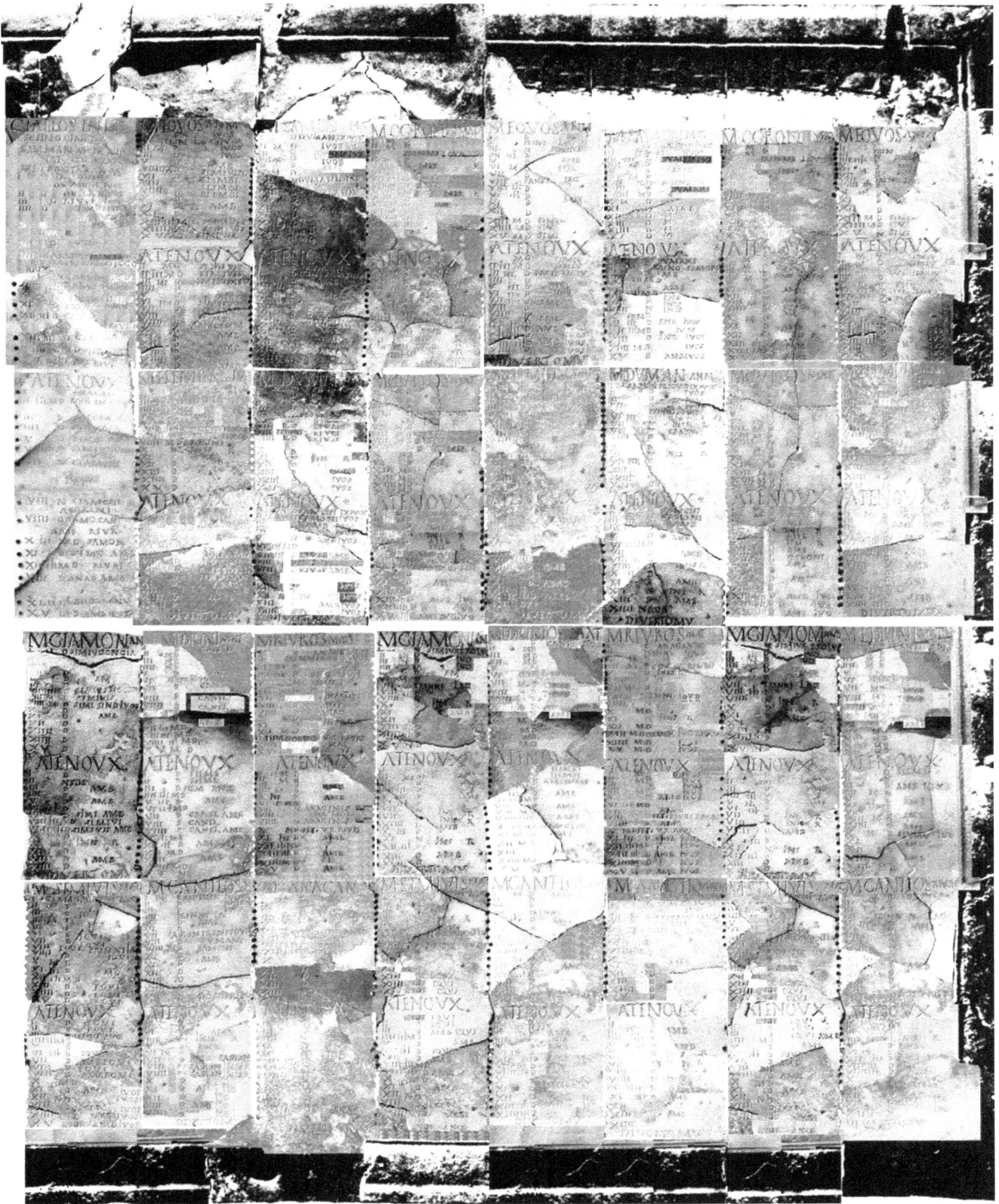

Plate 3 – Coligny Calendar. Right half.

probable original wording of the abbreviated terminology and the alignment of this notation on the calendar. In this sense it is technically more accurate, although the 1992 reconstruction just as accurately reflects the semantic content of the original calendar. Aside from verifying the adequacy of the 1992 transcript, one of the major results of this study is to bring to light new details about the engravers techniques and the minute linear and chronological units utilized on the calendar which previously had been unnoticed.

[M SAMON MAT]

[I	]	N	DVMAN]	IVO
[II	ITI	M D	]	IVOS
[IIII		D	DV]M ALE	IVO
[IIII		M D	AM]B	
[V		D		
[VI		M D		
[VIII		PRIN	]LOVD	
[VIIII		D	DV]MANI	
[VIIII	IIT	M D		
[X		M D		
[XI		D		AMB
[XII		M D		
[XIII		N		
[XIIII	ITI	M D		
[XV	IIT	M D		

[ATENOVX

[I		D	DVMAN	
[II	IIT	M D	TRI (TI) NVX	SAMO]
[IIII		D		AMB
[IIII	TII	M D		
[V	ITI	D		AMB
[VI	IIT	M D		
[VIII		D		AMB
[VIII		N	INIS	R
[VIIII	IIT	N	INIS	R
[X	{TII	M D}		
[XI	ITI	D	AMB	IVOS
[XII	IIT	M D		IVOS
[XIII		M D	AMB	IVOS
[XIIII		D		IVOS
[XV		D	AMB	IVOS

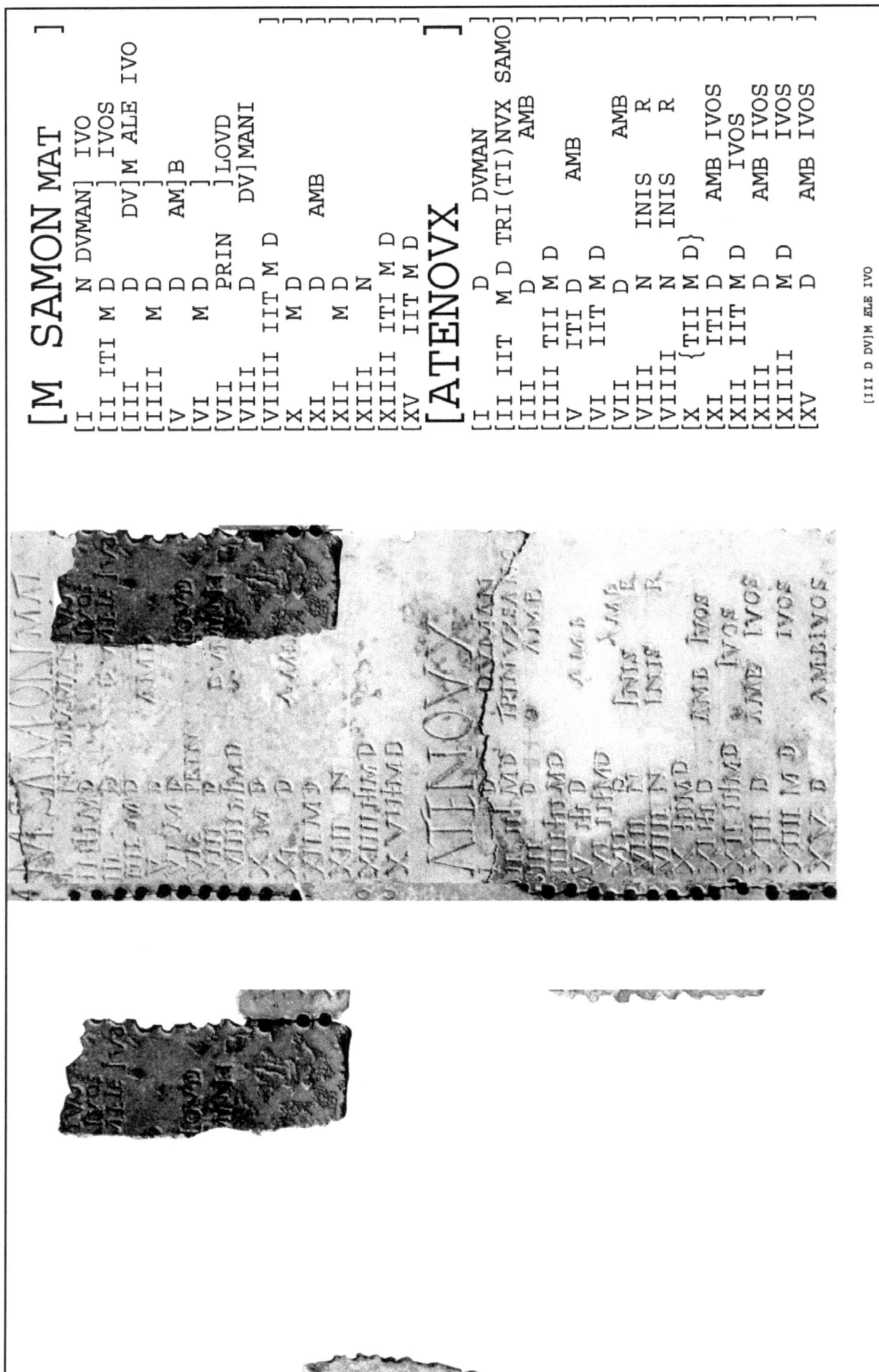

[IIII D DV]M ELE IVO

Plate 4 – Month-1 Year-3

THE ENGRAVERS' TECHNIQUES

The first task of this new study was to determine the measurement system utilized in ruling off the lines and columns of the calender, so that the measurements utilized in ruling off the original calendar plate could be preserved in the reconstruction. Measurements across multiple columns with interconnecting fragments yield the most consistent results indicating that a standard length was used to rule off the columns of the calendar. Ten measurements across from 2 to 5 different columns (ave. 3.2 columns), defined by the rows of Roman numerals set forth for the days of the calendar, give 8.27 .06 cm. or 3.26 .02 inches per column (8.20, 8.27, 8.40, 8.20, 8.24, 8.30, 8.27, 8.20, 8.30, 8.27 cm. per column). The average of fourteen individual measures from the full-scale photographs given in RIG: III give similar results of 8.29 .17 cm or 3.26 .07 in. (3.24, 3.18, 3.30, 3.34, 3.29, 3.23, 3.28, 3.16, 3.30, 3.34, 3.22, 3.38, 3.19, 3.26 in. per column) but with three times the margin of error.

The increased margin of error across individual columns is to be expected if the engraver used a ruler laid out across the plate and marked out the columns to plus or minus one fifteenth of an inch. If a movable block equal to one column in width had been used to establish the standardized column widths, the error across three columns would be increased by a factor of the square root of three times that found across single columns or .10 in., five times larger than that actually found. Assuming each column was marked off along the edge of a scaled ruler to a length of 3.0 Gaulish inches then gives 2.76 .02 cm per Gaulish inch for the more accurate multiple column widths (2.76 .06 cm. for the individual columns). Examination of the mean distance between columns and month names indicates that an "inch" equal to 2.76 .02 cm was utilized for all of the measurements on the calendar.

The Roman "foot" or *pes* was equivalent to 29.6 cm, yielding a "inch" or *uncia* (equivalent to one twelfth of a Roman foot) of 2.47 cm. (.97 English inches with 2.54 cm. per English inch). Clearly the calendar was not ruled off in standard Roman *unciae*. The long Greek foot of 32.6 cm. yields an "inch" of 2.72 cm., considerably closer, but still outside of the standard deviation of the most accurate measure of the unit apparently utilized in ruling out the calendar. However, the standard of Roman Gaul and Roman Germany during the late first century BC, the *pes Drusianus* of 33.0 cm., yields an inch of 2.75 cm. (1.08 English inches) (Price and Lang 1970: 659). Clearly this was the measurement unit most likely utilized on the Coligny calendar. Since the *uncia Drusianus* is only 1% larger than the Greek inch, it was probably adopted by the Gauls from a unit used by the Greeks in Massalia.

Operating under Tiberius, Drusus Germanicus subdued the Raeti and the Vindelici in 15 BC. In 13 BC he was put in charge of the three Gauls by Augustus. He dedicated an alter to Rome and Augustus at Lugudunum (now Lyons) on August 1 in 12 BC (Momigliano and Cadoux 1970: 365-6). Although the Coligny calendar plate is clearly a copy of an earlier calendar plate, it's present format was set up after 12 BC. Also since the calendar was found just outside of Lyons, it would make sense that it was ruled out in the standard of the *uncia Drusianus*. It seems likely that Drusus simply adopted the prevailing Gaulish inch, since otherwise he would have utilized the Roman standard. Thus the standard utilized on the calendar was most likely a Gaulish "inch" of 2.75 cm. or 1.08 English inches.

The Coligny engravers began with a bronze plate measuring 134. 8 cm. long (49.0 *unciae Drusianus*) by 78.0 cm. high (28.4 *unciae Drusianus*). With the rim attached the plate measured 52.0 by 32.0 *unciae Drusianus*. The engravers then began from the left side of the plate and measured off 15 columns each 3.0 *unciae Drusianus* wide, leaving the sixteenth column 3.5 *unciae Drusianus* wide. They began next at the bottom of the plate and measured up 6.5 *unciae Drusianus* for the bottom month-name line and 6.5 *unciae Drusianus* for each of the next two month-name lines. For the top month names they sometimes started a little above the standard line. The top month-name line averages about 2.5 *unciae Drusianus* below the edge of the top rim. The ANTENOVX lines are established at about 3.25 *unciae Drusianus* (midway) between the month-name lines. After making the month-name lines and the columns in this fashion, they filled in the numerals for the first 15 days in each month. Then they started at the top of the next month-name line and numbered backwards towards the middle for the ATENOVX days. They filled in ATENOVX in the space left between the two 15-day counts for each month.

The engravers then made all of the TII marks, followed by the M's. Next they made the left-hand lines for the D's, but stopping where N occurs in place of D or MD for more than one day in a row. For example in Cutios year-1, the D lines stop at ATENOVX IV and four N's are made, one at each of four the next five days. The D lines are then begun again at ATENOVX VIIII, but shifted slightly more to the left than previously. In other months the left line of each N, particularly starting in year-2, lines up with the left line of each D. Thus for each letter a line is simply ruled out for each day of the calendar and the rest of the N or D is left to be filled in afterwards. But one should note that the letter lines in ELEMBIV year-3 are rather poorly ruled out.

To the right of the D's or N's, the B's of the D AMB's and the R's of the N INIS R's often line up in a column, as if these were all made at the same time for a given month or column. The last items made were the drill holes for the movable pin or pins.

The reconstructed text of the Coligny calendar presented here followed these measurement patterns to the same degree observed in the surviving fragments. Thus the reconstruction can be seen to be one which is not forced upon the calendar, but one which is compatible with the actual design plan, engraving techniques, letter size, and word spacing patterns of the original engravers of the calendar.

MONTHLY AND YEARLY TIME RECKONING

Although the patterns apparent in the notation have already been outlined elsewhere (especially Olmsted 1992), a brief description of the function of the solar and lunar counting schemes found on the calendar is useful here as well. Before examining these other counting schemes, one must first give an outline of the arrangement of days on the calendar. In illustrating the sequence of variation of the 29-day and 30-day months on the Coligny calendar outlined here, double slanted lines // indicate a six-month division. I have used parentheses () around the intercalary month and brackets [ ] around Equos. The month of Equos is singled out for the following reason. Equos clearly has 30 days in years 1, 3, and 5, yet it strangely has the notation ANM, found elsewhere describing only the 29-day months. On the calendar all of the 30-day months have the notation MAT or MATV. For this reason most observers of the calendar have suspected that Equos had fewer than 30 days in either or both of years 2 and 4. In the first year of each five-year period except for the first year of a 25- or 30-year cycle, the Coligny calendar follows the following pattern in the lengths of the months: (30) //, 30, 29, 30, 29, 30, 30, // 29, 30, [30], 29, 30, 29. In year 3 the pattern is 30, 29, 30, 29, 30, 30, // (30) //, 29, 30, [30], 29, 30, 29. The addition of the intercalary months to years 1 and 3 causes each year to increase to 385 days, where they would otherwise contain 355 days. In addition to counting the actual days in these years, the notation at the beginning of the second intercalary month (in the middle of year 3) states that this year contains a total number of days (LAT) equal to CCCLXXXV and a total number of months (M) equal to XIII. Each of these years with intercalary months has an average of 29.6154 days in each month. Year 5 does not have an intercalary month so the pattern is 30, 29, 30, 29, 30, 30, // 29, 30, [30], 29, 30, 29 to give 355 days. The months in this year have an average of 29.5833 days each. If Equos had 28 days in year 2, year 2 would contain only 353 days. For year-2 the pattern would be 30, 29, 30, 29, 30, 30, // 29, 30, [28], 29, 30, 29. The months in this year would then have an average of 29.4167 days. If Equos had 29 days in year 4, year 4 would contain 354 days. For year 4 the pattern would be 30, 29, 30, 29, 30, 30, // 29, 30, [29], 29, 30, 29. The months in this year would average 29.5000 days. Of course if Equos had 30 days in each of the years 2, 4, and 5, each would contain 355 days to give the same pattern as year-5 above and an average monthly length of 29.5833 days, which is considerably longer than a standard lunar month of 29.5306 days and would cause the calendar to go out of whack with lunar time by around half a day each year. The situation would be even worse during years with intercalary months containing 385 days (13 months) and an average monthly length of 29.6154 days. To approach the lunar cycle, clearly Equos would have had to have fewer than 30 days in years 2 and 4.

In years 1 and 5 and presumably in year 3 (with lacunae) there are 5 IVOS days at the end of Equos, beginning on day 26 and continuing to day 4 of the following month Elembiu (years 1 and 3 extant) to give a total of 9 IVOS days for each of years 1, 3, and 5. However, the IVOS notation extends to day 5 of Elembiu in year 2 with the end of Equos missing because of lacunae. This extension of the IVOS festival suggests that Equos is missing some days in year 2, and the total length of this IVOS festival period would otherwise be foreshortened. The end of Equos and the beginning of Elembiu are missing in year 4. The

ending of the IVOS festival is unknown here. Remember also that Equos is listed as an ANM "incomplete" month even though years 1, 3, and 5 clearly have 30 days. This extra IVOS day in the beginning of Elembiu in year 2 and the notation ANM describing Equos is why previous observers such Mac Neill and Pinault have suggested that Equos had fewer than 30 days in year 2, and by extrapolation, year 4 as well, where the final part of Equos and the entire month of Elembiu are missing. As we shall see, if it were not the case that Equos had fewer than 30 days in these years, the calendar would go hopelessly out of whack with both lunar and solar time.

In the 30-year cycle after an initial 5-year phase of 1801 days in which solar time falls back by 25.21 days (5 X 365.2422 = 1,826.21 days), there follow five 5-year phases of 1831 days during which the sun regains 4.79 days in each 5-year period so that after 5 such 1831-day periods the sun has gained back 23.95 days. Thus in every 30-year period the sun falls back by 1.27 days with respect to the calendar. The calendar priests in their counting schemes would have assumed an initial fall back of 25 days during the first 5-year phase and that the sun gained back this fall-back by 5 days in each subsequent 5-year phase, giving a series of 5-year Intercalary-1 solstice dates occurring at the beginning of each 5-year phase of 1, 26, 21, 16, 11, 6. But notice that the sun actually is still one day later than the daily notation of the calendar so the next 30-year cycle would give intercalary-1 solstice dates of 2, 27, 22, 17, 12, 7 etc (see Olmsted 1992: tab. 24a).

However the counting schemes on the Coligny calendar actually show a progression of TII 5-year intercalary-1 solstice counts of 1, 25, 19, 13, 7 to be followed in the next 25- or 30-year cycle by ITI day counts of 2, 26, 20, 14, 8 and in the final cycle by IIT day counts of 3, 27, 21, 15, 9. To follow this progression one should consult plate 1, Sam 1 M, and one should also see month 1, year 3 (plate 4), where Samonios day 3 and the expected IIT mark have been transferred to Samonios 2a, labeled *tri(ti)nux samo* "the third night of Samonios" (also see Olmsted 1992: tab. 26a-28d). The TII marks and the N counting scheme, clearly indicated on the calendar, all show this same progression (see Olmsted 1992: tab. 43). Thus in Samain (plate1) we have *prinni loudin* 1, *prinni loudin* 7, TII 13, TII 19, TII 25 //; ITI 2, ITI 8, ITI 14, ITI 20, ITI 26 //; IIT 3, IIT 9, IIT 15, IIT 21, IIT 27. Notice in the scheme the count is completed with only 5 five-year solstice dates rather than the 6 five-year phases of the 30-year cycle and that each solstice date is separated by 6 days rather than the 5 days of the 30 year cycle. The only way this can happen is if the initial count is a 5-year phase of 1802 days during which the sun progresses 1,826.21 days falling back by 24.21 days, to be followed by four 1832-day five-year phases in which the sun gains back 5.79 days in each five year phase. Four of these 1832-day phases add up to 23.16 days (4 X 5.79), which is 1.05 days shorter than the initial fall back. Of course the calendar priests would have seen this as an initial 24-day fall-back to be recouped in four 6-day advances, one occurring in each new five-year phase. If the same 1-day overall fall-back in the sun was assumed in each 25-year cycle as the ITI marks' advancing by 1 day show (in Samain TII = 1, 25, 19, 13, 7; ITI = 2, 26, 20,

14,8; IIT = 3, 27, 21, 15, 9), then the whole scheme is error with the sun by only 0.05 days in a 25 year period. The N-count indicates the same dates as the TII scheme (Olmsted 1992: tabs. 20, 26a-b).

The lunar reckoning of this 25-year calendar is interesting as well. The 25-year calendar contains 9130 days (1802 + (4 X 1832)). 25 solar years contain 9131.05 days (25 X 365.2422), 1.05 days longer than the calendar. The 25-year calendar contains an initial phase of 61 months followed by four phases each of 62 months for a total of 309 months. 309 lunar months contain 9124.95 days days (309 X 29.5306), 5.05 days shorter than the calendar. Thus year-26 begins with the sun 1.05 days behind the calendar and the moon 5.05 days ahead of the calendar. These amounts total almost exactly 1 day behind for the sun and 5 days ahead for the moon, a solar accuracy equivalent to the Gregorian calendar. But notice that if the triple marks divide each 15-day period indicated on the calender into 3 periods of 5 days each (the Old Irish *cóicde*), then with each 25-year phase the moon would shift into the next 5-day week. Thus TII indicates not only the first 25-year phase but the first 5-day week of the moon as well. ITI indicates not only the second 25-year phase and falls appropriately one day later in the calendar (for the 1-day fall back in the sun), but it also indicates the second 5-day week of the moon. IIT not only indicates the third 25-year phase and falls later by an additional day from ITI, but also indicates the third 5-day week of the moon. With each 5-year phase the moon progresses by exactly one additional day within each week dominating the 25-year cycle.

Notice that this 25-year cycle has 1802 days and 1832 days in the 5-year phases rather than the 1801 days and 1831 days of the 5-year phases in the 30-year cycle. This extra day in each 5-year phase would arise by giving Equos 29 days in year 4 rather than the 28 days in year 4 necessary for the 30-year cycle. Equos would still have 28 days in year 2 accounting for the extra IVOS day in Elembiu year 2. Thus in years 1, 3, and 5, the IVOS count for the end of Equos and the beginning of Elembiu would be 9 days with 5 IVOS days at the end of Equos (30 days) and 4 IVOS days at the beginning of Elembiu. In year 4, 4 IVOS days would occur at the end of Equos (29 days) and 4 IVOS days would occur at the beginning of Elembiu for a total of 8 days. In year 2, three IVOS days would occur at the end of Equos (28 days) but now 5 IVOS days would occur at the beginning of Elembiu for a total of 8 days. Like MacNiell's scheme, the 25-year scheme still accounts for the extra IVOS day in Elembiu year 2. The ANM notation for Equos is assured in both counts since Equos has fewer than 30 days in years 2 and 4.

It is clear that the 25-year calendar was adapted from Plinius's 30-year Gaulish calendar by simply giving an extra day to Equos in year 4 making it 29 days long rather than the original 28 days. It is the completeness of these schemes and their accounting for the TII distribution that caused Pinault to call for the adoption of my 25-year scheme in his *Gnomen* (1996: 706 ff.) review.

Author's address

Dr. Garrett OLMSTED
Professor of Anthropology
Bluefield State College
Visiting Research Associate
University of Missouri-Columbia
E-mail: olmsted@netscape.net

Bibliography

BUCK, CARL D., 1933, Comparative Grammar of Greek and Latin. Chicago.

DUVAL, P.-M., 1962-7, Observations sur le Calendrier de Coligny, in Etudes celtiques, X, pp. 18-42, 372-412; XI, pp. 7-45, 269-313.

DUVAL, P.-M. and GEORGES PINAULT, 1986, Recueil des inscriptions gauloises (RIG): vol. III: Les calendriers, XLVth supplement to Gallia. Paris.

EVANS, D. ELLIS, 1967, Gaulish Personal Names. Oxford.

HAMMOND, N.G.L. and H.H. SCULLARD, 1970, Oxford Classical Dictionary (OCD). Oxford.

LAMBERT, PIERRE-YVES, 1995, La langue gauloise. Paris.

LAMOUREUX, CLAUDE, 1994, "Olmsted: The Gaulish Calendar" in Études celtiques: 30, 313-315.

NICHOLSON, E. W. B., 1898, Sequanian. First Step in the Investigation of a Newly Discovered Ancient European Language. London.

MOMIGLIANO, ARNALDO and THEODORE CADOUX, 1970, "Drusus", in OCD: 365-6.

MAC NEILL, EOIN, 1928, "On the Notation and Chronography of the Calender of Coligny", in Eriu, X, pp. 1-67.

OLMSTED, GARRETT, 1988, "The Use of Ordinal Numerals on the Gaulish Coligny Calendar", in The Journal of Indo-European Studies, XVI, nos. 3-4, pp. 267-39.

OLMSTED, GARRETT, 1992, The Gaulish Calendar. Bonn.

OLMSTED, GARRETT, 1994, The Gods of the Celts and the Indo-Europeans. Innsbruck.

OLMSTED, GARRETT, 2001, A Definitive Reconstructed Text of the Coligny Calendar: Journal Indo-European Studies Monograph No. 39. Washington, D. C.

PINAULT, GEORGES, 1961, Notes sur le vocabulaire du calendrier gaulois de Coligny, in Ogam, XIII, pp. 461-70.

PINAULT, GEORGES, 1962, "Notes sur le vocabulaire gaulois: les noms des mois du calendrier de Coligny", in Ogam, XIV, pp. 143-60.

PINAULT, GEORGES, 1996, "Olmsted: The Gaulish Calendar", in Gnomen, vol. 68, pp. 706-710.

PRICE, FREDERICK and MABEL LANG, 1970, "Measures", in OCD: 659.

ZWICKER, IOANNES, 1934, Fontes Historiae Religionis Celticae. Berlin.

FINDS OF ROMAN BRONZE WARE ON CELTIC SITES
IN EASTERN SLAVONIA

Marko DIZDAR & Ivan RADMAN-LIVAJA

Résumé : Plusieurs vases en bronze ont été trouvés dans les plus importants sites de l'époque de La Tène finale en Slavonie orientale, plus particulièrement dans les tombes et les grandes agglomérations fortifiées. Cette vaisselle appartient à la dernière phase de la culture matérielle des Scordisques, la fin du 2ème et la première moitié du 1 siècle av. J.-C. (La Tène D1). Les tombeaux contenaient de la vaisselle appartenant au service du vin. Certaines de ces pièces étaient sans doute produites sur place mais d'autres étaient importées d'Italie du Nord. Les routes commerciales allaient probablement d'Aquilée jusqu'à Siscia, d'où elles suivaient les cours des grands fleuves, la Sava et le Danube. Quelques-uns de ces sites avec des trouvailles de vaisselle en bronze allaient plus tard devenir des forts sur le limes (Dalj-Teutoburgium et Sotin-Cornacum) tandis que Vinkovci-Cibalae allait devenir une importante ville et un centre de production derrière le limes.

Abstract: Bronze ware has been found on the most important La Tène sites of eastern Slavonia, mostly in warrior graves of the late La Tène cemeteries, or in important fortified settlements of the same period. Those vessels belong to the final phase of the material culture of the Scordisci, i.e. the end of the 2nd and the first half of the 1st century BC (La Tène D1). Graves contained drinking ware, i.e. pails, saucepans, simpulums as well as sieves, cups and jugs. Some are considered to have been produced by the local Southpanonian craftsmen, while some were produced in Northern Italy. Trade roads probably went from Aquileia to Segestica and then followed the rivers Sava and Danube. Some of the sites where bronze ware has been discovered would eventually become Roman forts on the limes (Dalj-Teutoburgium and Sotin-Cornacum) while Vinkovci-Cibalae would become an important settlement and production centre behind the limes.

INTRODUCTION

The Celts settled in eastern Slavonia at the end of the 4th century BC. Soon, together with the autochthonous tribes, they started raiding Macedonia and Greece. After the battle at Delphi in 279 BC, one part of the defeated Celts returned to the middle Danube area and chose to settle in the area where the Sava River flows into the Danube. According to ancient historical sources, those Celts were called Scordisci.[1] They occupied the middle Danube area between the Slavonian hills in the west and the lower Morava valley in the east. Eastern Slavonia was thus the western border area of their territory. Many Celtic sites were discovered there but only a small number has been excavated. Mainly due to that fact, the exact frontiers of the Scordisci to the west and to the north are not well defined. Nevertheless, considering the available data, we can assume that the river Drava represented the northern frontier of their territory. As far as the western frontier is concerned, according to the archaeological finds, the Orljava river and the eastern parts of the Papuk and Dilj mountains (identified as the *Mons Claudius* mentioned by Pliny the Elder[2]) were most probably the borderline. The Sava River was probably the natural frontier to the south, although finds from northern Bosnia show that Scordisci could also have occasionally dwelled south of the Sava.

The archaeological research of the La Tène culture in eastern Slavonia started at the end of the 19th century,

when the Head of the Archaeological Department of the Croatian National Museum, J. Brunšmid, organised a network of regional deputies in charge of collecting and publishing archaeological finds in their respective areas of responsibility. The first discoveries and excavations of Celtic sites in eastern Slavonia, like Dalj, Sotin, Bogdanovci and Vinkovci, date from that period.[3] Research continued after the WWII, and in the fifties; during a rescue excavation at Lijeva Bara near Vukovar, the remains of a Celtic settlement belonging to the 1st century BC were discovered.[4] At the same time, a cemetery dated to the end of the early La Tène period and the middle period was excavated near Osijek.[5] In the following decades, many excavations took place near Vinkovci and Osijek, which enabled us to get a clearer picture of the typical Celtic settlements and their fortifications in eastern Slavonia.[6] According to the research results, it seems that the Scordisci in eastern Slavonia started building fortified settlements at the end of the middle phase of the La Tène period. Those settlements became, during the late La Tène period, the main political, economical and military centres of the Celtic culture in that area. They were built, as a rule, on the locations of the so called tell settlements, inhabited since the remote prehistoric times, on elevated positions near riverbanks. Such fortified settlements were situated in Sotin[7] and Ilok[8],

---

[1] Justin XXXII.3.6-8; Strabo VII.5.11-12.

[2] Pliny the Elder, Naturalis Historia 3.25.148; Pliny mentions that Mons Claudius as the frontier between the Scordisci and the Taurisci; Majnarić-Pandžić 1970: 76; Guštin 1984: 305; Popović 1992a: 96; Popović 1992-1993: 15.

[3] Brunšmid 1902: 122-123; Brunšmid 1909: 231-237

[4] Vinski 1953: 21-23; Vinski 1959: 99-109; Balen-Letunić 1996: 32-33

[5] Spajić 1954; Spajić 1956; Spajić 1962; Šimić 1997

[6] Majnarić-Pandžić 1972-1973; Majnarić-Pandžić 1984; Majnarić-Pandžić 1996; Dizdar 2001

[7] Majnarić-Pandžić 1972-1973: 70; Majnarić-Pandžić 1994: 75

[8] Some finds of Celtic pottery; excavations due to begin in 2001.

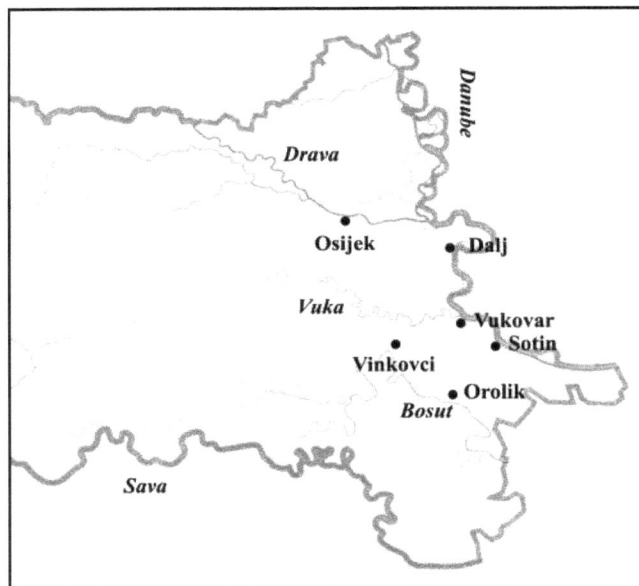

Figure 1.

on the Danube, in Sarvaš[9] on the Drava River, and in Donja Bebrina on the Sava River, where suburbs outside the fortified settlement were also located.[10]

The majority of fortified settlements in eastern Slavonia were found on the Bosut River and its tributaries near Vinkovci. During the excavations on the sites of Orolik and Privlaka, the La Tène layer was 1 m thick and contained the remains of house floors and a vast number of pottery shards and metal finds belonging to the second half of the 2nd century BC and the 1st century BC.[11] The biggest fortified settlement was located in Dirov brijeg, in the modern town of Vinkovci. Several smaller and non-fortified settlements, actually suburbs, were found around that settlement as well as cemeteries containing incineration graves.[12] Some fortified settlements were built on higher positions in plains subject to inundations (Otok and Slakovci), while one was built on the gentle slopes of a plateau near the Sava river (Damića gradina near Stari Mikanovci).[13] The fortifications of those settlements consisted of a large ditch filled with water from neighbouring rivers or streams (usually one side of the settlements was protected by the water course itself) and of earth ramparts whose top was burned.[14]

FINDS

The bronze vessels belonging to the wine-drinking ware appeared in the settlements and cemeteries of the Scordisci

at the end of the 2nd and the first half of the 1st century BC (La Tène D1).[15] In eastern Slavonia such bronze ware was found only in the most important La Tène sites like Dalj and Sotin on the Danube and Vinkovci and Orolik on the Bosut River.

A chance find was discovered on a spot named Planina, in the village of Dalj. It is a bronze handle of a sieve (T. 2, 2), or a *doigtier* as Guillaumet calls it.[16] An almost identical piece was found on a location called Blato (T. 2, 3), in the town of Vinkovci, during a field survey in 1998. That survey was undertaken on a spot where remains of La Tène pottery had been found in the 19th century, and it confirmed the existence of a Celtic graveyard on that location.[17] Many La Tène artefacts were found on several locations in Dalj, dating from the early to the late La Tène period. The importance of this place is emphasised by the fact that a Roman fort called *Teutoburgium* was built there in the 1st century AD, probably in the first decades of the century.[18] Such handles are a common find on late La Tène settlements, although the sieves themselves are usually not preserved because of their fragility. In the area inhabited by the Scordisci, handles of the same type were found at two sites in Serbia, and they were both dated to the 1st century BC.[19] Such sieves most probably belonged to the wine-drinking ware, and are dated from the end of the 2nd century BC to the time of Tiberius. It is believed that they were produced in Italian workshops[20] but we cannot exclude the possibility that some of them were made in Celtic workshops. Considering the total number of known finds in Europe and North Africa it is striking that only a very small percentage was found in Italy itself. Besides that, several pieces found in Celtic settlements seem to be unfinished, which would imply a local production.[21] Although the fact that this type of sieve was phased out of production approximately at the same time when a strong Romanization started in the areas inhabited by the Celtic population does not necessarily imply the Celtic origin of that type of sieve, it is certainly a proof of the popularity it enjoyed among them during their independence. It is also a strong argument for the thesis that it was also produced in their workshops.[22]

In the village of Sotin, on a spot called Zmajevac, local amateurs found late La Tène incineration graves in 1903. Unfortunately, the finds were sent to the National Museum in Zagreb lacking precise data about the circumstances of the discovery. Therefore, it was impossible to figure out with absolute certainty, which finds belonged to which grave. Some of the grave goods were assigned to three graves and published afterwards,

---

[9]   Majnarić-Pandžić 1978: 149

[10] Majnarić-Pandžić 1970: 57-58

[11] Majnarić-Pandžić 1969; Majnarić-Pandžić 1970: 55-57, T. LII-LIV; Majnarić-Pandžić 1981; Majnarić-Pandžić 1984; Majnarić-Pandžić 1996: 260, sl. 3.-5.

[12] Dimitrijević 1979: 144-146, sl. 4; Dizdar 1999: 45-47; Dizdar 2001

[13] Dizdar 2001: 27-33

[14] Majnarić-Pandžić 1984

[15] Popović 1992: 61

[16] Majnarić-Pandžić 1970: 22, TVIII. 11

[17] Brunšmid 1902: 123; Dizdar 1998: 38-43; Dizdar 2001a: 105-106, T. 15. 12

[18] Klemenc 1961: 19-20; Pinterović 1968: 67-69, 76-77

[19] Popović 1992: 61-62, fig. 1

[20] Guillaumet 1977: 244; Popović 1992: 61-62; Guštin 1991: 70-71

[21] Guillaumet 1977: 245-248; Guillaumet 1991: 92-95

[22] Guillaumet 1977: 245

while others are only known to have been found in that cemetery[23]. The grave I contained the cremated remains of the deceased placed in a bronze pail (thus serving as an urn) and covered with a bronze saucepan/casserole (T. 1, 1, 4). The pail has an iron handle terminating with stylised bird protomes. It seems that the fastening system of the handle is not the original one, and that the pail had been repaired at some time before having been placed in the grave. That pail is rather primitive and is certainly not a product of developed workshops like the Italic ones. It must have been produced locally and has no direct analogies among Pannonian finds. It is typologically closest to Radnóti's Bargfeld type.[24] The saucepan that was used to cover the pail has a long and thin handle, also terminating with a stylised bird protome (T. 1, 4). It is typologically somewhat related to the Aylesford type vessels, but considering her crude and unfinished look, we can reasonably suppose that it was most probably made in a local workshop imitating Italic bronze ware.[25] A fragmentary handle of a Pescate type simpulum was also found in that grave (T. 1, 5). It belongs to the A type according to Marina Castoldi's tipology.[26] The missing body of the simpulum was probably lost by the discoverers. It is the only find from that grave that can be attributed beyond doubt to an Italic workshop.[27] The grave I contained the usual combination of bronze ware, i.e. a pail, a saucepan and a simpulum, attested in several other excavated cemeteries of the Scordisci. When the grave goods were brought to the National Museum in Zagreb one fragmentary simpulum of the Aislingen type was listed as belonging to grave I, but that cannot be the case. That type dates from the Claudian-Neronian period and although found in the same location as the late La Tène graves, it must have been deposited in a much later grave from the Roman period. Anyway, this indicates a continued utilization of the site.[28]

Other grave goods attributed to the grave I include female La Tène jewellery (fibulae, bracelets, armlets, and a buckle) as well as an iron roasting-spit, a knife and a spur. Such grave goods would indicate that the remains of a man and a woman were buried together in the same grave, probably in the La Tène D1 period.

Fragments of two pails were found in grave II, together with their two handles, also terminating with stylised bird protomes (T. 1, 2, 3). They seem typologically close to the Bargfeld type, and considering their crude workmanship, we can also assume that they were produced locally. Other grave goods include an iron spear, fragments of a shield boss and an iron bracelet.[29] The grave III contained only weapons and no bronze ware. Just like in Dalj, the Romans

built a fort in Sotin, on the spot where the Celtic settlement used to be, and they called it *Cornacum*.[30]

During rescue excavations in Vinkovci, in 1957, on a location called Dirov brijeg, a bronze receptacle of the Pescate type simpulum was found in the remains of a fortified Celtic settlement (T. 2, 1).[31]

That simpulum type is the most common find of Italic bronze ware on Scordisci's sites in the middle Danube area. Usually, only the handle remains, either of the A or B type according to M. Castoldi's typology. As far as eastern Slavonia is concerned, we already mentioned the A type handle from Sotin. Another one was found in the fortified settlement in Orolik (that site is called Gradina by the locals). That fragment could belong to either the A or B type (T. 2, 5).

It should be pointed out that besides the sieve handle we already mentioned, the site of Blato has also yielded a late Republican tripod foot of the type Tassinari S1100.[32]

Further north from Dirov brijeg, in Vrtna street, 11 pieces of material were found in 1965. Researchers assume that those finds belonged to a hoard, but it seems more probable that those are remains from destroyed graves. Those are mostly spears and sword fragments, but among them are a bronze handle (T. 2, 6) and two fragments of a bronze vessel rim (T. 2, 4a-b). We were not able to find an analogy to the handle, but it has an impressed stamp with the name of the craftsman, *ABUDUS F*. The name *Abudus* is probably Italic but it is not mentioned anywhere.[33] However, since the stamp has the abbreviation *F* for *fecit*, there is no doubt that it was produced by an Italic workshop or perhaps by an Italic craftsman working in South Pannonia.[34] The finds probably date to the end of the 1st century BC or the beginning of the 1st century AD and they might be related to Tiberius' conquest of that area.

Those are all the bronze ware finds from eastern Slavonia: they were found either on the locations of important fortified settlements like Dirov brijeg in Vinkovci and Gradina in Orolik, or in late La Tène cemeteries like Planina-Dalj, Zmajevac-Sotin and Blato and Vrtna street in Vinkovci, although the last site might also be considered an early Roman cemetary.

CONCLUSION

Bronze ware used for drinking wine appears in the settlements and the cemeteries of the Scordisci at the end of the 2nd century BC and the 1st half of the 1st century BC (La Tène D1). Those vessels were produced in North Italy,

---

[23] Majnarić-Pandžić 1972-1973

[24] Radnóti 1938: 112-113; Majnarić-Pandžić 1996a: 27

[25] Majnarić-Pandžić 1972-1973: 61, T.I, 7; Majnarić-Pandžić 1996a: 27-28

[26] Castoldi&Feugère 1991: 64-66

[27] Majnarić-Pandžić 1996a: 28

[28] Majnarić-Pandžić 1972-1973: 62; Majnarić-Pandžić 1996a: 28

[29] Majnarić-Pandžić 1972-1973: 60-61, T.I., 6, T. III., 7-8

[30] Klemenc 1961: 20; Pinterović 1968: 70, 77

[31] Dimitrijević 1979: 173, T. 19., 2

[32] Božić 2002: 419-421, fig. 3

[33] The closest paralel is *Abudius*, c.f. Lörincz&Redö 1994: 6

[34] Majnarić-Pandžić 1996a: 32-33

Campania or locally, in south Panonnian workshops.[35] Certain types of bronze ware, like the Pescate type simpulums and Aylsford type saucepans, came from north Italian workshops, following the trade road going from Aquilea through Segestica and the Sava river valley. Strabo described that road[36], and he mentioned that the tribes living on the banks of the Danube traded their goods (slaves, cattle and hide) in Aquilea for wine and olive oil[37]. We can reasonably assume that the Scordisci emulated the drinking habits, which include the use of specific bronze ware, from the Mediterranean wine merchants. The road communication described by Strabo gained even more importance after Octavianus conquered Segestica in 35 BC. Thanks to that victory, the road to the Danube area was open.[38]

The trade roads from the Mediterranean to the middle Danube area can easily be followed by the finds of coin hoards, especially by coins from Apollonia and Dyrrhachium as well as Roman *denarii*. The money from Apollonia and Dyrrhachium is found all over the Balkans and south Pannonia, up to the Black Sea. The roads to the North, used by the traders carrying that money are the same roads that will later be used by the Roman armies. The drachmas arrived in larger numbers to the Danube area in the second quarter of the 1st century BC.[39] Large coin hoards of drachmas from those two towns are known in eastern Slavonia from Dalj and from Vukovar.[40] One of the two hoards from Vukovar also contained some Roman republican denarii, minted between 111 and 79 BC. Except those two sites, in eastern Slavonia drachmas were found at eight other locations and Roman republican denarii at nine locations. In the first half of the 1st century BC drachmas of Apollonia and Dyrrhachium are encountered more often then Roman coins, which became more numerous in the second half of that century.[41] According to the finds of coin hoards, three trade roads can be followed from the Mediterranean to the middle Danube. One road went through the valleys of rivers Neretva and Bosna to the Sava river. Drachmas are much more common finds on that road. The second road went from Greece through the Vardar and Morava valley to the Danube. Of course, finds of Roman republican coins are even less common on that road. They are found in large numbers on the third trade road, leading from North Italy and Aquilea through Segestica and the Sava valley to the Danube.[42] The same road was used for the trade of wine and bronze ware.

Such imported bronze ware is typical for the last period of the Scordisci's culture, i. e. the La Tène D1 period. It was an important sign of wealth and remains of vessels are usually found in rich warrior graves (with only one exception). In eastern Slavonia such an example comes from the graves in Sotin. We can suppose that chance finds from Dalj and Vinkovci also belonged to grave goods. Bronze ware was also found in important settlements like Dirov brijeg in Vinkovci and Gradina in Orolik. That period of wealth did not last for long: few decades later, the Scordisci lost their independence and their territory became part of the Roman Empire, as corroborated by finds from Vrtna street in Vinkovci.

After the Roman occupation of eastern Slavonia the autochthonous population started to gradually accept the Roman way of life, which was facilitated by the contacts already established in the past and by the fact that Roman settlements and forts were built near the most important late La Tène settlements like Osijek (Mursa), Dalj (Teutoburgium), Sotin (Cornacum), Orolik (Celena) and Vinkovci (Cibalae).

Authors' addresses

Marko DIZDAR
Institute of Archaeology
Ulica grada Vukovara 68
10000 Zagreb – CROATIA
E-mail: marko.dizdar@IARH.tel.hr

Ivan RADMAN-Livaja
Archaeological Museum
Zrinjevac 19
10000 Zagreb – CROATIA
E-mail: iradman@amz.hr

Bibliography

BALEN-LETUNIĆ, D., 1996, Pretpovijesna naselja i nekropola vukovarske Lijeve bare, In *Vukovar, Lijeva bara*. edited by A. Rendić-Miočević. Zagreb: Archaeological Museum, p. 32-33.

BOŽIĆ, D., 2002, Il vasselame bronzeo romano: grandi bacili e piccoli mestoli-colini, in *I bronzi antichi: Produzione e tecnologia*, Atti del XV Congresso Internazionale sui Bronzi Antichi, edited by Alessandra Giumlia-Mair, Montagnac, p. 419-428.

BRUNŠMID, J., 1895, Njekoliko našašća na skupu u Hrvatskoj i Slavoniji II. Našašće rimskih obiteljskih denara između Valpova i Osijeka. *Vjesnik Hrvatskog arheološkog društva* 1, Nova serija, p. 108-114.

BRUNŠMID, J., 1902, Colonia Aurelia Cibalae. *Vjesnik Hrvatskog arheološkog društva* 6, Nova serija, p. 117-166.

BRUNŠMID, J., 1909, Prethistorijski predmeti iz Srijemske županije. *Vjesnik Hrvatskog arheološkog društva* 10, Nova serija, p. 231-237.

BRUNŠMID, J., 1912, Njekoliko našašća na skupu u Hrvatskoj i Slavoniji XXXIV. Nahođej srebrnih ilirskih i rimskih novaca II i I stoljeća prije Kr. u Vukovaru. *Vjesnik Hrvatskog arheološkog društva* 12, Nova serija, p. 260-271.

CASTOLDI, M. & FEUGÈRE, M., 1991, Les simpulums. In *La vaisselle tardo-républicaine en bronze*, edited by M. Feugère & C. Rolley. Dijon: Université de Bourgogne, p. 61-88.

DIMITRIJEVIĆ, S., 1979, Arheološka topografija i izbor arheoloških nalaza s vinkovačkog tla. *Izdanja Hrvatskog arheološkog društva* 4, p. 133-282.

---

[35] Popović 1992: 61

[36] Strabo, IV.6.10

[37] Strabo, V.1.8

[38] Popović 1992: 73-74

[39] Popović 1987: 96-104, 155, sl. 29.

[40] Brunšmid 1912: 260-271; Dukat & Mirnik 1976: 196, 200, fig. 3; Dukat & Mirnik 1978: 198. fig. 1

[41] Brunšmid 1895: 108-114

[42] Popović 1987: 113, 125

DIZDAR, M., 1998, Nekropola keltsko-latenske kulture u Vinkovcima. *Obavijesti Hrvatskog arheološkog društva* 1/1998, p. 38-43.

DIZDAR, M., 1999, Željezno doba, In *Vinkovci u svijetu arheologije*, edited by S. Jozić. Vinkovci: Museum Vinkovci, p. 39-48., 111-121.

DIZDAR, M., 2001, *Latenska naselja na vinkovačkom području*. Dissertationes et Monographiae Zagrabiensis 3. Zagreb: University of Zagreb.

DIZDAR M., 2001a, Nalazišta latenske kulture na vinkovačkom području. *Prilozi Instituta za arheologiju u Zagrebu* 18, p. 103-134.

DUKAT, Z. & MIRNIK, I., 1976, Pre-Roman coinage on the territory of modern Yugoslavia, *Bulletin 13, Institute of Archaeology*, p. 175-210.

DUKAT, Z. & MIRNIK, I., 1978, Skupni nalazi novca u sjevernoj Hrvatskoj, *Izdanja Hrvatskog arheološkog društva* 2, p. 197-208.

GUILLAUMET, J.-P., 1977, Les passoires de la fin de La Tène en Gaule et dans le monde celtique. *Gallia* 35/2, p. 239-248.

GUILLAUMET, J.-P., 1991, Les passoires. In *La vaisselle tardo-républicaine en bronze*, edited by M. Feugère & C. Rolley. Dijon: Université de Bourgogne. p. 89-95.

GUŠTIN, M., 1984, Die Kelten in Jugoslawien, *Jahrbuch des Römisch-Germanischen Zentralmuseums* 31, p. 305-363.

GUŠTIN, M., 1991, *Posočje in der jüngeren Eisenzeit*. Ljubljana: Narodni muzej.

KLEMENC, J., 1961, Limes u Donjoj Panoniji. *Zbornik radova sa simposiuma o limesu 1960. godine*, Beograd, p. 5-34.

LŐRINCZ, B. & REDŐ, F., 1994, *Onomasticon Provinciarum Europae Latinarum, Vol. I: ABA – BYSANUS*. Budapest: Archaeolingua.

MAJNARIĆ-PANDŽIĆ, N., 1969, Gradina, Orolik – kasnolatensko naselje. Arheološki pregled 11, p. 79-81.

MAJNARIĆ-PANDŽIĆ, N., 1970, *Keltsko-latenska kultura u Slavoniji i Srijemu*. Acta Musei Cibalensis 2. Vinkovci: Gradski muzej.

MAJNARIĆ-PANDŽIĆ, N., 1972-1973, Kasnolatenski keltski grobovi iz Sotina, *Vjesnik Arheološkog muzeja u Zagrebu* 6-7, 3. Serija, p. 55-74.

MAJNARIĆ-PANDŽIĆ, N., 1978, Pregled istraživanja keltskolatenske kulture u sjevernoj Hrvatskoj, *Izdanja Hrvatskog arheološkog društva* 2, p. 149-158.

MAJNARIĆ-PANDŽIĆ, N., 1981, Gradina u Privlaci – utvrđeno kasnolatensko naselje, *Arheološki pregled* 22, p. 45-47.

MAJNARIĆ-PANDŽIĆ, N., 1984, Prilog problematici kasnolatenskih naselja u Slavoniji, *Opuscula Archaeologica* 9, p. 23-34.

MAJNARIĆ-PANDŽIĆ, N., 1994, Sjaj bronce i željeza u praskozorju povijesti. In *Vukovar – vjekovni hrvatski grad na Dunavu*, edited by I. Karaman. Zagreb, p. 65-80.

MAJNARIĆ-PANDŽIĆ, N., 1996, Einige Beispiele der spätlatènezeitlichen Siedlungen in Nordkroatien und ihre Beziehung zu den Zentren der frühen Romanisation, *Arheološki Vestnik* 47, p. 257.-266.

MAJNARIĆ-PANDŽIĆ, N., 1996a, CORNACUM (Sotin) and CIBALAE (Vinkovci) as Examples of the Early Romanization of La Tène Communities in Southern Pannonia. In *Kontakte längs der Bernsteinstrasse (zwischen Caput Adriae und den Ostseegebiet) in der Zeit um Christi Geburt*. Krakow, p. 23-33.

MIRNIK, I., 1981, Coin Hoards in Yugoslavia. Oxford: British Archaeological Reports, International Series 95.

PINTEROVIĆ, D., 1968, Limesstudien in der Baranja und in Slawonien. *Archaeologia Iugoslavica IX*, p. 55-82.

POPOVIĆ, P., 1987, *Novac Skordiska, Novac i novčani promet na Centralnom Balkanu od IV. do I. veka pr. n. e.* Beograd – Novi Sad.

POPOVIĆ, P., 1992, Italische Bronzegefässe im Skordiskergebiet. *Germania* 70/1, p. 61-74.

POPOVIĆ P., 1992a, Skordisci od pada Makedonije do rimskog osvajanja, In *Skordisci i starosedeoci*. edited by N. Tasić. Beograd, p. 95-110.

POPOVIĆ, P., 1992-1993, The Territories of Scordisci, *Starinar* 43-44, p. 13-21.

RADNÓTI, A., 1938, Die römischen Bronzegefässe von Pannonien. Budapest: Institut für Münzkunde und Archäologie der P. Pázmany-Universität.

SPAJIĆ, E., 1954, Nalazište mlađeg željeznog doba s terena Osijeka, *Osječki Zbornik 4*, p. 7.-18.

SPAJIĆ, E., 1956, Nalazište mlađeg željeznog doba s terena Osijeka, *Osječki Zbornik 5*, p. 47-53.

SPAJIĆ, E., 1962, Nalazište mlađeg željeznog doba s terena Osijeka, *Osječki Zbornik 8*, p. 37-55.

ŠIMIĆ, J., 1997, Kelti, in *Kelti i Rimljani na području Osijeka*. Osijek: Muzej Slavonije, p. 3-49.

VINSKI, Z. 1953, Arheološka istraživanja u Vukovaru. *Vjesnik muzealaca i konzervatora Hrvatske II/2*, p. 21-23.

VINSKI, Z. 1959, Ausgrabungen in Vukovar. *Archaeologia Iugoslavica III*, p. 99-109.

LA CÉRAMIQUE DACE TRAVAILLÉE A LA MAIN DE TIBISCUM

Doina BENEA

L'intégration culturelle de la population indigène de la province de Dacia dans les nouvelles formes d'habitat créées après la conquête romaine de 106 constitue l'un des domaines les plus intéressants de l'histoire de cette province.

La modalité la plus connue de dépister les éléments locaux daces dans les différents milieux provinciaux (camps, *vici militari*, villes, *villae rusticae* etc.) est la céramique. D'habitude, on étudie la céramique travaillée à la main, dans la manière La Tène spécifique à la population dace, céramique qui représente, par la pâte, les formes, les motifs ornementaux, des éléments d'attribution inconfondables.

La littérature de spécialité moderne européenne a depuis longtemps pris en discussion ce phénomène pour les provinces rhenanes, par exemple (Uslar 1934, 81-82).

Dans l'historiographie roumaine, c'est Constantin Daicoviciu qui a attiré, pour la première fois, l'attention sur l'importance de la céramique dace dans le milieu provincial romain de la Dacia, comme élément définitoire de la présence de la population indigène dans la vie sociale et économique romaine (1943, 103-105).

La céramique travaillée à la main en manière dace a été découverte dans de différents milieux provinciaux. Probablement, l'accent particulier accordé par la littérature de spécialité roumaine aux camps romains a fait que la plupart des découvertes publiées proviennent justement des fortifications romaines. Mais la céramique dace est attestée dans le milieu civil, dans les *villae rusticae*, dans les villages, dans les villes (à l'exception de Ulpia Traiana Sarmizegetusa).

Une analyse approfondie des découvertes de la Dacia Porolissensis a été réalisée il y a plusieurs années par N. Gudea et I. Moțu, qui ont synthétisé les découvertes plus anciennes de Orheiul Bistriței, Bologa, Buciumi, Râșnov et leurs propres découvertes de Porolissum (Moigrad), Gilău (Gudea, Moțu 1988, 229-250). Les auteurs ont essayé d'attirer l'attention sur la nécessité d'une étude complexe concernant la céramique travaillée à la main, d'après le lieu où elle a été découverte, le contexte stratigraphique général dans lequel cette céramique est apparue, la datation de certaines formes en fonction de la céramique provinciale romaine et, enfin, l'influence de la céramique romaine sur les formes de céramique travaillées à la main, la provenance des vases travaillés à la main. Ces critères facilitent, d'une manière évidente, une connaissance approfondie de cette catégorie céramique, fait confirmé par les découvertes de Buciumi, Porolissum, Bologa et, plus récemment, de Gilău (Gudea, Moțu 1988, 245-250; Marcu,

Țentea 1997, 235-267). A tout cela, il faut ajouter les recherches publiées récemment concernant Brâncovenești et Ilișua (Protase, Zrinyi 1994, passim; Protase, Gaiu, Marinescu 1996 passim).

La céramique travaillée à la main, découverte dans quelques camps de la Dacia Superior (comme *Drobeta, Praetorium, Tibiscum, Micia, Cumidava* (Râșnov) et de la Dacia Inferior (*Acidava, Buridava,* Brețcu, Olteni) a été présentée dans des études qui abordaient les fortifications respectives (Floca 1968, 49-58; Macrea 1967, 113-123; Tudor 1967, 655-656; Gudea 1980, 232-255; Petolescu 1986, 156-163; Marinoiu, Camui 1986, 138-158; Rogozea 1988, 165-173).

Quelques études ont abordé aussi la présentation de la céramique travaillée à la main dans les établissements civils situés à côté des camps, respectivement dans des *vici militaris*. Bien que peu nombreuses, les recherches entamées pour le moment sur les matériaux découverts à *Porolissum, Tibiscum, Acidava* (Enoșești), *Praetorium* (Mehadia) se sont limitées à présenter la typologie des formes de vases, leur origine dans le milieu préromain, l'évolution de certains types de vases dans l'époque romaine, qui ne différent nullement par rapport à ceux découverts dans le milieu militaire de la Dacie et dans celui des établissements autochtones, comme par exemple Locusteni, Obreja, Soporul de Câmpie etc.

Les découvertes sont beaucoup moins nombreuses dans les établissements situés à côté des camps (*vici militaris*). Ce fait est dû, en grande mesure, au manque des recherches systématiques dans ce type d'établissements à caractère semi-urbain. Nous considérons donc que la présence de quelques découvertes seulement représente une carence d'information archéologique, pour le moment.

Le camp et l'établissement civil d'à côté représentent, jusqu'à un certain moment de leur existence, une unité structurale du point de vue de la formation de l'établissement et de son administration, jusqu'à son détachement et la formation d'un centre urbain proprement-dit. Ce phénomène est connu seulement après le règne de Septimius Severus.

Dans l'étude de la céramique travaillée à la main de Tibiscum, nous allons soumettre à l'analyse tout le matériel découvert, tant dans le camp que dans l'établissement civil. A l'occasion de la publication de certains objectifs du vicus militaire et du camp, on a présenté aussi des fragments céramiques travaillés à la main (Benea 1982, 31 sq.; Bona, Petrovszky 1983, 410; Rogozea 1988, 165-178).

CÉRAMIQUE DACE SUR LE
TERRITOIRE DE TIBISCUM

III. siècle et postromaine

milieu II-ème siècle

TIMIŞ

0   20   40   60   80   100 M

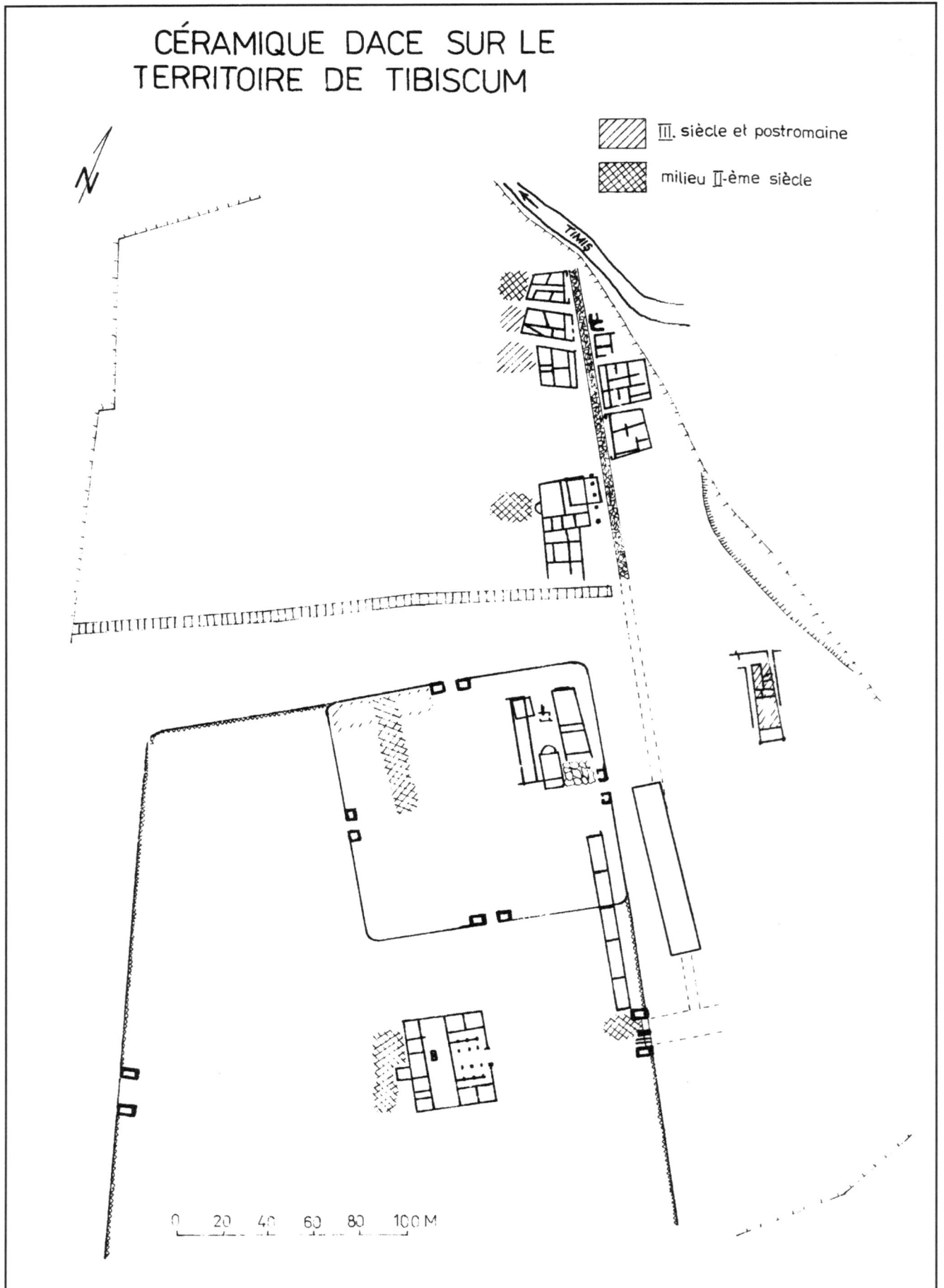

Plate I. Le camp et le vicus militaire de Tibiscum (Dacie).

Les camps de Tibiscum ont eu 6 étapes principales d'habitation. Initialement, il a existé un *castellum* en bois (60 x 60 m) avec deux fossés de défense, datable de la période des guerres de conquête de la Dacie. (Pl. I).

Un nouveau camp en terre, beaucoup élargi, a été élevé au même endroit après 106; il a été refait en pierre au temps de Hadrian et c'est ici qu'a stationné *cohors I Sagittariorum,* la phase Tibiscum II/1-2. Le camp avait les dimensions de 102 x 110 m. Au sud du camp II, ayant le fossé joint à cette fortification, on a construit un autre camp, dont l'existence a été courte - jusqu'au temps de Antoninus Pius-Marcus Aurelius. Après le nivellement de l'aire entière des deux fortifications, on a élevé le grand camp en pierre (IV), qui a reçu une forme particulière grâce à l'incorporation des deux fortifications (II et III) antérieures.

Le grand camp représente une reconstruction au temps des Severus, probablement Caracalla, et une autre au temps de Gallienus. La dernière étape d'habitation est celle post-romaine, caractérisée par des aménagements d'espaces d'habitation sous formes de huttes, l'emplacement d'annexes sur l'agger (des fours ménagers dans lesquels ont apparu aussi des fragments céramiques travaillés à la main, de facture dace). Le grand camp de Tibiscum a constitué le lieu de stationnement pour trois troupes auxiliaires: *cohors I Vindelicorum, numerus Palmyrenorum, numerus Maurorum* (Benea, Bona 1994, 38-60).

Dans le vicus militaire de Tibiscum on a étudié jusqu'à présent 10 édifices à caractère privé, respectivement des maisons avec une série de dépendances situées tout près. Dans le vicus militaire on constate d'habitude 4 grands niveaux d'habitation, qui souffrent des modifications spécifiques à chaque maison:

1. Les habitations sont caractérisées par des constructions en bois détruites par un incendie violent. Cette étape date des années 106-117.

2. Les premiers édifices en pierre sont construits à partir de l'époque de Hadrian; c'est toujours un incendie violent qui achève cette période, approximativement entre 158-167.

3. La fin de l'époque de Septimus Severus-Caracalla marque des perturbations dans la vie de l'établissement.

4. L'époque post-romaine, dans laquelle on constate l'utilisation des anciens bâtiments, mais avec une compartimentation plus réduite des espaces réalisée par des "murs secs".

La céramique travaillée à la main apparaît dans la plupart des objectifs étudiés jusqu'en 1999 (date limite pour la présente étude). Rarement, on a découvert des pièces entières, surtout des couvercles, des patères. (Nous préférons utiliser cette dénomination, à la place de celle de "terrines", utilisée dans certains travaux, ayant en vue justement la forme, empruntée à la céramique provinciale romaine). La majeure partie des pièces sont fragmentaires.

La céramique travaillée à la main a été découverte sur toute la surface étudiée à l'intérieur des camps (I, II/1-2).

Pour le grand camp (IV/1-3), on a constaté sa présence dans la zone de l'*agger*, de la *principia* et du bâtiment III (d'ailleurs, ce sont les seules zones que nous avons étudiées pour toutes ces phases d'habitation). La plus grande quantité de fragments céramiques travaillés à la main apparaît constamment dans les premiers niveaux d'habitation des camps de Tibiscum: sporadiquement dans *castellum* (1), dans le petit camp (II-1, 2) et dans les deux dernières étapes d'habitation du grand camp, datées du milieu du III-ème siècle et du siècle suivant.

La situation est presque similaire pour le vicus, avec un seul amendement. Dans le cas de certaines découvertes des édifices I, II, III, VII, VIII, de tels fragments apparaissent surtout dans les ateliers des artisans (ateliers de poterie, de bijoutier, de verrerie etc), et moins dans les habitations privées. Nous mentionnons la présence des couvercles travaillés à la main en pâte grossière brun-roussâtre avec des traces de scorie ou de métal fondu, découverts dans les ateliers no. 1 et no. 3 de Tibiscum (Benea, Bona 1994, 96-100). Ils attestent l'utilisation de la main d'oeuvre indigène dans les ateliers locaux du vicus militaire.

En échange, dans le bâtiment X, qui représente une simple maison privée, une telle céramique n'apparaît pas dans la phase en bois du bâtiment; elle n'y apparaît qu'à partir du IV-ème niveau d'habitation du bâtiment en pierre, daté de la première moitié du III-ème siècle.

La céramique travaillée à la main a une pâte qui est toujours mélangée au sable et à des cailloux ayant le rôle de dégraissant, parfois aussi au mica. La cuisson est inégale, comprenant une palette de couleurs allant du brun-roussâtre jusqu'au gris-brunâtre, et même jusqu'au noir. Dans les niveaux correspondant au II-ème siècle - début du III-ème siècle, on constate une amélioration de la qualité de la pâte, ce qui entraîne l'obtention des formes plus sveltes des récipients.

Les motifs ornementaux sont ceux caractéristiques, connus déjà à l'époque La Tène: la bande entaillée et celle alvéolaire, qui couvrent parfois la partie ayant le diamètre maximal du pot; le bord décoré d'entailles. De tels éléments de décoration apparaissent seulement sur les pots, le reste des formes ne présentent aucune décoration. Dans le dernier niveau d'habitation du camp on a trouvé aussi un pot décoré de boutons.

La céramique travaillée à la main de facture dace découverte à Tibiscum s'inscrit généralement dans le répertoire des formes caractéristiques pour la province de Dacia.

Du point de vue typologique, il y a quatre catégories céramiques: des pots (I), des patères (II), des couvercles (III), des tasses (IV).

I. LES POTS ont plusieurs variantes:

1. **Pots** (Pl. II/ 1-2) au bord à peine retroussé, au corps globulaire et à la partie bombée maximale sous le bord. Le fond en est plat. Les dimensions sont moyennes. La

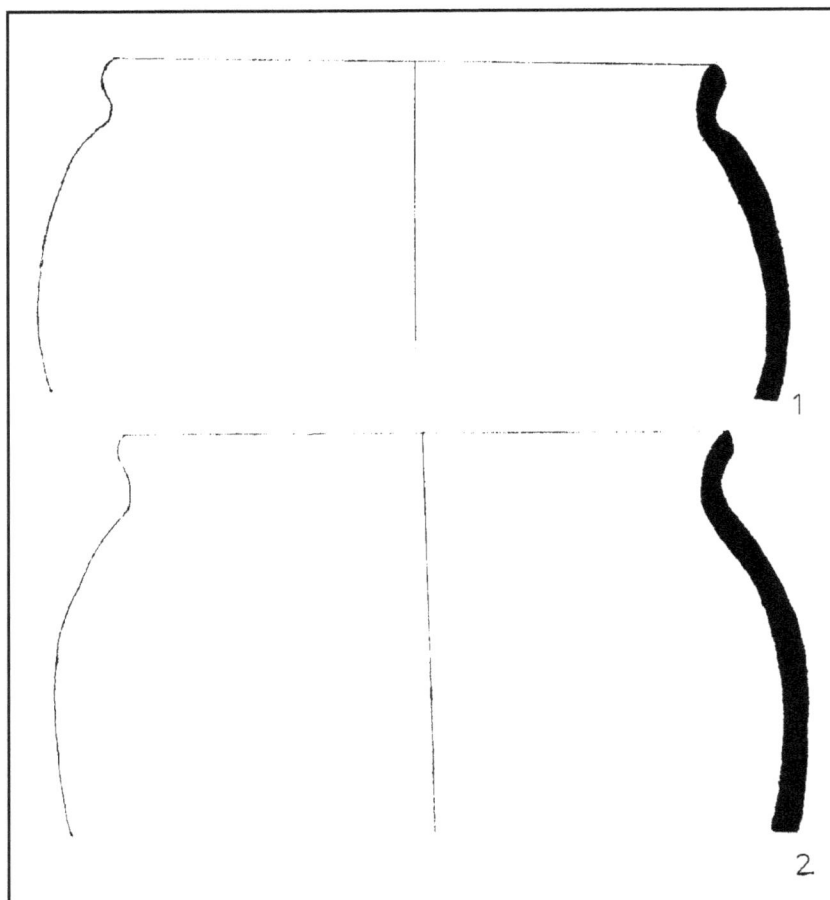

Plate II. 1-2 Pots daces de type 1 découverts à Tibiscum.

décoration manque. La datation, réalisée d'après le contexte, tant dans le vicus que dans le camp, est de la première moitié du II-ème siècle.

2. A. Pots (Pl. III/ 3) au bord droit ou un peu évasé, au corps ovale. Sur les fragments gardés, la décoration manque.

B. Pots (Pl. III/ 4-7, 9) au bord fortement retroussé en dehors et aux parois courbées. Ce sont des formes typiques déjà à partir du I-er siècle après J.-Ch. (Des analogies: Crişan 1969 Pl. .99, Glodariu 1981, type 27; Marcu-Ţentea 1997, 236-237, type I a/ 2). La datation est réalisée par des analogies dans la phase Gilău I. La forme existe jusqu'au III-ème siècle.

A Tibiscum, la datation est réalisée d'après le contexte, surtout de la première moitié du II-ème siècle (les pièces 4, 6 à l'époque Trajan-Hadrian, et les pièces 5, 6, 7 - de la première moitié du III-ème siècle.)

C. Pot (Pl. IV/ 10, 12) au bord retroussé, décoré parfois d'entailles, ayant le corps allongé et bombé dans la partie inférieure, avec un aspect piriforme. La décoration manque. Il est caractéristique à Tibiscum pour les derniers niveaux d'habitation, datables du III-ème siècle, vers le milieu (les bâtiments II, VII, X, par exemple). On en trouve des analogies à Gilău, dans la

dernière phase d'habitation (Marcu-Ţentea 1997, Pl. 6/3). L'origine du type se trouve dans l'époque préromaine (Glodariu 1981 Pl. 2/ 24; Bichir 1984, Pl. 9/ 1).

3. Pot (Pl. III/ 8) ayant le corps globulaire, le bord petit et retroussé, beaucoup épaissi dans la zone du cou. C'est un pot de petites dimensions. Il n'est pas décoré. Selon le contexte stratigraphique, dans le camp de Tibiscum, il appartient au niveau 2 d'existence du grand camp (de la première moitié du III-ème siècle).

4. A. Pot (Pl. IV/ 13,14, 15.) ayant l'aspect d'un bol, au corps rond, au bord à peine évasé, à la bouche large de petites dimensions, ce qui a déterminé son inclusion dans la catégorie des bols (Popilian 1976, type 5; Brukner 1981 Pl. 78, 79, 80, 81, 85). Des analogies: fréquemment dans les niveaux Gilău II et III. A Tibiscum, il est attesté surtout dans le vicus militaire (le bâtiment VIII datable du milieu du III-ème siècle; le bâtiment X de la première moitié du III-ème siècle (v. Rogozea 1988, Pl. 2/ 3, 3/ 2).

B. Pot (Pl. IV/ 11) aux parois minces, à la bouche large, au bord à peine retroussé, au fond plat, de couleur brun-rougeâtre; la cuisson est inégale. La pièce a été découverte dans le vicus, le bâtiment I (atelier de verrerie) à 0,40-0,70 m; daté du III-ème siècle.

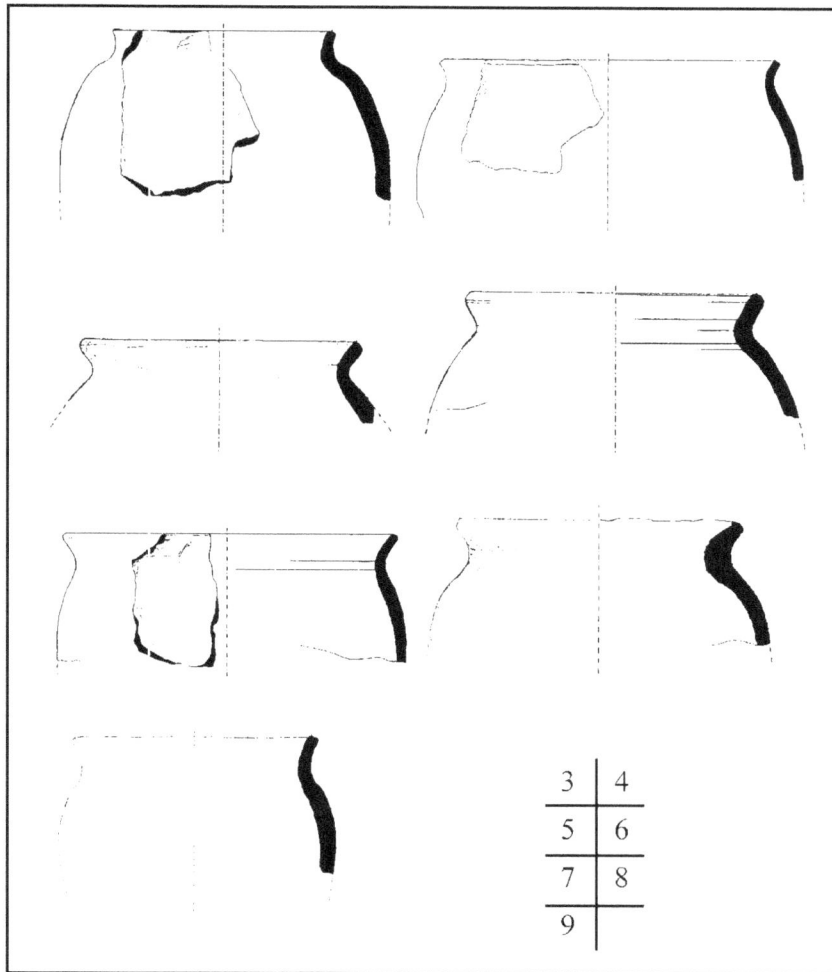

Plate III. 3. Pot dace de type 2 A découvert à Tibiscum ; 4-7. Pots de type 2 B; 8. Pot dace de type 3.

Les pots travaillés à la main présentent des variantes intéressantes, déterminées surtout par la courbure du corps du récipient; la hauteur en est moins réduite, en échange l'ouverture de la bouche a un diamètre plus grand. A de rares exceptions près, le pot est ornementé dans la partie supérieure du corps de la pièce avec une bande alvéolaire. Par leurs dimensions, les pots travaillés à la main découverts à Tibiscum ont dû servir surtout à préparer les aliments et moins à les garder.

Le répertoire des formes de pots est relativement pauvre. En grande mesure, il continue, en tant que formes et même en tant que motifs ornementaux, ceux de l'époque pré-romaine. D'une manière certaine, on remarque une amélioration dans la qualité de la pâte, qui est mieux travaillée, même si elle contient des cailloux, du sable fin et du mica dans sa composition.

II. LES PATERES (Pl. VI/ 1-2 ; Fig. 2) sont des récipients confectionnés en pâte grossière gris-noirâtre, ayant pour dégraissant, dans leur composition, le mica, le sable et même des caillloux. La pâte est mieux pétrie et le finissage extérieur et intérieur du vase est fait plus soigneusement. Les pièces sont réalisées simplement d'une

plaque ronde qui constitue le fond du récipient, auquel on "attache" une bande large de 3-5 cm, appliquée en position verticale ou oblique. La partie la plus fragile des vases est le point de jonction de la bande à la plaque constituant le fond, ce qui détermine la détérioration du récipient. Parfois, la partie supérieure se termine avec un bord épaissi à l'extérieur, droit ou oblique à l'intérieur. Pratiquement, le répertoire des formes est unique, avec plusieurs variantes déterminées par la hauteur des parois et leur caractère oblique.

Comme type de vase, la patère (dont la dénomination est peut-être impropre) a été empruntée à la céramique provinciale romaine où elle se rangeait parmi les vases utilisés à servir la nourriture. Les dimensions des pièces à des diamètres variables, utilisées dans le monde romain, suggère l'existence de services de table. Les découvertes de Tibiscum, avec un diamètre de 15-20 cm, suggèrent une catégorie moyenne de tels récipients.

Des pièces similaires sont attestés dans les camps de Gilău (les phases I-III), Buciumi, avec une datation générale dans les siècles II-III (Marcu-Ţentea 1997, 238; Gudea 1970, 306; Gudea, Moţu 1988, 233). Selon le contexte stratigraphique, les découvertes de Tibiscum apparaissent

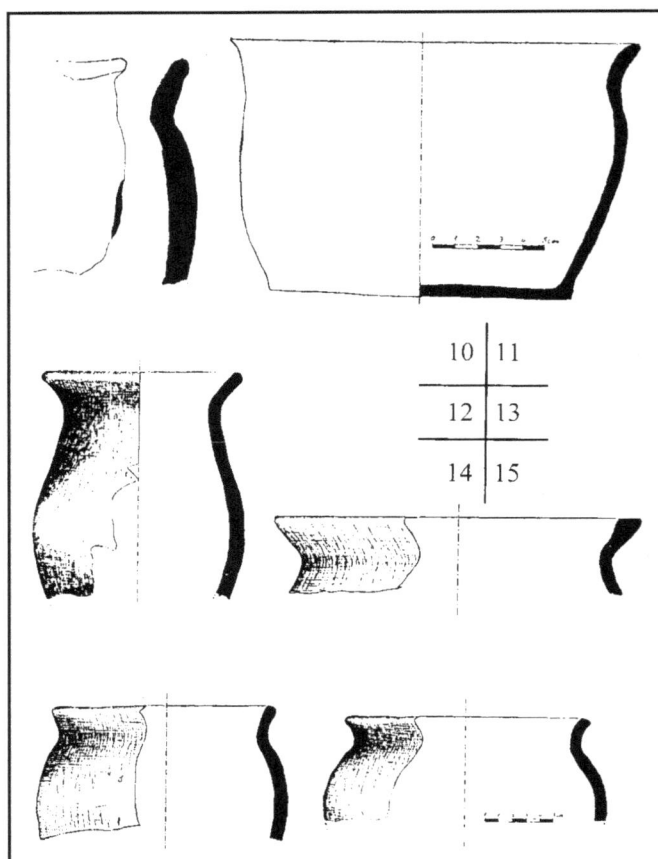

Plate IV: 10, 12 Pots de type 2 C découverts à Tibiscum ; 13-15. Pots de type 4.

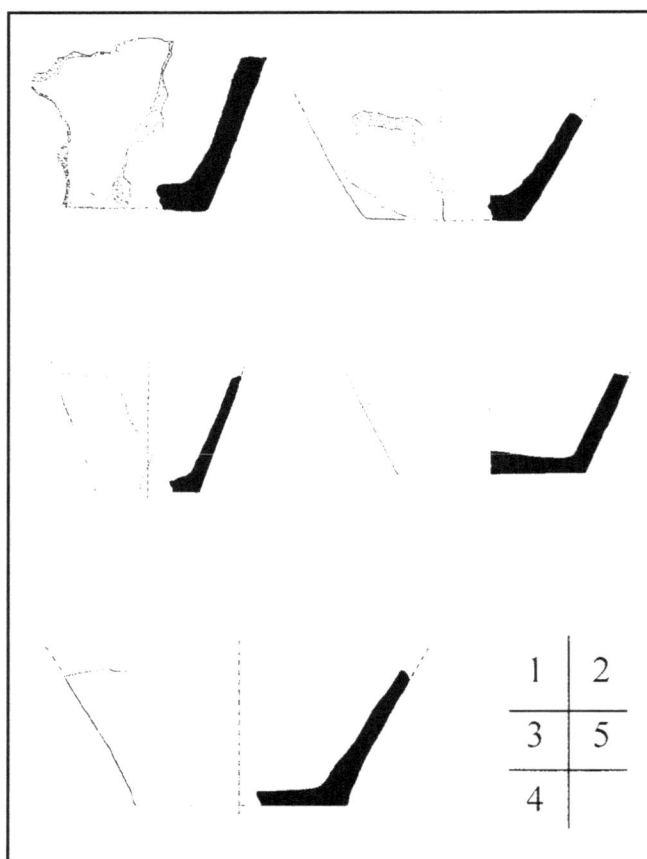

Plate V. 1-5 Fonds de pots découverts à Tibiscum.

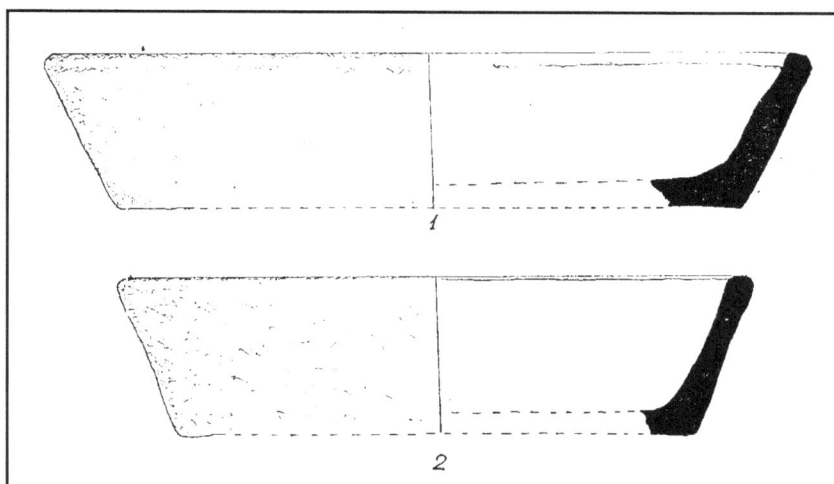

Plate VI. Patères découvertes à Tibiscum.

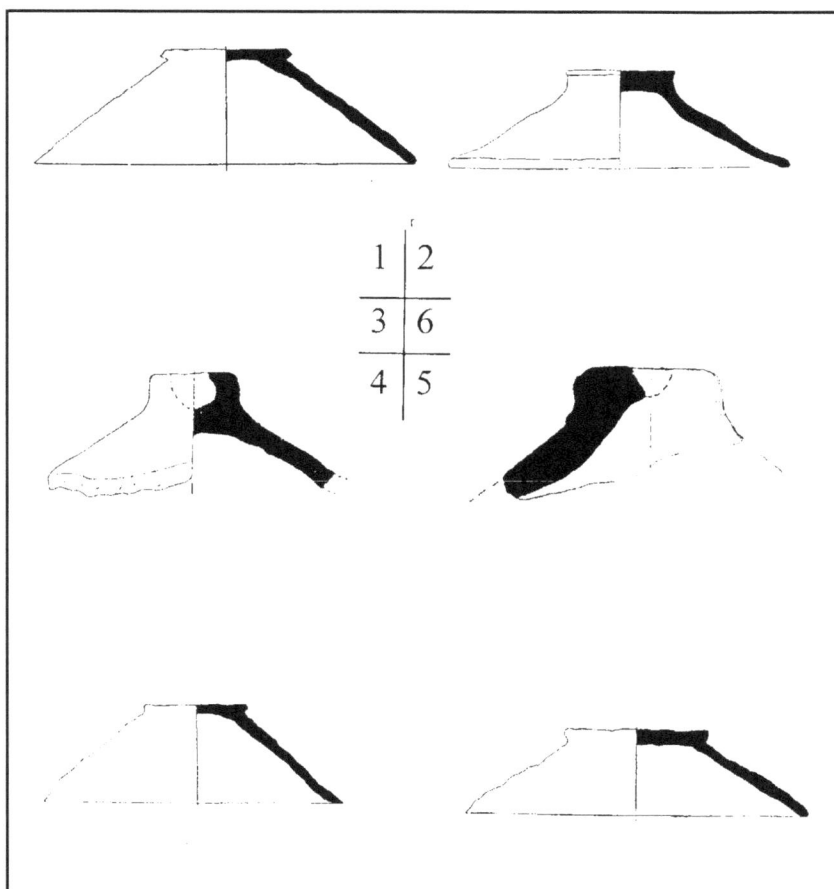

Plate VII. 1-6. Couvercles découverts à Tibiscum.

surtout dans le vicus militaire; parmi celles-ci, seulement 2 exemplaires sont entiers et 24 sont fragmentaires. Ils ont été découverts dans: le bâtiment I dans le premier niveau d'habitation; le bâtiment VII dans le niveau datable de la première moitié du III-ème siècle; le bâtiment II (le premier niveau d'habitation de l'édifice en pierre, à l'époque de Hadrian); dans les ateliers des artisans découverts dans le vicus, situés à l'ouest des bâtiments: I,

II, III, VII, VIII et dans les aménagements romains tardifs situés sur le côté nord du grand camp, découverts en 1989. Des découvertes similaires sont attestées dans les camps de Bologa, Buciumi, Gilău.

III. LES COUVERCLES (Pl. VII/ 1-6 ; Fig. 4/ 1-6) étaient confectionnés en général en pâte brun-roussâtre,

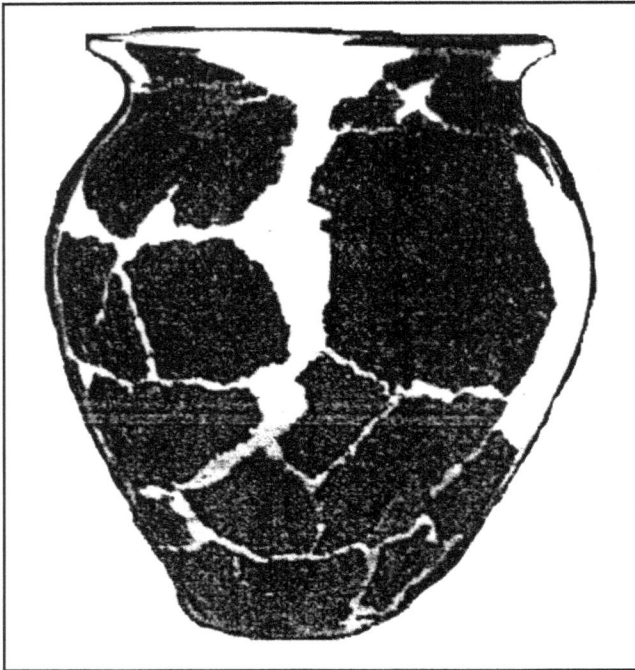

Figure 1. Pot de tradition celtique découvert dans le camp de Tibiscum.

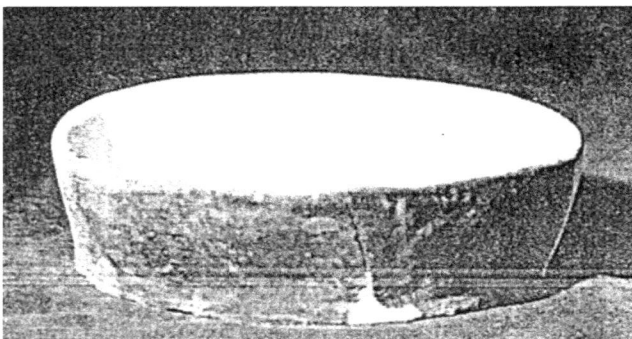

Figure 2. Patère travaillée à la main découverte dans le bâtiment VII du vicus militaire de Tibiscum.

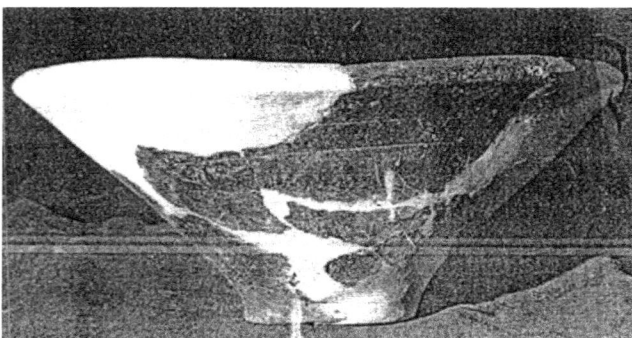

Figure 3. Tasse dace travaillée à la main découverte dans le bâtiment II du vicus militaire de Tibiscum.

mieux travaillée, du même type que la pâte dont on réalisait les patères. À l'époque romaine, elles on les a

utiliseés en tant que lampe, pour l'éclairage. Les analogies pour de telles pièces sont attestées dans les camps de Gilău, Bologa, Buciumi etc. Elles aparaissent tant dans le milieu militaire que dans le vicus.

Les couvercles présentent une seule forme avec des variantes qui se ressemblent beaucoup. (forme tronconique, dimensions variables, des boutons ronds). Les couvercles de Tibiscum travaillés à la main n'ont pas de seuil intérieur. Ils ne sont pas décorés.

IV. LES TASSES DACES (Fig. 3). Du point de vue de la technique de réalisation, les tasses daces sont travaillées dans une pâte brun-roussâtre, ayant dans la composition des impuretés, du sable fin et même du mica. Les pièces sont fumées à l'intérieur. Tous les exemplaires ont des parois fortement obliques en dehors et la base large. A l'époque romane, on les a utilisées en tant que lampes, pour l'éclairage. Il paraît que les pièces diminuent en hauteur.

Dans une étude récente consacrée aux tasses daces travaillées à la main, Mircea Negru a réalisé une typologie de cette catégorie céramique, en fonction du nombre d'anses, en apportant aussi des précisions concernant la datation des formes en fonction du contexte de la découverte (1998, 26-42). Les exemplaires découverts à Tibiscum ne comportent pas d'anses.

Ces exemplaires sont apparus presque tous dans les bâtiments du vicus militaire, respectivement: une pièce a été découverte dans *le bâtiment I,* utilisée dans l'atelier où l'on produisait des perles de verre; 2 exemplaires dans le *bâtiment II* (atelier de verrerie). Ces exemplaires, datés, d'après le contexte stratigraphique, du milieu du II-ème siècle, étaient utilisés dans le processus de production, ayant des traces de scorie à l'intérieur et à l'extérieur de la pièce. On a découvert 2 exemplaires dans *le bâtiment X,* dans le niveau d'habitation de la demeure (1,10-1,40 m); ils peuvent être datés de la première moitié du III-ème siècle.

Le nombre d'exemplaires découverts à Tibiscum est réduit pour cette catégorie de vases. Pour le moment, il manque dans le camp des fragments de tasses daces; en échange, ceux-ci apparaissent dans le vicus militaire, dans presque tous les bâtiments étudiés. Il faut remarquer la présence de certains fragments céramiques travaillés à la main dans les ateliers de poterie, de verrerie (le bâtiment I), de bijoutier et de production du bronze. Des exemplaires similaires ont été découverts à Gilău (les phases I-II) (Marcu-Țentea 1997, 238).

Le type de tasse sans anse aparaît déja à l'époque La Tène dace tardive. Son origine a été précisée, dans le cadre des formes de céramique daces, par I. Glodariu (1981, 161) et plus récemment par Gh. Bichir (1984, 31).

Nous devons signaler une catégorie à part de pièces céramiques travaillées à la main en pâte grossière avec du sable, du mica et des cailloux: il s'agit des tasses aux parois très obliques, avec un support annulaire détaché,

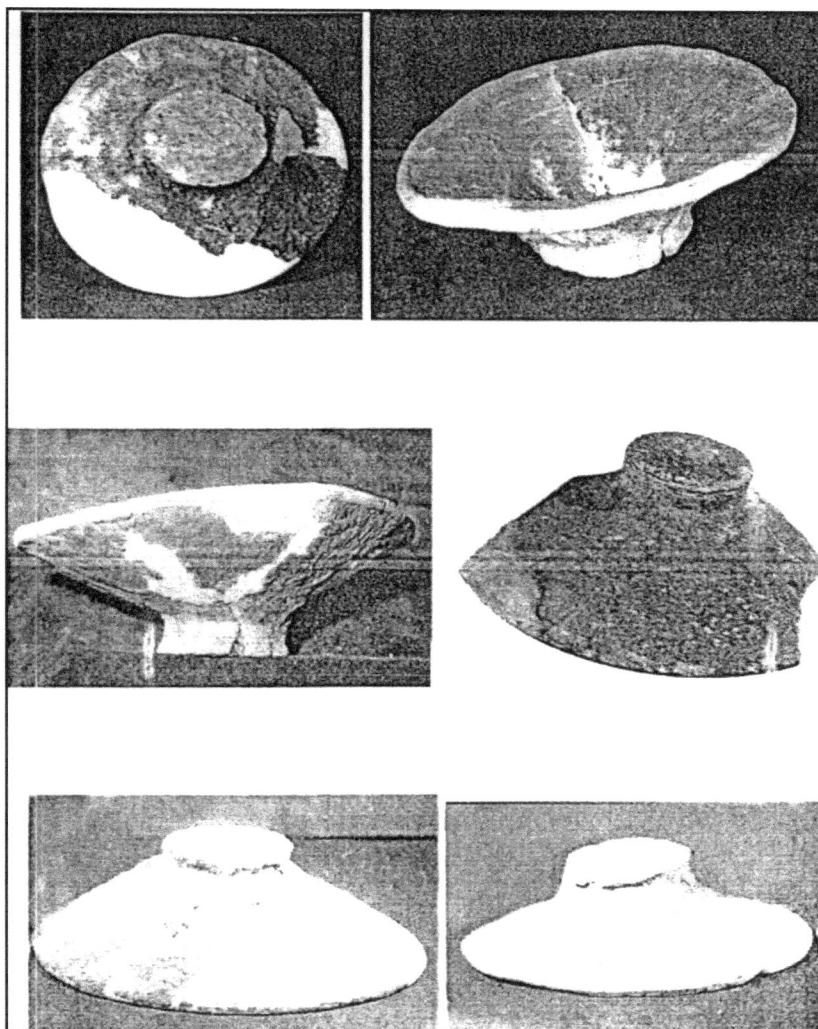

Figure 4. Couvercles de pots découverts dans le camp et le vicus militaire de Tibiscum

utilisées dans les ateliers des artisans du vicus militaire de Tibiscum. (Fig. 1). Elles présentent sur le côté extérieur un enduit de scorie métallique en tant que couche protectrice; à l'intérieur, il y a des traces de bronze fondu. De telles pièces, entières ou fragmentaires, ont été découvertes dans l'atelier identifié en 1986, près du bâtiment VII. Dans le même atelier, on a découvert, à côté de fragments de creusets ordinaires tronconiques, un bol semi-circulaire réalisé dans une pâte grise bien travaillée avec un dégraissant plus fin, ayant une couche protectrice extérieure de scorie métallique. (D. le diamètre de la bouche 8,5 cm; la hauteur 4,2 cm).

Dans le cadre de la céramique travaillée à la main on peut mentionner aussi un pot et un couvercle confectionnés dans une pâte grossière travaillée à la main, de couleur gris-noirâtre. Le corps du vaisseau est couvert de raies fines incisées verticalement, réalisées avec le peigne ou avec un petit balai. La facture des pièces est différente par rapport à celle connue habituellement pour la céramique dace de Tibiscum ou d'autres sites de la Dacie Romaine. Les pièces ont été découvertes dans le bâtiment X dans le premier niveau d'habitation appartenant à l'édifice en

pierre (à une profondeur de 1,10-1,30 m). Le type d'ornement est connu dans l'époque La Tène dace tardive (Rogozea 1988, passim; Crişan 1969, 210, Pl. 107/9; Glodariu 1981, Fig. 2, nr.16, 39 etc.), mais il aparaît surtout dans le milieu norico-pannonien. Selon E. Bonis, ce type de décoration aurait son origine en Gaule, d'où il aurait pénétré en Pannonie (Bonis 1942, 35-37). Cette dernière opinion suggère la possibilité de la pénétration de cette catégorie de céramique dans l'espace de la province nord-danubienne, apportée par les colons établis en Dacie. La découverte de Tibiscum vient s'ajouter à d'autres, déja connues, de Ulpia Traiana Sarmizegetusa, Tihău et Gilău, où une telle céramique est apparue dans des camps dont les troupes provenaient de la province voisine, la Pannonie (Ardeţ 1991, 138; Marcu-Ţentea 1997, 242).

En guise de *conclusion:* à la fin de ce travail, nous allons reprendre brièvement les conclusions formulées le long de notre exposé.

La présence de la céramique travaillée à la main en manière dace a été constatée sur le territoire du camp et du vicus militaire de Tibiscum, notamment dans les premiers

63

niveaux d'habitation et ensuite dans les derniers, caractéristiques au III-ème siècle. L'analyse de la pâte et même des formes a permis une différenciation nette des variantes, à travers les 6 étapes d'habitation dans le camp et les 4 étapes dans le vicus militaire de Tibiscum.

La présence du mica en tant que dégraissant dans la composition de la pâte dont la céramique de tradition dace travaillée à la main découverte à Tibiscum est confectionnée représente une caractéristique pour la céramique romane locale des ateliers de Tibiscum aussi, ce qui suggère une production locale.

L'existence de la céramique dace dans les ateliers militaires du vicus suggère la possibilité de ceux-ci d'utiliser la main d'oeuvre locale indigène dans leur activité. On peut affirmer ausssi, avec certitude, la présence dans le vicus des colons d'origine celte, norico-pannonienne, venus à Tibiscum avec les premières troupes (cohors I Sagittariorum). La présence, dans le même édifice, de la céramique travaillée à la main de tradition celte, à côté de celle autochtone, ne peut constituer un simple hasard. Elle est due aux contacts humains, qui s'établissent entre le milieu indigène situé près du camp et la population du vicus, implicitement, l'armée qui y stationnait. Ces contacts humains présupposent *les obligations de la population locale de participer à des prestations de travail sur l'aire habitée du camp et du vicus, de s'enrôler dans l'armée et de pénétrer ainsi dans l'élite locale, d'engager des relations économiques avec la population du vicus militaire, en assurant soit la force de travail nécessaire, soit les produits agricoles pour le marché local.*

La présence de la céramique autochtone dans le milieu militaire et civil romain doit être mise en relation, d'une manière évidente, avec les éléments de la population autochtone qui y activaient, d'une façon ou d'une autre.

Il est difficile de démontrer maintenant la manière dont la céramique locale a pu influencer la céramique romaine, quoique certains éléments de décoration, tels la bande entaillée, soient reproduits sur certains types de pots travaillés à la roue, rencontrés à Tibiscum-même.

De toute façon, l'influence romaine sur la céramique locale s'est fait ressentir pleinement par l'amélioration de la qualité de la pâte, par la réalisation des formes plus sveltes du corps des vases. De même, les parois des vases deviennent plus minces et plus finement aplaties. Nous croyons que l'adoption de la patère à des diamètres différents, comme forme prédilecte de vase destiné à servir la nourriture, (récipient tellement typique pour la céramique des baraques romaines), représente la preuve la plus éloquente du fait qu'on avait accepté des innovations dans la céramique propre.

La datation de certaines catégories de récipients d'après le contexte stratigraphique de leur découverte à Tibiscum a contribué tout d'abord à un encadrement chronologique plus rigoureux des types respectifs. L'évolution de certaines formes de pots peut être suivie le long des siècles II - III et cela représente l'un des aspects de l'intégration culturelle, économique des autochtones dans le milieu

provincial romain. Attirer les indigènes dans le circuit de la vie romaine était nécessaire pour un meilleur contrôle de leur communauté.

Dans les derniers niveaux d'habitation on constate la présence plus marquante des fragments céramiques daces à Tibiscum, fait qui *pourrait* être dû à une éventuelle colonisation de daces libres, ce qui est parfois mentionné par les sources littéraires.

De toute façon, la céramique travaillée à la main, à côté de celle travaillée à la roue, en manière locale, tout comme certains types d'ornements confectionnés en argent constituent des preuves archéologiques certaines de l'intégration des autochtones daces dans le monde provincial romain de la Dacie.

Adresse de l'auteur

Doina BENEA
Université d'Ouest Timisoara
bd Vasile Parvan, 2-4
1900 Timişoara ROUMANIE

Bibliographie

ARDEŢI A., 1991, Ceramica dacică şi de tradiţie celtică la Ulpia Traiana Sarmizegetusa,Thraco- Dacica, 12, 138-141.

BENEA D., 1981, Cercetările arheologice de la Tibiscum, Materiale şi Cerc. Arh, 15, 305-312.

BENEA D. & Bona P., 1994, Tibiscum, Editura Museion, Bucureşti.

BICHIR G., 1984, Geto-dacii din Muntenia în epoca romană, Bucureşti.

BONA P., PETROVSZKI R. & PETROVSZKI M., 1983, Tibiscum–cercetări arheologice (II), ActaMN, 20, 405-432.

BONA P., PETROVSZKI R., ROGOZEA P., 1982, Tibiscum-cercetări arheologice (II) (1980-1981), Studii şi Comunicări Etnografie şi Istorie Caransebeş, 4, 185-207.

BRUKNER O., 1982, Rimska Keramika u jugoslovenskom delu provincije Donje Pannonia. Diss.et Monogr., 24, Beograd.

CHIRILĂ E., GUDEA N., LUCĂCEL V., POP C., 1972, Das Römerlager von Buciumi, Beiträge zur Untersuchung des Limes der Dacia Porolissensis, Cluj.

CRIŞAN I.H., 1969, Ceramica geto-dacică. Cu privire specială la Transilvania, Bucureşti.

DAICOVICIU C., 1943, La Transilvania nell'antichita, Bucarest.

FLOCA O., 1968, Pagus Miciensis, Sargeţia, 5, 49-58.

GLODARIU I., 1981, Aşezările dacice şi daco-romane de la Slimnic, Bucureşti.

GLODARIU I., 1981a Contribuţii la cronologia ceramicii dacice din epoca Latène târzie, Studii Dacice, Cluj-Napoca, 146-165.

GUDEA N., 1970, Ceramica dacică din castrul roman de la Buciumi, SCIV, 21, 2, 299-311.

GUDEA N., Pop I. 1970a, Castrul roman de la Râşnov-Cumidava, Braşov, 14, 57-60.

GUDEA N., 1977, Materiale arheologice din castrul roman de la Bologa, Apulum, 15, 169-185.

GUDEA N., 1980, Castrul roman de la Breţcu, ActaMP, 4, 255-332.

GUDEA N., MOŢU I., 1988, Despre ceramica provincială lucrată cu mâna din castre. Observaţii arheologice cu specială privire la câteva castre din Dacia Porolissensis, ActaMP, 12, 229-250.

GUDEA N., 1989, Porolissum.Un complex arheologic daco-roman la marginea Imperiului Roman(I), ActaMP, 13.

MACREA M., GUDEA N., MOŢU I., 1993, Praetorium. Castrul şi aşezarea romană de la Mehadia, Bucureşti.

MACREA M., PROTASE D., DĂNILĂ St., 1967, Castrul roman de la Orheiul Bistriţei, SCIVA,18, 1, 113-123.

MACREA M., GLODARIU I., 1976, Aşezarea dacică de la Arpaşu de Sus, Bucureşti.

MARCU F., ŢENTEA O., 1997, Ceramica lucrată cu mâna din castrul roman de la Gilău, Römer und Barbaren, ActaMP, (Festschrift für Limes Kongress), Zalău, 1997, 235-268.

MARINOIU V., CĂMUI I., 1986, Castrul roman de la Bumbeşti-Jiu,. Probleme de restaurare, Litua, 3, 138-158.

NEGRU M., 1997, An introduction to the Study of native hand-made Pottery from Dacia, Acta 35 RCRF, Ephesus, 97-106.

NEGRU M., CIUCĂ I., 1997, Ceramica dacică lucrată cu mâna descoperită în aşezarea civilă a castrului roman de la Enoşeşti-Acidava, Arhivele Olteniei, s.n., 12, 23-39.

NEGRU M., 1998, Consideraţii privind ceştile dacice modelate cu mâna descoperite în Dacia romană, Arhivele Olteniei, s.n., 13, 27-42.

PETOLESCU C.C., 1986, Cercetări arheologice în castrul roman de la Cătunele, Litua, 3, 156-158.

POPILIAN G., 1976, Ceramica romană din Oltenia, Craiova.

POPILIAN G., 1976a, Traditions autochtones dans la céramique provinciale romaine de la Dacie Méridionale, Thraco-Dacica, 1, 279-286.

POPILIAN G.,1980, Necropola daco-romană de la Locusteni, Craiova.

PROTASE D., 1976, Soporul de Câmpie. Un cimitir dacic din epoca romană, Bucureşti.

PROTASE D., 1980, Autohtoni în Dacia Romană, Bucureşti.

ROGOZEA P., 1988, Ceramica dacică din aşezarea dacică de la Tibiscum (I), Tibiscum VII, 165-179.

TUDOR D., 1967, Depozitul de vase dacice şi romane de la Stolniceni, SCIV, 18, 4, 655-670.

v. USLAR R., 1934, Saalburg Jahrbuch, 8, 81 non vidi, apud N. Gudea, I. Moţu, 1988, 229-230.

DES PRODUITS ALIMENTAIRES ET DES AMPHORES DE SELLIUM (TOMAR, PORTUGAL)

Salete da PONTE

Résumé : Les fouilles que nous avons réalisées à Sellium (Tomar – Portugal) en 1981 et 1996 ont mis au jour environ 260 amphores pour les produits vinaires, a huile, a garum, a salaisons et sauces de poisson. Elles représentent la circulation de ces produits dans la cité-capital de Sellium et surtout la vie économique de cette civitas de Lusitanie romaine. Les amphores découvertes dans ce site permettent établir aussi une économie de marché de type urbain; d'ailleurs les dolia sont aussi trop répresentatives comme des grands vases pour la conservation de céréales et certainement d'autres productions alimentaires secondaires. Nous avons rencontré de nombre uses amphores qui transportaient du vin de Bétique (Haltern 70; Dressel 28), Tarragone (Dressel 2-4), Narbonne (Gauloise 1-4) et du Méditerranée Orientale (Rhodes et Agora M 54) sous Auguste et pendant presque la première moitié du IIe siècle de notre ère. La prodution locale est attestée par les amphores lusitaniennes des vallées du Tage et du Sado attribuables au Haut (Almagro 51 a-b) et Bas Empire (Almagro 51c). Les amphores a huile d'importation sont nettement peu répresentatives ce qu'elles témoignent, sans doute, une production locale probablement d'une qualité moyenne. Il s'agit des amphores Dressel 20, 23 e 25 qui transportaient leur produit de Bétique (vers le milieu du Ie et IIe siècle). Plus nombreux sont les tessons tardifs et le nombre élevé de dolia qui apportent des traces évidences du produit transporté. Il s'agit probablement d'une production locale et regionale (vallées du Tage, Sado, Algarve) par sa qualité et pour répondre aux besoins du marché locale. Pour terminer sont plus nombreuses des amphores lusitaniennes, pour les salaisons et sauces de poisson, typiques du Haut (Dressel 14) et Bas Empire (Almagro 50, Almagro 51c et Beltran 72). Il y a aussi um certain nombres d'exemplaires à garum de Béltique, surtout les amphores Dressel 7/11 et Dressel 14. L'examen au microscope pétrographique des pâtes céramiques des amphores et des camparaisons avec des autres exemplaires d'origine connue vont permettre distinguer les productions des ateliers d'amphores lusitaniennes dans le vallée du Tage, du Sado et du Algarve.

Abstract: The excavations which we carried out in Sellium (Tomar, Portugal) from 1981 until 1996 provided approximately 260 amphorae for wine, oil, garum and other fish sauces. They represent the circulation of these products in the city-capital of Sellium and especially the economic life of this civitas of Roman Lusitania. The amphorae discovered in this site make also possible to assume a market economy of the urban type; on the other hand, the dolia are also very representative, like those large vessels for cereal conservation and certainly other secondary food productions. We found many amphorae which transported wine from Baetica (Haltern 70; Dressel 28), Tarraconensis (Dressel 2-4), Narbonensis (Gallic 1-4) and the Eastern Mediterranean (Rhodes and Agora M 54), dated from August and almost the first half of second century AD. Local production is testified by the Lusitania type amphorae from the Tagus and Sado basins, ascribable to the Early (Almagro 51 a-b) and Late Empire (Almagro 5c). The imported oil amphorae are not very represented, this meaning that they testify undoubtedly a local production, probably with an average quality. We are dealing with the amphorae Dressel 20, 23 and 25, which transported their product from Baetica (in the middle of the first and the second centuries AD). More numerous are the late shards and the high number of dolia which yield clear traces of the transported product. It is probably a local and regional production (from the Tagus and Sado basins and the Algarve), due to its quality and to solve the needs of the local market. The Lusitania type amphorae for fish products are more numerous, and they are typical of the Early (Dressel 14) and Late Empire (Almagro 50, Almagro 5c and Beltrán 72). There is also a certain number of examples for garum from Baetica, especially the amphorae Dressel 7/11 and Dressel 14. The petrologic analysis of the amphorae pastes and the comparisons with other specimens coming from known sources will make possible to distinguish the productions from the Lusitania type amphorae workshops along the Tagus and Sado basins and the Algarve.

INTRODUCTION

Cette étude permet un itinéraire probable de ces produits de terre et des produits marins.

Il y a sur le site de *Seilium* une abondance et variété des amphores destinées à la circulation des dofférents produits agricoles et piscicoles. Des nombreuses et des différents types d'amphore présents sur le *territoire de Seilium*, entre l'époque de l'empereur Auguste et Vᵉ siècle, permettant connaître la vie économique de marché et l'alimentation de ces populations; d'ailleurs ceux récipients suggèrent des innombrables peines sur les contenus des plusieurs amphores et la frontière chronologique qui est

signalée par la production hispanique des amphores et des même produits[1].

Les 52 fragments[2] recueillis sur le site de *Seilium*[3] a permis par le méthode d'analyse statistique[4] de définir les produits

---

[1] ALARCÃO & MAYET 1990, p. 306.

[2] Ces échantillons seilienses sont formes DRESSEL 2-4, DRESSEL 7-11, DRESSEL 14, HALTERN 70, DRESSEL 20, DRESSEL 23, DRESSEL 25, PASCUAL 1, OBERADEN 81 et 83, BELTRÁN I-II, BELTRÁN 85, ALMAGRO 50 et ALMAGRO 51.

[3] PONTE 1993, p. 452; *ID.*, 1999, pp. 339-360; PONTE *et alli* 1993, pp. 413-415; BANHA 1998, pp. 165-190.

[4] L'étude analitique de 52 échantillons des amphores provenants de Seilium fut éffectué par Doutora Isabel Prudêncio de l'Instituto Tecnológico e Nuclear (Lisbonne).

qu'elles transportaient et, dans cette optique, les différents provenances.

Cet étude permet constater le type d'alimentation des populations *seilienses*.

LE GOÛT DE NOURRITURE

Les sources littéraires, épigraphiques et des documents archéologiques sont, en effect, les fondements disponibles pour mieux connaître des habitudes alimentaires du monde romaine.

Des récipients et des ruines de *Seilium* découvertes[5] nous permettent identifier et définir la vie économique et le quotidienne de ce site romain; des nombreuses tessons en céramique, surtout des différents amphores vinaires, à huile et à *garum*, reflètent la vie familiale, le goût sur la table et les activités de type urbain et rurale des habitants de *Seilium*.

Il y a, pourtant, un ensemble de problèmes sur les contenus d'importation et d'exportation des produits de Hispanie romaine et de la région méditerranéenne[6].

Le commerce lointain est signalé par les sources antiques et assuré par les épaves des bâtiments marchands avec des produits alimentaires; des informations archéologiques et paleogéographiques des établissements rurales, des fours, des fabriques de poisson et des nonbreuses amphores découvertes dans les autres centres urbains nous permettent proposer et établir certes modèles alimentaires dans la suite de la ocupation romaine dans la Hispanie romaine.

Des amphores de *Seilium* nous donnent aussi une contribution précieuse sur la structure économique de ce site; nous permettent de mieux comprendre des productions des amphores et leurs produits alimentaires; elles révèlent des renseignements importants sur la structure de marché[7] et le commerce entre Haute Ribatejo et le Moyen Tage.

SITUATION GÉOMORPHOLOGIQUE

Le territoire de *Seilium* date de l'époque de l'empereur Auguste[8]. La région se situe entre le Haute Ribatejo et le Moyen Tage. La cité est traversée par le fleuve Nabão, sub-affluent du Tage.

Le climat est tempéré et les sols sont riches en général, présentant une fertilité élevée donnant lieu a un ensemble des activités agricoles et industrielles[9]. Ces caracteristiques géographiques permettent établir une idée du niveau de vie en *Seilium* par rapport a Hispanie romaine et à Rome.

DES PRODUITS

Des différents types d'amphores et des *dolia* trouvées sur le site de *Seilium* présentent des éléments importants pour l'étude du *modus vivendi* des populations seilienses. Des histogrammes illustrés nous donnent une vision partial des importations des produits et sur leur consommation, surtout du vin, à huile et des salaisons de poisson.

PLINE observe que "il y a deux liquides particulièrement agréables au corp humain: le vin, dans l'intérieur et à huile, dans l'extérieur". Ces deux produits liés aux céréales, aux potagers et a l'arbres à fruit[10] constituaient le dénominateur commun de la vie économique de *Seilium*.

Des amphores de *Seilium* réprésentent un impact économique du système de marché de type urbain[11] dans la région nord de la vallée du Moyen Tage. Le commerce et la consommation des produits alimentaires entre *Seilium* et des autres sites du monde romain sont assurés surtout grâce aux amphores et la rôle des *dolia* de production locale. D'un autre côté, il y a les sources littéraires[12] et des documents archéologiques[13] qui attestent un commerce fort et local dans le territoire de *Seilium*.

Des objects réflètent d'une habitude de la vie quotidienne et une économie perceptible à partir des amphores, des jarres et des *dolia* que transportaient et contennaient des produits de terre, des denrées liquides et des autres biens alimentaires[14], comme des pièces de viande et de poisson. Ces amphores vinaires (Fig. 1) témoignent des différents rythmes de circulation du vin qui elles mêmes transportaient: les unes contenaient le vin de Bétique, de Tarraconaise, de Narbonnaise et des sites méditerranéens pour le Haute Empire (Ier et IIe siècles de notre ère); les autres plus tardives, dans notre optique, transportaient le vin lusitanien local ou régional. Ce produit était diffusé en barriques[15] et conservait en *dolia*.

La culture de la vigne dans le territoire de *Seilium* ne devait dépasser pas une qualité suffisance par le marché local, comme nous semble témoigner la bonne pourcentage des amphores vinaires d'importation pendant le Haute Empire. Pourtant, nous semble que le nombre élevé de *dolia* et la suffisance production des amphores lusitaniennes entre le IIe siècle et le Ve siècle, pouvaient répondre aux besoins des populations rurales et urbaines de *Seilium*.

Bien plus, *Seilium* correspond a une zone viticole antique, oú il y a nombreux registres d'une culture méditerranéenne dans

---

[5] PONTE 1993, pp. 450-451; *ID.*, 1999, p. 339; ID., 2000.

[6] PONTE 1999, p. 360.

[7] GEORGES 1988, pp. 91-113.

[8] PONTE 1993, pp. 447-449; *ID.*, 1996, p. 194.

[9] *ID., ibidem.,*1996, pp. 193-197.

[10] AULO-GÉLIO, III, 4.

[11] ALARCÃO *et alli* 1990, pp.231-233.

[12] CONDE 1999, p. 17; VIANA 1998, p. 42.

[13] MANTAS 1999, p. 287.

[14] ÉTIENNE & MAYET 1997, p. 52.

[15] ÉTIENNE & MAYET 2000, p. 12.

TYPOLOGIE	Insulae	Macellum	Forum	·
Haltern 70	42	15	1	58
Dressel 28	3	2	0	5
Gauloise 1	1	0	0	1
Rhodes 1	2	0	0	2
Lusitanien 1	12	0	0	12
Man‡/C‡diz	1	0	0	1
Lusitanien 4	9	0	0	9
Gauloise 5	4	0	0	4
Agora M54	1	0	0	1
Pascual 1	7	9	0	16
Dressel 2-4	6	0	1	7
Dressel 7-11	3	6	0	9
TOTAL=	91	32	2	125

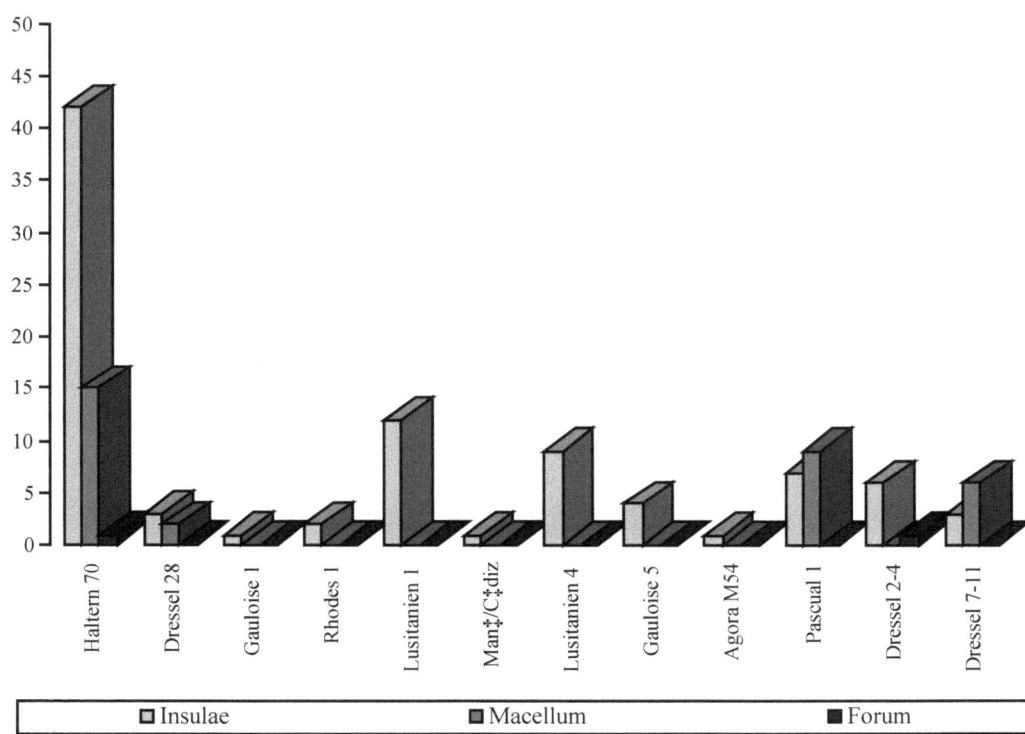

Figure 1. Évaluation quantitative des différents types d'amphores vinaires trouvées sur l'aire urbaine de *Seilium*.

le *Conventus Scalabitanus*[16]. Par ordre décroissant des témoignages amphoriques, la pièce HALTERN 70 est l'une des amphores à vin de Bétique qui transportait *vinum* et aussi *defructum* et *sapa*[17].

On atrouvé un fragment de l'anse et de col d'une amphore HALTERN 70 avec un timbre rectangulair vermillone, mais pas encore déchiffré, qui identifiait le type de produit vinaire. Cette amphore apparait au côté des autres types (PASCUAL 1 et DRESSEL 2-4, de TARRACONAISE)

que transportaient, entre l'époque augustéenne au début des Flaviens, le même produit.

Les textes anciens nous en donne la formule du *defructum* et de *sapa* qui nous éclairent sur la panoplie de ses utilisations, soit la vinification[18], soit la conservation des fruits[19], comme des olives noires[20] ou blanches[21], soit la

---

[16] VIANA 1998, p. 18.

[17] PONTE 1999, p. 343.

[18] PLIN., N*H.,* XIV, 80, 121; COLUMELLE, XII, 19, 1 et 12; PALLADIUS, I, 11 et 18; CATON, 23, 2.

[19] COLUMELLE, XII, 44, 2 (des raisons); XII, 48, 5 (des coings); XII, 10, 3 (Des prunes et des cronouilles); XII; 10,4 (des poires).

[20] COL. XII, 50, 2 et 3.

cuisine comme ingrédient ou qu'il soit un liquide alcoolisé[22]. Ce produit pouvait être un liquide simple, vin cuit ou la sauce au vin[23], transporté par les amphores HALTERN 70 de Bétique. En effect, tous les *tituli* communs sur HALTERN 70 font référence a *defructum*, *sapa* ou *oliva ex defructo* ou *ex dulcis*[24].

Le *defructum* et le *sapa* appartenaient à la catégorie des vins cuits. Ils étaient une sorte de liqueur et non sirop, ou soit, des substances non alcooliques, sucrées et sirupeuses[25]. Le réduction du moût on fait aujourd'hui dans la région du *Conventus Scallabitanus* pour obtenir un liquide adoucé non alcoolique et qui servait pour boire, comme liqueur ou comme conservation des olives.

Les raisons sont encore sèches au soleil pour obtenir une pâte douce non alcoolique[26]. Le *defructum* et le *sapa* auraient des qualités semblables. Les textes anciens non éclairent cette question, présentant des différences sur les pourcentages du moût obtenu par fermentation en ce cas-ci[27].

Les agronomes latins recommandent l'addition de *defructum* au vin pour lui enlever sa dureté (*ferocia*) et qualité[28], ce qui non empêche son consommation (*defructum-boisson*), ou comme le *defructum-conservateur*. Le *sapa* serait un sirop, mot connu en latin sous la désignation de *sucus*[29]. En fait, la vinification et ses sous-produits permettent fabriquer un produit alimentaire, agricole, médical et industriel[30]. Dans la même région de Bétique ont importé également des plusieurs produits vinicoles en autres amphores avec en faible quantité que le type HALTERN 70.

Les beaucoup trop des tessons fragmentaires recueillis en *Seilium* datent du Ier et IIe siècle après J.C. Nous sommes sûrs que des vins cuits provenaient aussi de Tarraconaise. Ces produits sont identifiés par les amphores PASCUAL 1 (Dressel 1b), DRESSEL 2-4 et DRESSEL 7-11. L'amphore PASCUAL 1 est la plus abondante a *Seilium*, provenant de contextes augustéens. Il est difficile confirmer l'origine du vin importé par les formes PASCUAL 1, qu'il soit originaire d'Italie ou bien de la Tarraconaise[31]. Pourtant les amphores DRESSEL 2-4 apparait dans les contextes du milieu du Ier siècle après J.-C. jusqu'au IIe siècle de notre ère. Ceux-ci présentent un certain nombre de traits communs celles des amphores de

Tarraconaise[32]. Celles pouvaient contenir une double gamme de produits[33] : des vins de Tarragone qui concurraient les vins italiens (*copia*) et les autres (*balista-cocolobis*); des vins grossiers cultivés en *Laletania*. Ce la dernière type du vin présentait des caractéristiques semblables au vinagre (*acetum*).

Les amphores DRESSEL 2-4 trouvées a *Seilium* peuvent ajouter à annoncer l'existence du moût ou de la lie (*faex laletana*) de Léetanie[34]. D'un autre côté l'abondance et variété de ces amphores dans les dernières années au règne d'Auguste et surtout à partir du règne de Tibère a *Seilium* démontre l'expansion du vin de Tarraconaise et des autres productions qui rivalit les vins italiens. L'extrême faiblesse des amphores vinaires provenants de Narbonnaise et de la région méditerranéenne et trouvées sur le site de *Seilium*, témoignent davantage du goût des certaines familles de *Seilium*, qui possédaient des habitudes sur leur table.

Seilium révèle en travers des amphores vinaires d'importation un déclin significatif, surtout à partir du milieu du Ier siècle après J.C. Je juge qu'il y aurait une diffusion du vin hispanique et une production significative des amphores lusitaniennes et de *dolia*, soit ces les dernières pour l'exportation, soit pour la conservation du vin. Les amphores lusitaniennes découvertes en *Seilium* réflètent non seulement de la consommation du vin et des produits vinicoles de l'origines différents, mais encore une vision partielle de produits locaux et régionals. La région de *Seilium* est trop fameuse par la consommation et l'exportation de *passum* et des figues sèches. En outre, l'abondance des amphores lusitaniennes en *Seilium* et *Villa Cardilio* (Torres Novas) témoignent qui celles-ci véhiculaient du vin hispanique et des produits de terre pour certains sites extra-péninsulaires[35].

Le nombre des amphores à huile est moins élevé que le pourcentage de tessons vinaires. Ils se détachent les amphores DRESSEL 20, DRESSEL 23 et DRESSEL 25 qui transportaient l'huile de Bétique (Fig. 2). En effet, un fragment DRESSEL 20 retouvé dans les fouilles de cette cité porte une marque du période claudien, identifiée comme Q. C. C.. Nous jugeons que ce *tria nomina* pourrait être interprété comme les initiales de *Q. Coelius Cassianus, diffusor olearius olisiponense* ?[36]. Ces pourcentages de tessons témoignent davantage du goût des gens de qualité de *Seilium*, qui réclamaient leur table des meilleures huiles du monde romain, surtout de Bétique. La prépondérance de *dolia* et la faiblesse des amphores à huile d'importation nous faisons penser sur la suffisance qualité de la production locale à huile destinée a une économie de marché du type urbain. Le fait qu'il existait encore depuis peu dans la région[37], une production à huile,

[21] *ID., ibidem.*, XII, 49, 6 et 49, 7.

[22] ÉTIENNE & MAYET, 2000, p. 97, note 38.

[23] APICIUS, I, 378.

[24] GARCÍA VARGAS 1998, pp. 203-204, note 76.

[25] *ID., ibidem.*, p. 203.

[26] SEALEY 1985, p. 63; PLIN, *NH*, XIV, 93.

[27] ÉTIENNE & MAYET, 2000, p. 95.

[28] SEALEY, 1985, p. 39.

[29] ÉTIENNE & MAYET, 2000, p. 95; APIC., I, 23.

[30] AMOURETTI 1993, pp. 472-473.

[31] Voir *supra*, p. 125.

[32] *id. ibidem.*, p. 127.

[33] *id. ibidem.*, p. 108.

[34] MARTIAL I, 26, 9 et VIII, 53, 6.

[35] ÉTIENNE & MAYET 2000, pp. 230-235; DIAS DIOGO 1999, pp. 201-214.

[36] PONTE *et alli*, 1993, pp. 349-350; FABIÃO 1993-94, pp. 219-245.

[37] GUIMARÃES 1979, pp. 9-17; *ID., ibidem.*, 1998.

TYPOLOGIE	Insulae	Macellum	·
Beltr‡n 85	4	0	**4**
Dressel 20	19	5	**24**
Dressel 23	4	7	**11**
Dressel 25	5	0	**5**
TOTAL=	**32**	**12**	**44**

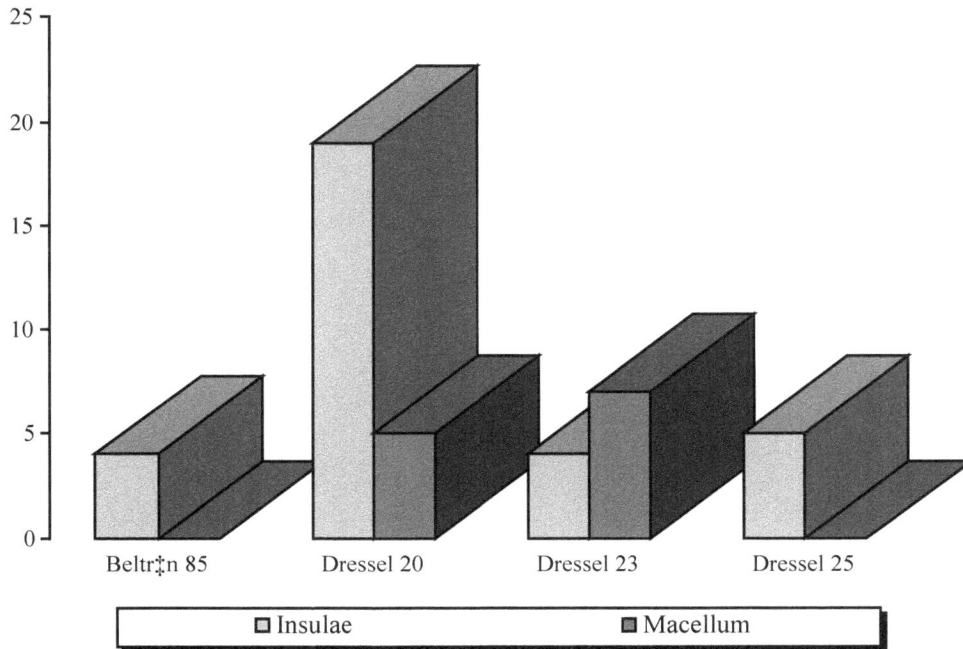

Figure 2. Évaluation quantitative des différents types d'amphores à l'huile trouvées sur l'aire urbaine de *Seilium*.

à quelle les propriétaires utilizaient des vases de grand taille (*dolia*) et des jarres ou des autres récipients de différents capacités pour mieux à faire et à conserver l'huile d'olive[38].

L'étude des *dolia* et des autres vases en céramique poissées de *Seilium* permettent observer que tous les récipients pouvaient être destinés dans plusieurs produits de terre. Enfin, *Seilium* a permis de composer un histogramme sur de nombreuses amphores des salaisons ou des sauces de différents types qui précisent l'alimentation des populations de ce site urbain.

Seilium révèle que les nombreux fragments d'amphores piscicoles (Fig. 3) contenaient des plusieurs des salaisons ou des sauces. Elles transportaient évidemment du *garum*, la *sardina Pilchardus L.*, *liquamen*, la *muria*[39] et également des autres produits de la sauce de poisson, comme *scomber*

(cabale), le *ballex*, *allec* ou *allex*, soit poisson marin[40]. Nous reconnaissons, pour instant, l'extrême faiblesse de tessons d'importation réprésentés par les amphores OBERADEN 83, DRESSEL 7-11 e BÉLTRÁN IIb de Bétique du Ier siècle après J.-C.; il y a exceptionnellement un fragment de lèvre et d'un col très long du type MAÑA C2b[41] du milieu ou dernier Ier siècle avant du Christ, provenant de *Cartagena*. Ce fragment s'inspire des amphores pseudo-coennes datées entre la première moitié du Ier siècle après J.-C. et la fin du Ier siècle ou le début du IIe siècle après J.-C.[42]. Notre exemplar apparaît dans la couche daté du règne d'Auguste.

C'est rarement facile de déterminer le contenu de cet'amphore importée, mais nous pensions qu'elle

---

[38] VAZ PINTO 1997, pp. 112-115.

[39] ÉTIENNE 1990, pp. 16-17.

[40] GARCÍA VARGAS 1998, pp. 199-200.

[41] GUERRERO AYUSO & ROLDÁN BERNAL 1992, pp. 12 et 30, Lam. XV, n° 15; GARCÍA VARGAS 1998, pp. 66-67.

[42] ABADIE-REYNAL 1999, p. 257.

TYPOLOGIE	Insulae	Macellum	Forum	.
Oberaden 83	2	0	0	2
Dressel 7-11	8	0	1	9
Beltr‡n IIb	2	0	0	2
Dressel 12	1	0	0	1
Lusitanien Garum 1	52	15	4	71
Lusitanien 2	11	0	0	11
Lusitanien 3	14	0	0	14
Lusitanien 4	61	19	7	87
TOTAL=	151	34	12	197

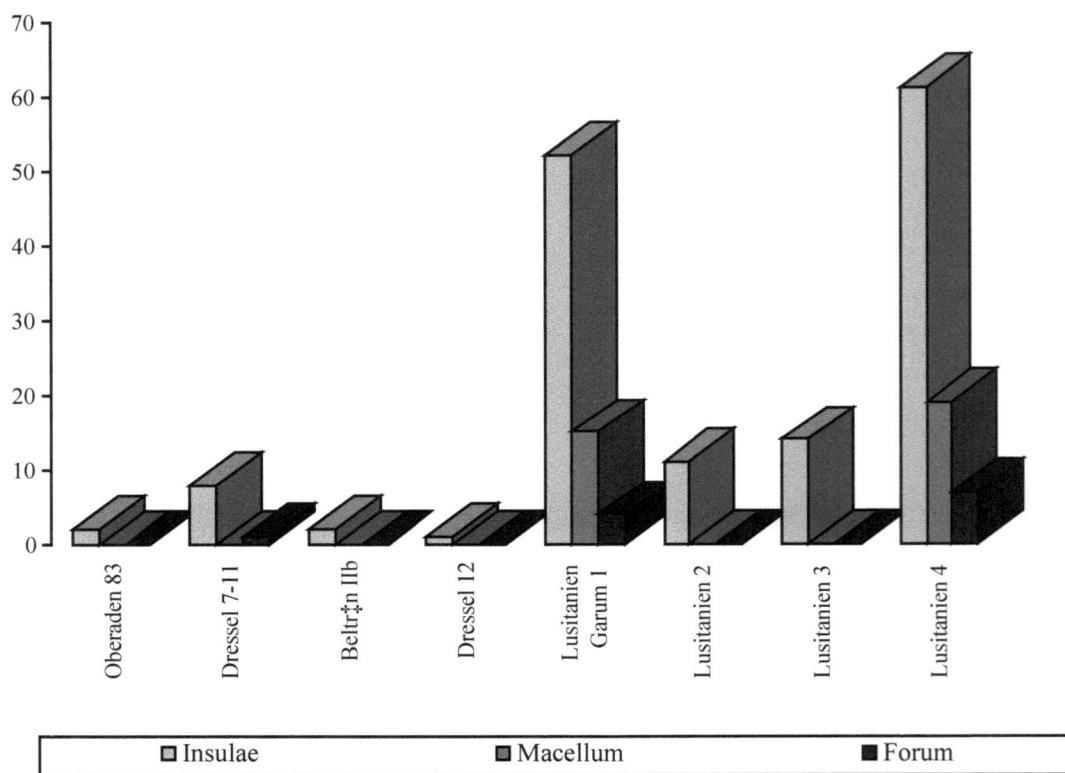

Figure 3. Évaluation quantitative des différents types d'amphores à salaisons et sauces de poisson trouvées sur l'aire urbaine de *Seilium*.

transporterait des viscères de thorine, de *garum*[43] ou de *salsamenta*[44]. Des formes de l´Haute Empire, prevenants de Bétique sont bien moins que les productions lusitaniennes de la même époque chronologique. Il s´agit de l´amphore DRESSEL 14b (Lusitanie 1) qui nous apparaît une production particulière de la DRESSEL 14 de Bétique. *Seilium* fournit un fragment qui porte une marque sur l´anse:RVMA[45]. Elle correspond depuis l´époque claudienne ayant les autres trouvées encore dans la seconde moitié du IIe siècle, mais plus du tout au IIIe siècle. Nous pouvons dire que la pâte et la caractéristique morphologique de ces nombreuses tessons permettent mettre de la différence entre celles de Bétique et celles de production lusitanienne. Des autres amphores du Bas Empire, comme certains exemplaires de ALMAGRO 50 (Lusitanie 2), ALMAGRO 51a-b (Lusitanie 3) et ALMAGRO 51c (Lusitanie 4), des productions de Lusitanie romaine, présent une chronologie assez longue, aux alentours du milieu du IIe siècle et dans la première moitié du IIIe siècle[46], vers le milieu du Ve siècle.

---

[43] *ID., ibidem.*, pp.199-201; GUERRERO AYUSO & RÓLDAN BERNAL 1992, p. 31.

[44] BEN LAZREG *et alli.*, 1995, pp. 103-132.

[45] PONTE 1999, p. 353.

[46] *ID., ibidem.*, MAYET 1990, p. 31.

TYPOLOGIE	xi	Production	Type
Haltern 70	58	Ba˜tique	Vin
Dressel 28	5	Ba˜tique	Vin
Man‡/C‡diz	1	Ba˜tique	Vin
Beltr‡n 85	4	Ba˜tique	Huile
Dressel 20	24	Ba˜tique	Huile
Dressel 23	11	Ba˜tique	Huile
Dressel 25	5	Ba˜tique	Huile
Oberaden 83	2	Ba˜tique	Poisson
Dressel 7-11	9	Ba˜tique	Poisson
Beltr‡n IIb	2	Ba˜tique	Poisson
Gaulesa 1	1	Narbonnaise	Vin
Gaulesa 5	4	Narbonnaise	Vin
R—dio 1	2	M˜d. Orientale	Vin
Agora M54	1	M˜d. Orientale	Vin
Pascual 1	16	Tarraconnaise	Vin
Dressel 2-4	7	Tarraconnaise	Vin
Dressel 7-11	9	Tarraconnaise	Vin
Lusitana 3	12	R˜gionale	Vin
Lusitana 4	9	R˜gionale	Vin
Dressel 12	1	R˜gionale	Poisson
Lusitana Garum 1	71	R˜gionale	Poisson
Lusitana 2	11	R˜gionale	Poisson
Lusitana 3	14	R˜gionale	Poisson
Lusitana 4	87	R˜gionale	Poisson
TOTAL=	366		

BA□TIQUE	121
NARBONNAISE	5
M□DITERRAN□E ORIENTALE	3
TARRACONNAISE	32
R□GIONALE	205
TOTAL=	366

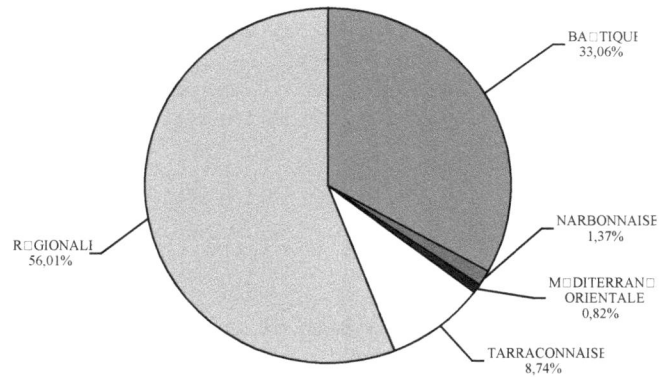

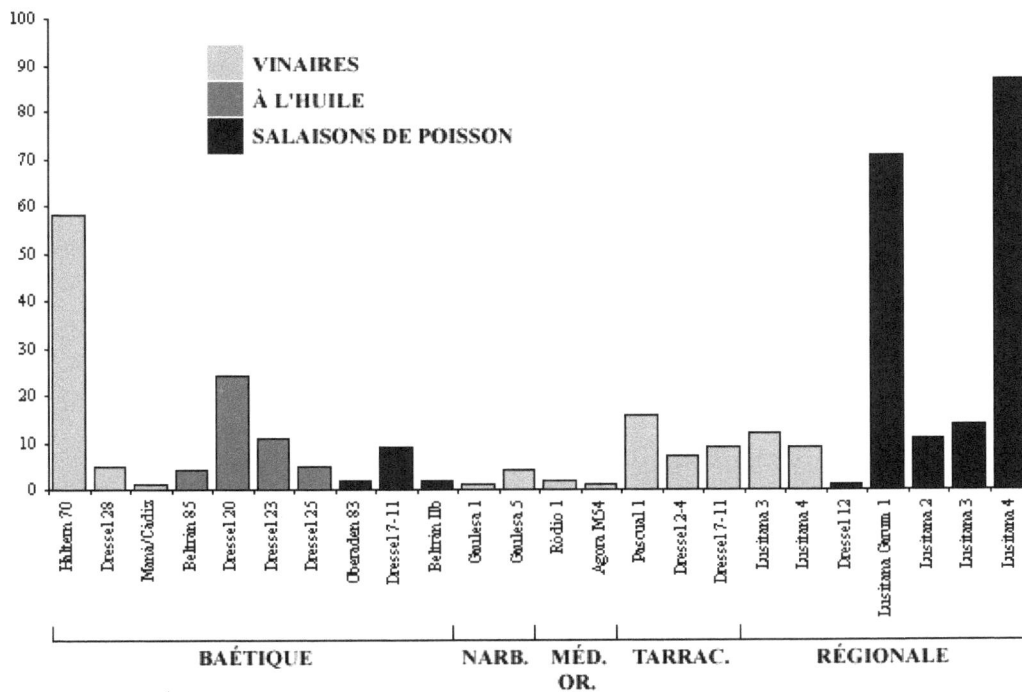

Figure 4. Évaluation quantitative des amphores vinaires, à l'huile, à *garum* et salaisons de poisson trouvées sur l'aire urbaine de *Seilium* ; des provenances et des pourcentages des amphores de *Seilium* pour les principaux produits commercialisés.

Il y a à *Seilium*, comme a São Cucufate[47], a Troia[48], a *Abul*, en Alcácer do Sal[49], de Pinheiro, district de Setúbal[50] et à plusieurs sites lusitaniens[51], une préponderance des amphores a salaisons et sauces de poisson, soit d'origine exterieur, soit d'origine lusitanienne. Les amphores à *garum* de Bétique et lusitaniennes sont constituées par les DRESSEL 7-11, DRESSEL 14, BÉLTRÁN IIb, ALMAGRO 50 et ALMAGRO 51. Elles, cependant, transportaient des produits fabriqués dans les usines lusitaniennes (valée du Sado et du Tage), comme les thons, les sardines portugaises, maquereaux ou des tout petits poissons, surtout au Bas Empire[52] C'est probable que ces amphores pourraient exporter le sel provenant de l'estuaire du Sado.

CONCLUSION

À partir de l'abondance des amphores du vin, à huile, a salaisons et sauces de poisson trouvées dans le site de *Seilium* nous pouvons démontrer le goût alimentaire des populations *seilienses* (Fig. 4). Ces habitants avaient une alimentation méditerranéenne. Ces amphores nous donnent la connaissance du commerce du vin, à huile et des salaisons produites dans le monde romain. Nous pouvons démontrer que sur ce site de consommation effectuait une économie de marché de type urbain. Au début l'approvisionnement et la commercialization des produits de terre et des piscicoles prouvenaient surtout de la province de Bétique, la province de Tarraconaise et de Narbonnaise; depuis il y a dans le Ier siècle après J.-C. une fort concurrence entre les produits importés et les lusitaniens. Dans le Haute Empire au début il y a une prépondérance des produits de Bétique, surtout du vin, à huile et des salaisons; depuis, à partir du milieu du IIième siècle après J.-C. les amphores lusitaniennes portent des plusieurs produits locaux et régionaux[53], soit pour l'approvisionnement du marché intérieur, soit pour l'exportation de ceux-là.

Ces histogrammes nous donnent, soit les pourcentages des types amphoriques lusitaniens et des marchés extra-péninsulairs, soit les contenus de l'origine locale ou provinciale. Les amphores non lusitaniennes permettent rétrancher que les populations seilienses en général tenaient une nourriture aussi variée. À partir du milieu du Ier siècle après J.-C., les amphores trouvées sur le site de *Seilium* permettent distinguer produits lusitaniens et produits importés des provinces voisines. Nous constatons aussi qu'il y a une fort concurrence dans la production et

diffusion dans le monde romain des types de conteneurs et la nature des contenus-du vin, à huile et encore les produits dérivés ou sous-produits; le *garum, liquamen, muria, sardina pilchardus* ou sardine de l'Atlantique[54].

Ces amphores et l'autre matériel exhumé permettent les derniers années du Ier siècle avant du Christ au milieu du Ve siècle de notre ère reconnaître deux temps différents et correspondent à les deux phases d'activité économique et par conséquent au *modus vivendi* des populations *seilienses*: une, sous le Haute Empire et l'autre, sous le Bas Empire; la première correspond à large diffusion des amphores vinaires (HALTERN 70), à huile (DRESSEL 20) et de poisson (DRESSEL 14); la seconde correspond a des moments des changements dans les productions de conteneurs et des techniques de fabrication des produits de terre et de pêche. Enfin, il faut noter que à Troia, à *Olisipo*, à *Caetobriga* ou à *Balsa*, en Algarve, il y avait une grande concentration de nombreuses unités de production des amphores, qui transportaient le vin, l'huile, les salaisons et sauces de poisson.

Des plusieurs fragments amphoriques permettent déduire que pour la consommation du vin et d'huile, *Seilium* faisait leur importation de Bétique; les salaisons et sauces de poisson provennaient probablement des usines lusitaniennes[55].

Adresse de l'auteur

Salete da PONTE
Instituto Politécnico de Tomar
Avenue Cândido Madureira, n° 13
2300-517 Tomar PORTUGAL

Bibliographie

ABADIE-REYNAL, C., 1999, Les amphores romaines en mer noire (Ier-IVe siècle, in *The Production et Commerce des amphores anciennes en Mer Noire*, Aix-en-Provence, pp. 255-264.

ALARCÃO, J., ÉTIÈNNE, R., & MAYET, F., 1990, *Les villas romaines de São Cucufate (Portugal)*. Paris.

ALARCÃO-MAYET, F. (dir.)., 1990, Ânforas Lusitanas:Tipologia, Produção e Comércio, in *The Conimbriga/Paris*, edited by Museu Monográfico de Conimbriga/Diff. de Boccard, p. 305-308.

AMOURETTI, M.- C., 1993, Les sous-produits de la fabrication de l'huile et du vin, in *The ECH, suppl. XXVI*, pp. 463-476.

AULO-GÉLIO, III, 4 (CARCOPINO, J.,), 1978, *A vida quotidiana em Roma no apogeu do Império*. Roma.

BANHA, C. M. S. & ARSÉNIO, P. A. M., 1998, As ânforas romanas vinárias de Seilium (Tomar), Conventus Scallabitanus, in *The Revista Portuguesa de Arqueologia* 1 (2), pp. 165-190.

BEN LAZREG, N.; BONIFAY, M.; DRINE, A., & TROUSSET, P., 1995, Production et commercialisation des *salsamenta* de l'Afrique ancienne, in *The Productions et Exportations*

---

[47] MAYET & SCHMIT 1997, pp. 75-84.

[48] ÉTIENNE *et alli.*, 1994, p. 100.

[49] MAYET *et alli.*, 1996.

[50] MAYET & SILVA 1998.

[51] EDMONDSON 1966, pp. 255-269; DIAS DIOGO 1996, pp. 61-71; GUERRA 1996, pp. 267-282; FABIÃO 1996, pp. 329-342; MANTAS 1996, pp. 343-368; DIAS DIOGO & CAVALEIRO PAIXÃO 2001, pp. 117-140; DIAS DIOGO *et alli.*, 2000, pp. 81; FABIÃO 1997, pp. 35-58; BUGALHÃO 2001.

[52] MAYET & SCHMIT 1997, pp. 203-204.

[53] PONTE 1999, pp. 358-360.

[54] BEN LAZREG *et alli* 1995, p. 117.

[55] ÉTIENNE *et alli*, 1994, pp. 163-166.

Africaines Actualités Archéologiques en Afrique du Nord Antique et Médiévale, Aix-en-Provence, pp. 103-132.

BRUN, J.-P., 1997, Production de l'huile et du vin en Lusitanie Romaine, in *The Conimbriga* 36, pp. 45-72.

BUGALHÃO, J., 2001, A indústria romana de transformação e conserva de peixe em *Olisipo*. Núcleo arqueológico da Rua dos Correeiros, in *The Trabalhos de Arqueologia* 15, Lisboa.

CONDE, M. S. A., 1999, *Horizontes do Portugal Medieval. Estudos Históricos, (Patrimonia Histórica)*. Cascais.

DIAS DIOGO, A., 1996, Elementos sobre ânforas de fabrico lusitano, ocupação romana dos estuários do Tejo e do Sado, in *The Actas das Primeiras Jornadas sobre Romanização dos estuários do Tejo e do Sado* (APJRETS), pp. 61-71.

DIAS DIOGO, A. M., 1999, Ânforas romanas de *Villa Cardílio*, Torres Novas, in *The Conimbriga* 38, pp. 201-214.

DIAS DIOGO, A. M.; CARDOSO, J.P. & REINER, F., 2000, Um conjunto de ânforas recuperadas nos dragados da foz do rio Arade, Algarve, in *The RPA* 3 (2), PP. 81-118.

DIAS DIOGO, A. M., & CAVALEIRO PAIXÃO, A., 2001, Ânforas de escavações no povoado industrial romano de Tróia, Setúbal, in *The Revista Portuguesa de Arqueologia (RPA)* 4 (1), pp. 117-140.

EDMONDSON, 1996, *Two Industries*.

ÉTIENNE, R., 1990, Que transportaient donc les amphores lusitaniennes?, in *The Les Amphores Lusitaniennes.Typologie, Production, Comerce*, pp. 15-19.

ÉTIENNE, R., & MAYET, F., 2000, *Le vin Hispanique*. Paris.

ÉTIENNE, R.; MAKAROUN, Y., & MAYET, F., 1994, *Un grand complexe industriel a Tróia (Portugal)*. Paris.

FABIÃO, C., 1993-94, O azeite da Bética na Lusitânia, in *The Conimbriga* 32-33, pp. 219-245.

FABIÃO, C., 1996, O comércio dos produtos da Lusitânia transportados em ânforas no Baixo Império, *APJRETS*, Lisboa, pp. 329-342.

FABIÃO, C., 1997, A exploração dos recursos marinhos, in *The Portugal Romano. A exploração dos recursos naturais*, Lisboa, pp. 35-58.

GARCÍA VARGAS, E., 1998, *La producción de ánforas en la Bahía de Cádiz en época romana* (siglos II a. C.-IV d. C.). Cádiz.

GEORGES, J.-G., 1988, Villes et villas de Lusitanie (Interactions-Échanges-Autonomies), in *The Les Villes de Lusitanie Romaine. Hiérarquies et Territoires. Table Ronde International du CNRS* (Talence, le 8-9 Décembre 1988), Paris, CNRS, pp. 91-113.

GUERRA, A. E., 1996, Marcas de ânfora provenientes do Porto dos Cacos (Alcochete), in *The Actas das Primeiras Jornadas sobre Romanização dos estuários do Tejo e do Sado*, Lisboa, pp. 267-282.

GUERRERO AYUSO, V. M. & ROLDÁN BERNAL, B., 1992, *Catalogo de las anforas prerromanas*. Cartagena, 1992.

GUIMARÃES, M. S., 1998, *A oliveira e o azeite na região de Tomar. Usos e Costumes*.Tomar.

MANTAS, V. G., 1996, Comércio marítimo e sociedade nos portos romanos do Tejo e do Sado, in *The APJRETS*, Lisboa, pp. 343-368.

MANTAS, V. G., 1999, Cidades e História Económica na área de influência da estrada *Olisipo-Bracara*, in *The Anejos AespA* 20, pp. 279-298.

MARTIAL, *Epigrammes*, I & VIII.

MAYET, F., 1990, Typologie et Chronologie des amphores lusitaniennes, in *The Les amphores lusitaniennes.Typologie. Production. Commerce*, Paris, pp. 29-36.

MAYET, F.; SCHMIT, A., & SILVA, C. F., 1996. *Les amphores du Sado (Portugal)*, Paris.

MAYET, F., & SCHMIT, A., 1997, Les amphores de São Cucufate, in *The Itinéraires Lusitaniens*, Paris, pp. 75-84.

MAYET, F., & SILVA, C.T., 1998, L'atelier d'amphores de Pinheiro-Portugal. Paris.

PALLADIUS, *Traité d'Agriculture*, I.

PLINE L'ANCIEN, *Histoire Naturelle*, XIV.

PONTE, S., 1993, Achegas sobre a estrutura urbana de Sellium (Tomar), in *The Actas del XXII Congreso Nacional de Arqueologia*, Vigo, pp. 447-459.

PONTE, S., 1996, Vestígios antigos dos hidrossistemas de Tomar, in *The Conimbriga* 35, pp. 189-205.

PONTE, S., 1999, Importação de produtos vinários de Sellium (Tomar, Portugal) no Alto Império. Notícia de outros bens alimentares, in *The Économie et Territoire en Lusitanie Romaine*, (Collection de la Casa de Vélazquez 65), Madrid, pp. 339-360.

PONTE, S., 2000, Projecto de Sellium Romana: orgânica do princípio de urbanidade présenté in *The IIième Congresso de Turismo Cultural, Lusofonia e Desenvolvimento, Déc./2000*, Pelotas (Brasil).

PONTE, S., GUIMARÃES, M., PESSOA, M., & MARQUES, A., 1993, La production de l'huile et du vin au Portugal durant l'antiquité et le moyen-âge, in *The La Production du vin et de l'huile en Méditerranée (Bulletin de Correspondance Hellénique, supl. XXVI)*, Paris, pp. 413-421.

SEALEY, P. R., 1985, *Amphoras from the 1970 Excavations at Colchester Sheepen* (Oxford 1985).

VAZ PINTO, I., 1997, Dolia de São Cucufate e jarres modernes de l'Alentejo: essai d'etnoarchéologie, in *The Itinéraires Lusitaniens*, pp. 111-156.

VIANA, M., 1998, Os vinhedos medievais de Santarém, (Patrimónia Histórica). Cascais.

PRELIMINARY ARCHAEOLOGICAL AND TOPOGRAPHICAL NOTES ON CLASSICAL AND MEDIEVAL SETTLEMENT PATTERNS IN THE MERSIN AREA OF CILICIA (SOUTHERN TURKEY)

Ergün LAFLI

Abstract: Working on ancient Cilician societies, archaeology and history has a great importance, since it gives us first hand information about several subjects, i.e. objects of ancient settlement, their patterns, functions, dynamics and distribution in the Near East. In this contribution the author has attempted to report about his topographical observations in Mersin, a selected "test" region in the middle part of ancient Cilicia in southern Turkey. He presents an exemplary model for understanding subjects related to settlement patterns, such as settlement continuity, function, roads and their impact in classical and medieval Cilicia. Thus, a brief insight will be given into possible regional and international trading contacts in the eastern Mediterranean. This report is also a preview of a forthcoming archaeological field survey project, which is planned to be directed by the author in this geographical area in 2004.

INTRODUCTION: DESCRIPTION AND A SURVEY OF EXISTING RESEARCH

Cilicia is an ancient definition of a landscape, located on the south-eastern Anatolian coast of the eastern Mediterranean. It consists of two geographically definitive parts: Cilicia Campestris, a well-watered fertile plain bounded by the Taurus, Antitaurus and Mediterranean, and Cilicia Aspera, the rugged region of the southern Taurus stretching west to Pamphylia. During antiquity, in part due to its location on the highway from Constantinople to northern Syria via the Cilician Gates, this region prospered. Ancient cities in Cilicia were therefore centres of population, culture, trade, manufacture and administration. By the fourth century A.D. Cilicia contained more than 80 densely populated cities, of which the greatest were Tarsos, Seleuceia and Pompeiopolis. A large Cilician city might extend *c.* two km in its greatest dimension and have a population of 50,000, but most were much smaller. Through the sixth century A.D., urban wealth was based on agriculture, but trade and manufacture of linen were significant. Thus, settlement patterns of these cities and their "dependents" should be based on agrarian, security and other purposes. Pompeiopolis and Zephyrion, classified under Cilicia Prima, were quoted in the council list of A.D. 451, by Hierocles at A.D. 530, and later at *Notitiae*.[1]

While in the past scholars were often uninterested in the settlement patterns of classical and medieval Cilicia[2], its legacy has recently attracted increased attention[3]. At the terminus of one of Cilicia's countless classical and medieval sites of "middle Cilicia", today's Mersin, surprisingly boasts an impressive complex of ruins and monuments that speak clearly of the region's prosperity during these periods. The term "middle Cilicia" used in this paper, covers the whole city of Mersin of contemporary Turkey. Nature has placed middle Cilician topography in the pathway of almost all the commerce of the eastern Mediterranean. Archaeological data from this region preserve an economic system based on the maritime periphery of this region with Cyprus, northern and western Syria, the Levant and Egypt. Written sources as well as archaeological finds brought forth evidence that the classical and medieval Mersin region was connected with these neighbouring regions through maritime commerce, more exclusively through grain trade from Lycaonia to the Near East via its harbours. During antiquity, there were two principal coastal cities and their peripheral dependents in this area: Pompeiopolis and Zephyrion as well as other settlements between Tarsos (or Kydnos river) in the east and Kalanthia (or Lamos river) in the west. The ports of these cities were thriving centres of sea borne commerce. Particularly in the late Roman period, the grain trade from central Anatolia to Cyprus, Syria and especially to Egypt, brought special advantages to these coastal middle Cilician settlements, which were situated at the heads of the main roads into the interior. The development of the settlements from this point on affords examples of processes working concurrently: a natural Christianisation. The seventh century and the Arabian attacks, however, caused a considerable decline; thus middle Cilician settlements were maintained until the seventh century. After 1071 Byzantium lost middle Cilicia to Philaretos Brachamios; thereafter, it constantly changed hands between Byzantium, Arabs, Crusaders, Seljuks, Armenians and eventually Turks.[4]

Settlements in the peripheral area and hinterland of Pompeiopolis and Zephyrion were numerous. In the hinterland of these two cities, there were two possible main

---

[1] Hild/Hellenkemper 1990, p. 2ff.

[2] A full list of former researches on Cilician settlement patterns can be found at: Laflı 2001a and 2004a. Also V. Seton-Williams article at Anatolian Studies 4 as well as Hellenkemper/Hild 1986 and Hild/Hellenkemper 1990.

[3] Most recent studies on Cilician settlement patterns are H. Hellenkemper's and Mitford's articles at *ANRW* as well as S. Durugönül's paper at *Adalya* and Blanton 2000. K. Hopwood has questioned same subject at western Rough Cilicia: Hopwood 1991.

[4] Rother 1971 and 1972; Blumenthal 1963.

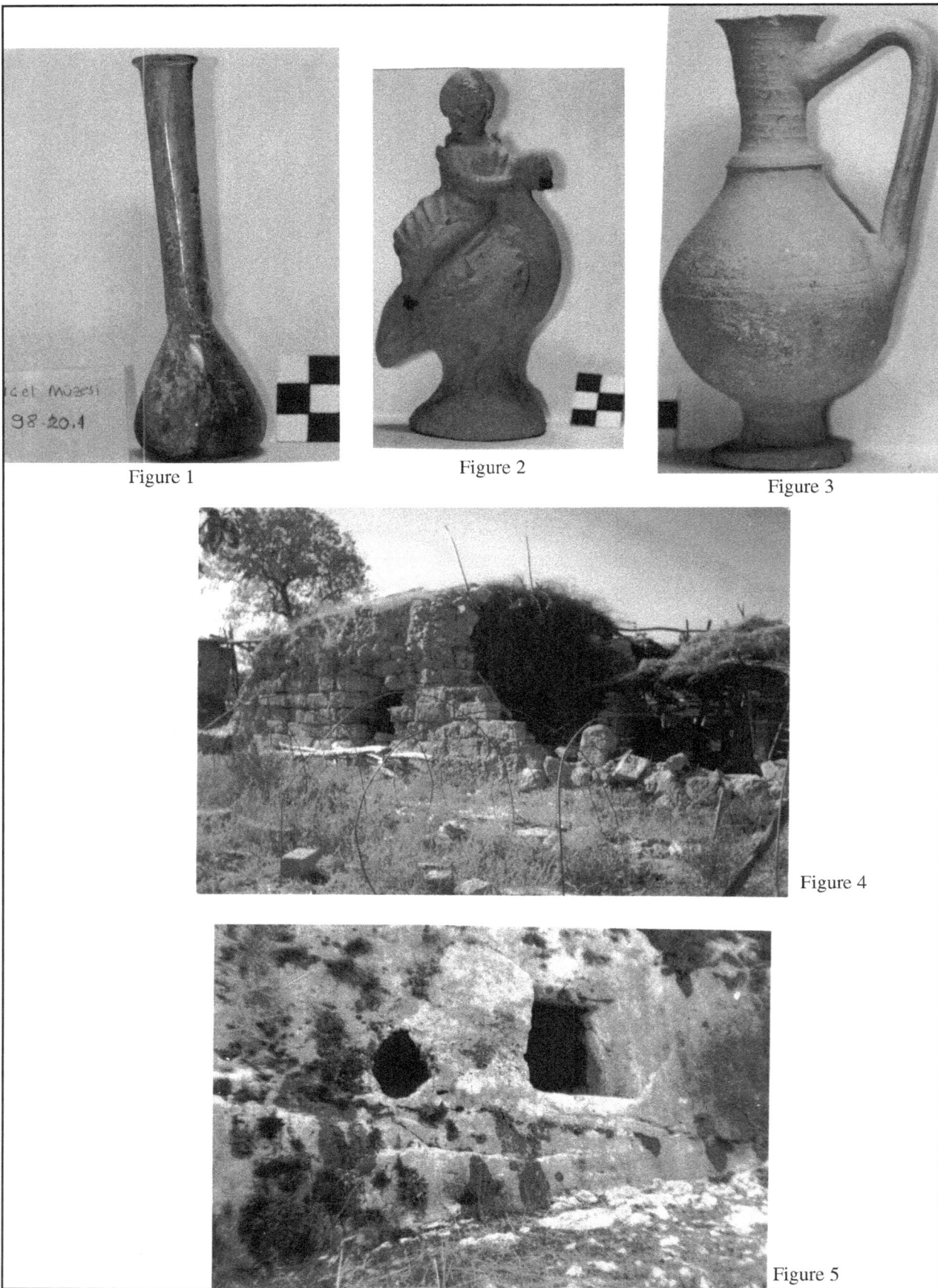

Figure 1. A Roman glass *unguentarium* from Gayrettepe at the Museum of Mersin (Inv.-Nr. 98.20.1).
Figure 2. A Roman terracotta figure from Mersin coastal area at the Museum of Mersin.
Figure 3. A late Roman terracotta jug glass from Gayrettepe at the Museum of Mersin.
Figure 4. An early Byzantine cistern at Eski Mezitli (view from the east).
Figure 5. First rock-cut grave at Mersin-Gözne/Arslanköy road, *c*. 10 km. north of Mersin (view from the south).

routes through some local rivers to the north which served for the transportation of goods from the harbour to the interior or from the interior to the harbour, and thus connecting Pompeiopolis and Cilician coast with central Anatolia. Most recently these routes and their major junctions were reconstructed by F. Hild.[5] The first road, which could be the same route as in the Tabula Peutingeriana, passes from Pompeiopolis, heading in the direction of Tetrapyrgia and thus connected the site with Laranda, an important southern Cappadocian grain production centre in the hinterland of Mersin.[6] It passes thus through Laranda, İbrala, Manazan, Büyükkoraş, Küçükkoraş, Ad Fines, Tetrapyrgia, Arslanköy, Fındıkpınarı, and Kuzucubelen, and eventually arrives at Pompeiopolis. The second stems from a road from the coastal site Zephyrion to the interior. It encompasses the river of Müftü (or Efrenk) and then Arslanköy Deresi whose valley extends to Dümbelek Yayla at the Cappadocian border. Its route is thus Zephyrion, Gözne (Armenian Mlic) or Yeniköy, Evcili, Tırtar and Tetrapyrgia. The importance of these routes lies in their position, affording a relatively narrow passage via the Taurus mountains (more specifically Bolkar Dağları), between Lycaonia-Cappadocia and the Mediterranean-Cilician Sea. Pompeiopolis dominates the intersection of these roads at the east exit from rough Cilicia, which is bounded by a serpentive and rough coastline. The Cilician Gates, a narrow pass located at an altitude of 1.050 m, offer the easiest crossing of the Taurus Mountains between central Anatolia and the Cilician plain, and thus were always the route of a major highway. Our two routes were also connecting with *Pylai Kilikiai*, the Cilician Gates. The mountainous northern part of Mersin is likely have formed one of the main communication and trade corridors between the Cilician coast and the interior of Asia Minor: after the discovery of a building, established in a natural cave and with an excellent position for possible control of the Müftü-Deresi valley,[7] I have realized that the medieval fortifications and buildings were established for the preservation of these ancient trade routes (cf. below). Their possible links with sites in central Anatolia, however, cannot be traced back through the archaeological evidence, since an archaeological inventory of this region is almost completely lacking. What products might be expected from hinterland by means of the coastal cities? These could include timber, sheep, goats, other forestry sorts, grain productions etc. Cilician timber was considered good for ship-building and exported to timberless Egypt throughout the Hellenistic period (Strabo XIV, 5.3). Thus, one can assume that the links between the coast and hinterland in this part of Cilicia were based on economic interdependence, since middle Cilicia was also an important access to the Anatolian plateau.

Pompeiopolis, formerly Soloi, lies 12 km west of Mersin city centre, in the district of Mezitli, in the small village of Viranşehir. It is situated on the west bank of a river called the Liparis in antiquity (today Mezitli Çayı). Since it is situated where the Cilician plain ends and upland Cilicia starts (i.e. western border of the Cilician plain), Pompeiopolis was the last large city of this area. It is located in a higher fertile area than most of the regions west of it and at the head of some major inland routes. Its hinterland, the Taurus Mountains, is an extremely rugged area, rising to some 2000 metres in the interior, rise steeply just 2 km north of the city, along the Cilician sea coast. The routes to Pompeiopolis were passable by pack animals which probably constituted the major form of transport in this area. The extension and borders of Pompeiopolis and its topographical as well as political influence on its peripheral area (i.e. its chora; for instance to Kuyuluk on its north) still remain unknown.[8] Today it became a part of Mersin metropolitan area.

More is known about the earliest history of Pompeiopolis, during which time it was called Soloi. On its earliest areas of occupation, probably on the höyük called Viranşehir Höyüğü in the east bank of the city, some seals and weapons supposedly from the Middle Bronze Age were recovered, which were taken to the State Museum of Berlin. According to the literary tradition, the city was founded by Argives and Rhodians from Lindos, although the site was settled much earlier, which can be proved by Iron Age pottery, found by J. Mellaart and Middle Bronze Age materials (among other a Hittite stamped item) found by the recent Turkish excavators of Viranşehir Höyük. At these Turkish excavations it has been documented that this höyük at the core of ancient city was occupied at Hellenistic, Classic, and Archaic periods, as well as Iron Age and second millenium B.C.[9] Soloi was an influential coastal city in the eastern Mediterranean trade as early as in the eighth century B.C. It was under Persian rule from the mid-sixth century B.C. until the arrival of Alexander the Great in the fourth century B.C. According to Xenophon, the city was fined 200 talents in 333 B.C. by Alexander for siding with Persia. The measure of autonomy of the city during the period of Persian rule is reflected in the city's minting of its own coinage. The golden age for Soloi was during the Seleucid era. The poets Philemon and Aratus (quoted by St. Paul), and the philosopher Chrysippos were natives of Soloi. That "solecisms" are derived from the atrocious Greek spoken in Soloi is perhaps untrue. Ravaged in the mid 70s B.C. by Tigranes the Great of Armenia during the Mithridatic war, many inhabitants were deported to Tigranocerta; their city remained almost deserted until 67 B.C. when it was resettled with ex-pirates by Pompey and renamed in his honor.[10] Under Roman rule the city once again achieved vitality. The Emperor Hadrian on a tour of Anatolia in A.D. 130 visited the province of Cilicia and gave monetary support to work on the harbour. Although there is no clear textual or archaeological evidence of the first appearance

---

5   Hild 1977 as well as 1991; Schaeffer 1903; and Hellenkemper/Hild 1986, pp. 86-89.

6   Ibid., p. 310. A small part of this road was found by myself in Çamlık, 5 km north of Pompeiopolis; it is, however, Ottoman in character

7   Laflı 2001b.

8   M. H. Sayar has re-found the border inscriptions of Pompeiopolis in a area 3 km north of Viranşehir: Sayar 1995, pp. 46-47. A further find spot of border inscription was found by myself in Süvarik Mevkii near Görpınar, where some rock-cut tombs were also documented.

9   Yağcı 2003, p. 32.

10   Strabo 8.7.5; 14.3.3; 14.5.8. There are, however, other Pompeiopoleis in Asia Minor, which was the subject of a paper by U. Klein on Paphlagonian and Cilician Pompeiopoleis.

Figure 6

Figure 7

Figure 8

Figure 6. Second rock-cut grave at Mersin-Gözne/Arslanköy road, *c*. 10 km. north of Mersin (view from the east).
Figure 7. First rock-cut grave at Doruklu (view from the south).
Figure 8. Second rock-cut grave at Doruklu (view from the south).

of Christianity, the earliest persecution of Christians was attested from the third century A.D. What we know is that the bishops of Pompeiopolis had resided in this city since A.D. 381 and that perhaps an earthquake destroyed the city in A.D. 527. As a bishopric Pompeiopolis was visited by Egeria, but succumbed to the Arabs in the seventh century.

The quantity of Roman and Byzantine material from this site is overwhelming, because the documentation and the ruins are so various and abundant. In the 19th century numerous European travellers visited Pompeiopolis and mentioned an ancient theatre on Viranşehir Höyük, to the East, which has now almost gone, a temple, a bath, aqueducts and a necropolis.[11] From the 19th century some travellers have documented the city plan; these former plans cannot be, however, taken as evidence of full documentation of this city, they are rather reflecting what has been preserved until the 19th century.[12] So far, however, very little has been done on the topography and city planning of Pompeiopolis. The city has been settled on the coastal plain and enlarged to the East. Formerly the dimensions of this city were not being investigated in detail; only some approximate numbers (*c.* 35 hectares) are available. According to some researches, a city wall was documented, traces of which are today almost completely gone, and a very little part of which is visible on southern part of the city. In Pompeiopolis today only foundation level remains of *c.* 20 buildings of unknown function are visible (fig. 9). Beside these heavily ruined buildings only two structures and their function can be identified clearly. The most significant and attractive structure of the ancient town is a Roman colonnaded street with 33 columns still standing, which still remains as a very problematic structure in its architecture and chronology. This structure was studied in the 1970s, but new archaeological excavations in this area have provided more conclusive information.[13] The outline of the ancient harbour from the Roman and late Roman period is the second most noticeable structure of Pompeiopolis.[14] It consists of two breakwaters 200 m apart. It was first documented and illustrated by Captain General F. Beaufort, though today it is silted up and robbed of its stone facing, leaving only the concrete core. The western breakwater is better preserved. The huge dimension of the harbour indicates the size of the town during the Roman times. It is one of the best

investigated structures of Roman Pompeiopolis. Current excavations concentrate on the colonnaded street as well as *höyük* of ancient Soloi.

One building with marble slabs carved with crosses (probably an early Byzantine church) is located on the northern extention of the city. Also in Viranşehir numerous architectural elements of different periods as well as some buildings could be observed. Since constantly urbanized Mersin city was enlarged in its western, northern and eastern limits extremely, numerous archaeological sites and monuments belonged to Pompeiopolis and its peripheric area are being destroyed.

The Roman and Byzantine inscription corpus of Pompeiopolis were not being studied in detail yet. One of the noteworthy formerly unpublished inscriptions was found in a field north of the harbour. This Late Roman inscription is a simple marble plate with a dimension of 49 x 50 and a thickness of 20 cm. Letters are 4 cm; only one line is preserved: TOY MAI MAPIA.

The location of the necropolis of ancient Pompeiopolis still remains a question. Formerly there had been no research in terms of burials of Pompeiopolis and its environs. Therefore a specific location in the regards of Pompeiopolitan burial sites is lacking. What we know is only some positions in the surroundings of Pompeiopolis with references of sporadic and scattered burial evidence: R. Heberdey and A. Wilhelm report a "necropolis" at the west side of the city, exterior of the "city walls". A sarcophagus was mentioned and illustrated by V. Langlois, which had been identified as the grave of "Aratus - Pomponius Mela". This supposedly grave was later referred to by Heberdey/Wilhelm and described in detail.[15] Local authors describe, furthermore, another location called Çamlık, *c.* 5 km north of Viranşehir. In this woody location we have observed numerous Roman and even earlier (prehistoric?) sherds as well as medieval glazed pottery. Very simple graves were also documented in this area. Further graves were reported by Heberdey/Wilhelm, especially from Kuyuluk, a small town 3 km north of Viranşehir. According to oral information by the staff of Mersin Museum there had been rescue excavations at Kuyuluk in the 1980s by this museum's directory. The Mersin Museum possesses numerous pieces from Kuyuluk in its collections, which reflect a rich and interesting burial inventory (fig. 2-3). Terracotta coffins of Late Hellenistic-Early Roman period displayed at Mersin Museum are said to originate from the Kuyuluk district. A part of grave inventory of these burials, among others *alabastra*, were formerly studied by H. Çorbacı at Mersin University; the rest I have analysed for my Ph.D. thesis. A further burial location called Tavşan Ören was reported by R. Heberdey and A. Wilhelm where they have discovered numerous burials as well as a huge structure with *c.* 90 m diameter. Only very recently M. H. Sayar has searched on the Pompeiopolitan territorial area north of it. In this peripheral area a cultic rock-cut structure was re-discovered by M. H. Sayar at Çevlik-Merdivenlikaya.[16] Similar ones were also observed at Yalınayak. In 2002 in a

---

[11] Erten 2002. Also Dagron/Feissel 1987, pp. 57-64 (extensive information on former and current researches of the inscriptions).

[12] The city plan of Soloi was done by F. Beaufort in 1818 and Trémaux: Erten 2002, pp. 121-122. The plan of Trémaux, however, was not completely accurate.

[13] In 2001 a shop with mosaic pavement and in 2002 a Hellenistic layer were recovered at the colonnaded street. Through excavations it was also ascertained that colonnaded street was used until the sixth century: Yağcı 2003, p. 32. In 2000 four life-sized marble sculpture of drapped Roman governors and noblemen as well as six further figured capitals were found in this street: figs. 10 and 13. In 1995 a bust of a statue of Hadrian was found here, which is today at Mersin Museum and already published by A. Çalık. Furthermore, some sculptures were already published by L. Frey and R. Özgan as well as by A. von Gladiss and a classical stele in book of G. Dagron and D. Feissel. We do not know, however, if we can see these pieces associated with the colonnaded street

[14] Vann 1995.

[15] Heberdey/Wilhelm 1896, p. 75.

[16] Sayar 1995, p. 47.

Figure 9

Figure 10

Figure 11

Figure 12

Figure 13

Figure 9. Ruins of a possible bath building northwest of Pompeiopolis (view from the south).
Figure 10. A figured column capital from the colonnaded street of Pompeiopolis; at the Museum of Mersin.
Figure 11. An architectural element with a figure, found south of the colonnaded street of Pompeiopolis;
at the Museum of Mersin.
Figure 12. A column capital from an unknown location; today at the garten of "Karayolları Lojmanları"
at Dumlupınar quarter, west Mersin.
Figure 13. A second figured column capital from the colonnaded street of Pompeiopolis
at the Museum of Mersin.

area of 10 x 10 m 50 graves from different periods were recovered in a street called Milli Egemenlik, north of colonnaded street and west of Mezitli.[17] This should be a public necropolis on the road to Pompeiopolis. Nine different type of burials were founds; 24 of them were tile graves, similar to those of Tarsus-Gözlükule.[18] Numerous unguentaria (especially of glass) as well as other burial goods were collected. It is surprising to find this cemetery immediate north of actual city core of Pompeiopolis.

Zephyrion, today Mersin's town centre, is about 48 km west of Adana towards the end of the alluvial Cilician plain where the mountains of the Taurus range begin closely to approach the Mediterranean. The city's history is elusive, though archaeology suggests a very ancient settlement, Yumuktepe (or Soğuksu Tepe), an actual core of the city of Mersin, including, in its pre-Islamic phase, an unbroken pottery sequence from the Neolithic to classical times. Literary evidence is scanty, though Zephyrion seems to have changed hands frequently in the Hellenistic period, from Seleucid to Ptolemaic, and then back to Seleucid control. A short period of semi-autonomy ended with Pompey's Cilician settlement, and like Mopsuestia and Alexandria ad Issum the city chose 67 B.C. as the opening of a new era. It was aparently a relatively small and unimportant coastal city, but was nevertheless a bishophric under the Metropolitan of Tarsus in the Christian period. Its modern successor is capital of the province Mersin.

The core of ancient Zephyrion should have been today's town centre of Mersin; because of highly urbanization of Mersin its traces are today almost completely gone.[19] Only very few architectural elements of various periods are visible in the streets of Mersin city centre. Some of these found in reuse were probably taken from the ruins of Pompeiopolis. We furthermore are aware of the finds recovered at the excavations of the Opera building of Mersin in the 1940s, during which activity an archaic marble kouros (?) was also found (today in the Museum of Mersin). In 2002 when Cumhuriyet Square (in front of Opera building) in Mersin city centre was being sanitised, numerous 6th-7th century *amphorae* (one with painted inscription) were collected.[20] One column with an early Byzantine capital is still standing in a shopping centre in Mersin town centre. This is one of the very few known monuments belonging to ancient Zephyrion. In the city centre of Mersin at a drainage dig one was able to find glazed medieval pottery of good quality and in large quantities. Thus, one can assume that Mersin city centre was continued to be settled during the medieval period by Armenians and later by Turks. This is one of the very sparsely evidence of medieval urban occupation on the plain area by Armenians and Turks in Mersin area.

Middle Cilicia, identified by myself as the "Mersin coastal and rugged area", is notoriously less explored. Our knowledge about the classical and medieval periods of this area is scanty and based on a limited number of literary sources and finds of former travellers and geographers of various periods, who have visited this region and left documentation. Nevertheless very little archaeological field surveys were made in order to clarify our actual knowledge. The basic geographical and historical information on the ancient topography of Mersin area were formerly collected by among others Captain F. Beaufort, V. Langlois, C. Texier, P. Trémaux, V. Cuinet, G. Alishan, Th. Bent, F. X. Schaeffer, P. Paribeni and P. Romanelli, R. Hederbey and A. Wilhelm, E. Kirsten, E. Blumenthal, P. Verzone, R. Edwards as well as F. Hild and H. Hellenkemper. In the 1960s, the geography of western Cilician plain and coast was intensively studied and described by E. Blumenthal on a theoretical geographical scale. His aim was to search the relationships between the topographical and historical features of this region. On the settlement patterns of Mersin and rest of Çukurova, L. Rother analysed urbanisation of this area geographically. In 1980s H. Hellenkemper and F. Hild observed numerous unknown settlements in Mersin; they compared their records with the results of researches of the 19th and 20th century, as well as ancient literary sources. But this research was not systematic, and they neglected to report about the sites between Arslanköy and Pompeiopolis in detail. They rather report about the travel results of their nationals R. Heberdey and A. Wilhelm and F. X. Schaeffer. Work initiated by former researchers, especially that of R. W. Edwards, reveals that in the rugged area of north Mersin in the medieval period 12 small fortresses were protected by their natural position and by defensive walls.[21] With the exception of the unpublished works of the local museum in Mersin, only five archaeological excavations have been done in this area: the prehistoric researches on Yumuktepe, Kazanlı, Tırmıl and Çavuşlu by J. Garstang, and subsequently an excavation of Pompeiopolis by a team from the University of Mersin. Only two of them achieved any results on the occupation of the medieval period: the first one is Yumuktepe, which is now being re-excavated by a Turco-Italian archaeological expedition. Although the present excavations at Yumuktepe focus on the Neolithic period, later material is also being considered and recorded. This has provided intriguing information on höyük settlement use in this region during the late antiquity and the medieval period (10th-13th centuries A.D.).[22]

Although a moderate number of classical and medieval sites have been discovered by several scholars in the surroundings of Pompeiopolis, detailed information about this period in this region is very poor. Roman and Byzantine road systems of the hinterland of Pompeiopolis and Zephyrion were studied by F. X. Schaffer and R. Heberdey/A. Wilhelm. These roads were connecting Roman and Byzantine settlements in Mersin area, among others Akkent, Ankyra, Ankhiale, Askora (?), Arpaç, Aulai (Karaduvar I), Çiftlikköy, Davultepeköy, Erçel-Bağören, Gayrettepe, Hristiyan Köy, Kale Köy,[23] Karaduvar II

---

[17] Yağcı 2003, p. 33.

[18] Goldman 1950, fig. 64-66.

[19] In the 19th century numerous archaeological structures were reported; today most of them are lost.

[20] Anonymous 2002, p. 7.

[21] Edwards 1987. For those medieval structures in Mersin area: Gottwald 1941.

[22] Köroğlu 1997; and Garstang 1953, pp. 260-262.

[23] Laflı 1995a.

Figure 14

Figure 15

Figure 16

Figure 14. An architectural element with animal and human figures, found at Fındıkpınarı; at the Museum of Mersin.
Figure 15. A lion type of sarcophagus lid from Rough Cilicia; at the Museum of Mersin.
Figure 16. A lion; at the Museum of Mersin (Inv.-Nr. 93.91).

(Hagios Dimitrios?), Kuyuluk, Kazanlı, Pompeiopolis, Tece, Tömük, Yaka Kalesi and Zephyrion. In the hinterland of Zephyrion and Pompeiopolis archaeo-logycally known settlements are as follows: Akarca, Arslanköy, Başnalar (Zipken Kaya), Belenkeşlik, Buluklu (ancient Kestel?), Cemilli, Çukurkeşlik, Dikilitaş,[24] Erçel, Fındıkpınarı (fig. 14), Gideği Kalesi, Gözne (Armenian Mlic), Hebilli, Hisar Kale, İçme, Kuzucubelen, Menevşe and Yavca. After our researches more settlements were discovered at their hinterland: among others environs of Akbelen, Çifte Sakız, Doruklu-Çavak, Doruklu-Ören, Eski Mezitli (fig. 4),[25] Evcili, Evcili-Harçgediği and Kuyuluk-Çamlık.[26] Characteristic features and functions of these settlements as well as their ancient name and identity are mostly unknown and need to be studied in detail. Ancient literary sources report about numerous site names in this region, such as Ankhiale[27] and Kyinda; no research, however, has been done for matching these names with these sites. Also inscription evidences of this region were not studied in detail.[28]

SURVEY RESULTS AND INTERPRETATIONS

The patterns of settlement distribution and the topography of this area vary considerably and significantly. These ancient settlements in character of dumping areas, single buildings, temporary markets, small harbors, fortified enclosures and buildings (single towers, castles), garners (especially those of by large *pithoi*), burial sites, manufactury or industrial areas, stone quarries, farms, villages, small towns, cities, estates and road stations tended to be small, near-by village or a modern settlement and were not very impressive. The large number of these sites indicated how thickly the area was populated especially towards the sea where the sites were mostly small farmsteads. Thus, the majority of ancient Mersin inhabitants were peasants and sheperds. The hinterland region of Mersin in the Taurus Mountains was an area of scanty agricultural resources which was unable to support its population without considerable ingenuity and diversification. This region had sufficient resources to support its own-population by peasant-farming and could therefore be expected to import. In nearly all cases the sites are situated in well watered areas close to both agricultural land and also to hills or mountains. Most of these settlements also overlook the main routes. The topographical evidence confirms that settlements on the coast were populated densely than others in mountainous areas. In none of former researches, however, was the relationship between the topographical core and periphery of Cilician cities postulated.

In the Mersin area, the ancient settlement pattern is based on two main basic elements: höyüks and plain settlements.

A further type of structure is medieval castles on strategic points of Mersin. Most important höyük sites in Mersin are Yaka Kale, Karaduvar I, Karaduvar II, Kazanlı, Tırmıl, Yumuktepe, Çavuşlu, Viranşehir Höyüğü and Tömük. The distribution of these höyük sites concentrates on alluvial floors on Mersin plain. The northernmost extension of höyük sites is Çavuşlu, a "Hittite", extremely damaged site, where sondages made by J. Garstang in 1952, with so far very weak later occupation on its summit, whereas further researches have to be taken in order to comprehend its topographical characteristic. A further observation of the höyük sites is their later occupation: So far only Yumuktepe has been investigated according to its later occupation; but, as at above mentioned, this research has been in limited scales. It seems archaeologically that in most cases summit of höyüks were occupied for fortification or observation purposes by the medieval inhabitants of Mersin plain, whereas so far a very small number of medieval settlements with human habitation or housings were discovered or researched both in the coastal plain or rugged hinterland area. According to the surveys of V. Seton-Williams at Tırmıl Hellenistic painted and Roman red glazed ware and at Kazanlı I, south of Mersin-Tarsus road, and *c.* 4 km east of Mersin, beside sea, on right track of Kazanlı, and Karaduvar II, north of village Karaduvar, Hellenistic black glazed, megarian and Roman red glazed ware were found. These are the sole evidences for the classical occupation of these ancient höyüks. One further topographical issue is related to distribution pattern of these höyüks. Obviously höyüks were settled on important political, military or economic routes; for numerous reasons the degree of importance of these routes were changed. Researches on topographical shiftings on this "test" area are therefore very valuable to comprehend the degree and pattern of these changes in a chronological scale. A still unknown feature related to höyüks in Mersin is the position of their associated burial sites. One proof comes from Karaduvar I that some prehistoric urn burials were found in front of the settlement of Karaduvar I.

The coastal line between Pompeiopolis and Zephyrion were filled out mostly with burial sites, *amphorae* and other coarse ware dumping areas, estates, harbors, single buildings, small settlements as well as farms. These locations were spread out continually, but irregularly on a coastal line of *c.* 200 m wide between these two ancient cities. One specific location is Muğdat quarter in western part of Mersin, where we have documented a large *amphorae* workshop or dumping areas,[29] building structures as well as an oil press. A further site is the garden of one of the Mersin University's campus, so-called "Öğretmen Okulu", where we have found a large amount of re-used and deformed dumped glass as well as huge amount of coarse ware dumpings, with specific and consistent vessel forms.[30] These coarse ware dumpings

---

[24] Heberdey/Wilhelm 1896, p. 3. Langlois has also published an illustration of this stone; Paribeni/Romanelli refer it too.

[25] Laflı 1995b.

[26] Laflı 1995c, 1999, 2001a, 2001c, 2002a-2004b, 2005 and 2006.

[27] Most recently: Kalkan 2002.

[28] Heberdey and Wilhelm as well as Langois have published most extensive literary evidence of Mersin region.

[29] Y. Garlan (or J.-Y. Empreuer) has published some sites west of Mersin at *"Recherches sur les amphores romaines"* (Collection de l'Ecole française de Rome 10; Rome 1972); perhaps he has taken his pictures from Muğdat. Today these dumping areas are today in the territory of park of Muğdat Mosque.

[30] One type of *amphorae* from these dumps I have observed at Troy, where they have been classified by pottery analysts as "southern Asia Minor originated".

Figure 17

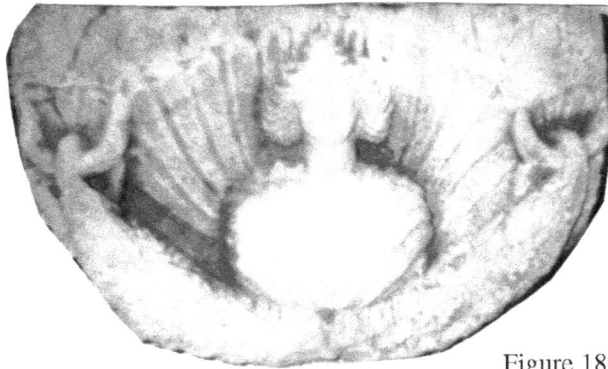

Figure 18

Figure 19

Figure 20

Figure 17. A Roman sarcophagus at the Museum of Mersin.
Figure 18. A Roman grave stone from Mut area; at the Museum of Mersin.
Figure 19. A Roman statue with a drapped female with two children at her each side (Hera or Kybele?) from Rough Cilicia; at the Museum of Mersin.
Figure 20. A theather frise block from Rough Cilicia; at the Museum of Mersin.

continue to the west and associate with some later (5th-7th centuries A.D.) burial sites in Eğriçam quarter. In Akkent quarter at west of Mersin we have documented numerous small sites, each of them with different characteristics. In this area especially farm houses and farming sites are numerous, where one was able to document late Roman column capitals, building foundations etc. These settlements continue from Akkent through Girne Plajı upto Pompeiopolis. One of the most attractive sites between Pompeiopolis and Zephyrion is Kaleköy, where we have found remains of a medieval building as well as numerous earlier re-used architectural elements, among others, columns, capitals and inscribed blocks. Two medieval blocks reused at the gate of the modern cemetery are the sole evidences on the approximate chronology of this medieval building. Some 5th century column capitals, architrave and frieze blocks as well as huge columns, some of them with inscribed letters (such as BO) should have been transported from Pompeiopolis and reused here. At this medieval building I was also able to observe medieval glazed pottery. This settlement also contains some burials. In the 1980s and 1990s numerous conglomerated buildings were destroyed through new building activities of Mersin urban centres at their western extension. A congrolometa building situated in front of Yumuktepe, on the other side of Müftü river. One further example was observed west of quarter Pozcu, near Dumlupınar High School, where a rescue excavation has been undertaken in a late Roman cemetery by Mersin Museum. Also Byzantine communication towers are observable in Mersin plain: one is in Tece (documented first in 1893), where a Roman bridge on Tece Deresi was also documented; another on this road exists at Yaka Höyük, c. 10 km east of Mersin. These small settlements continue to exist to the village Elvanlı, where we have documented a further early Byzantine settlement. At Davultepe small late Roman settlements were observed at the quarter of Anayurt. A small fortification called "Çürücek Kalesi" is also located in Davultepe area. North of Davultepe two villages, Doğulu and Takanlı (late Roman) as well as Cırmantepesi and Eski Camili (medieval) are further ancient settlements. At the road between Tece and Davultepe in 1975, Adana Museum undertook a small scale rescue excavation. In Erdemli (ancient Kalanthia) in a small forest, called Alata Çamlığı, an early Byzantine burial site was discovered and a rescue excavation by former Erdemli Museum undertaken. Some decorated terracotta oil lamps have been found in this cemetery, some of which today are displayed at the Museum of Mersin. At Çeşmeli at the quarters Barboros and Atatürk, some archaeological structures were found, where in 1994 Adana Museum undertook a rescue excavation and found a marble column. In the eastern extension of our research area, there are three main sites: Hebilli, a medieval fortification site, called Kalah-el-Habilleh, Dikili Taş, a burial site with a settlement, and Yaka, also a höyük site with a medieval fortification. Thus, it would not be misleading to assume that during antiquity and the medieval period, the coastline between Pompeiopolis and Zephyrion, Pompeiopolis and Kalanthia in the west and Zephyrion and Tarsos in the east was filled with various sites of human activities.

Numerous place names in Mersin region indicate an archaeological location: for instance "Kapılı Ören", 5 km northwest of Mersin is a name for a "ruin with doorway", although we did not find here any traces of archaeological occupation. Mostly Turkish names of this region such as Höyük (or Hüyük), Kale, Kilise, Ören, Asar (or Eser), Kule, Tepe, Virane, Manastır, Harabe, Tell, Zindan, Şehir, Ziyaret, Kuyu, Mezar, Kabristan, İn, Mağara etc. are the indicators of an ancient settlement or archaeological feature. In some cases one can observe the survival of ancient names in modern toponyms, such as Tarsus, Adana, Namrun, Lamos, Gözne, Silifke, Anamur, Gilindire, Misis, Anazarba, Seyhan etc.

One of the most important and common feature in Mersin's settlement patterns is extensive burial sites of various periods. So far no archaeological study has been done to characterize burial types and their typologies. In the 1980s and 1990s there has been some archaeological rescue excavations at some burial sites located at the western and northwestern peripheral areas of Pompeiopolis. These burials are mostly from the 5th to 7th centuries A.D. and their inventory were documented by me. The sole archaeologically documented and published burial site of this region is Gayrettepe 3 km north-east of Pompeiopolis. At the rescue excavations in Gayrettepe by the Museum of Mersin, numerous pithoi and chamber burials from Hellenistic to late Roman periods with very well preserved grave inventory (Hellenistic to late Roman terracotta and glass unguentaria; fig. 1) were recovered (Ünlü/Gürkan 2001). A further burial site with early Byzantine graves was discovered 3 km north of Kaleköy.

An important and formerly insufficiently researched area is the northern rugged part of Mersin, where the junction of two important roads constitutes the settlement pattern mainly (cf. above). In numerous locations in the northern Mersin area, as well as the northern part of Kuyuluk, I have observed stone quarries from Roman and Byzantine periods. These places are easy to recognise because of their artifically shaped rocky surfaces. Agrarian activities at these mountainous sites north of Mersin are very obvious through oil presses at various locations, such as Evcili, Başnalar and a site at Arslanköy-Gözne road (10 km north of Mersin city centre).[31] A further location with simple burials engraved in a rock floor is Gavur Kuyusu near Çukurkeşlik. In a previous short report I have mentioned late Roman and early Byzantine ruins and monuments in Çukurkeşlik region as well as a further cave structure at the other side of Çukurkeşlik valley. A church was also observed at this small site. South of Gavur Kuyusu, at a place called Seyreğin Bağı I have observed a large building with an excellent carved façade. At this site four cisterns were also documented. In Mersin region pottery dumping areas do not only concentrate to the coastal line, but also existing in mountainous places: a dumb with tons of medieval glazed pottery was observed at medieval fortified enclosure near Evcili.

In the hinterlands of the Pompeiopolis area, 15 medieval fortification structures were discovered and studied. Only at Çandır (Paperon) and Sinap no Late Roman-Early Byzantine occupation was discovered, even though the

---

[31] At this site I have also observed a destroyed monumental gate.

main occupation of these fortifications are exclusively medieval. At the rest of the ruins an earlier occupation has been ascertained. These fortifications are as follows: In the rugged area Arslanköy, Başnalar, Belenkeşlik, Çandır, Evcili, Fındıkpınarı, Gözne, Hisar, Kuzucubelen, and Sinap; on the plain Yaka, Tırmıl, Hebilli and Tece. Two further medieval fortification sites were found in Emirler (İnsu Kalesi) and north of Mezitli. These medieval fortification systems or watch towers are indicating the main roads in this region, since they have been built on main routes. At the same time we do not know if they were protecting some settlements in this region, while very few urban occupation of later medieval period is known in Mersin. Obviously, security of these routes was very problematic; therefore in this area some hoard finds were formerly recovered. The importance of this region goes back to the Iron Age; in a place called Şıh Bağı at Korum Yolu near Gözne, probably also formerly a Greek settlement, an Aramaic border inscription was found by the American traveller J. W. Montgomery in 1907.

Since the end of 19th century German speaking travellers, such as R. Heberdey and A. Wilhelm, F. Hild and H. Hellenkemper, as well as M. H. Sayar reported some of these sites and monuments, among others also burials. The most common group is the rock-cut simple chamber tombs, which were engraved into the natural rock. Their relationship to a specific settlement in the surroundings is very difficult to determine. Formerly known rock-cut graves were reported from Akarca, Başnalar (Zipken Dağı), Cemilli, Çukurkeşlik, Davultepeköy, Erçel, İçme, Menevşe (chamosoria), Kuzucubelen and Kuyuluk-Kovanlık. At the abstract booklet of this congress I have reported the rock-cut graves in Mersin area briefly. After my surveys more unknown examples of such monuments were found in following settlements: one in Çukurkeşlik, one from northwest side of Şamlar Dağı south of Çukurkeşlik, four from Doruklu (figs. 7-8), two Çifte Sakız and two from Kirazlı Boğaz (i.e. Kerimler Mevkii) and two from one location at the street Arslanköy-Gözne (figs. 5-6). These graves have a rectangular, oval or sometimes even round entrance. In these graves most of the time one or two basins for burials were engraved. Doors of these graves were at none of these examples preserved in situ. None of them were recorded with an inscription. Only one example of these graves was ornamented at its door; this is from Doruklu, ornamented in a form of a house with a roof. Most of these examples have a view to the south. It is difficult to distinguish which of these settlements had posessed these graves and what their chronology is. Possibly these graves were used for many centuries continually. For instance rock-cut graves in the area of Kuyuluk could be belonged to the chora of coastal metropolis Pompeiopolis. At the north of Tarsus Namrun Yaylası and its environs cover numerous archaeological sites and monuments; for instance a Roman rock-cut grave at Keşbükü on Tarsus-Namrun road as well as further graves in İndibi near Namrun-Erdoğdu.

PRELIMINARY CONCLUSIONS

A systematic archaeological field survey project, undertaken in whole Mersin area between the ancient cities Tarsos and Kalanthia will involve topographical reconstruction, more detailed mapping of settlement patterns and a complete inventory of the region. This "test" survey could thus create a firmer base for emergence and functions of settlements in this part of Anatolia during the antiquity and Byzantium. There are advances to be made both by work in the field and by careful study of texts and inscriptions. More surface exploration in this area will help fill out not only our skeletal knowledge of middle Cilician cities, but also their relation to the coastal and rugged settlements in their environs. With this idea in view, an archaeological field survey project was planned by the writer of this paper for the year 2004. The primary object of this survey should be to examine and record classical and medieval structures and settlements in the area within a radius of about 40 km around ancient Pompeiopolis and to determine as accurately as possible relationships between the cities and peripheral settlements. The topography, which will be the object of this forthcoming project, however, should be defined both in ancient and modern terms. To sum up, following objectives should be considered in this forthcoming survey:

1. Important position held be Cilicia on land and maritime routes in the eastern Mediterranean in antiquity and the middle ages.

2. Urban centres and rural sites.

3. Trade and local production.

4. Funerary remains.

5. Prosperity and power/autonomy. It seems that the region prospered most when it was part of a larger empire with peaceful conditions, not when it could exercise a certain degree of independence.

Author's address

Ergün LAFLI
Eğriçam Mah., 2246 sok. 10
TR-33160, Mersin, TÜRKEI
E-mail: elafli@yahoo.ca

Bibliography

ANONYMOUS, 2002, Mersin Cumhuriyet Alanı 2002 Yılı Düzenlemeleri. *San Kulüp. İçel Sanat Kulübü Bülteni* 115 (Eylül), p. 7.

BLANTON, R. E., 2000, *Hellenistic, Roman and Byzantine Settlement Patterns of the Coast Lands of Western Rough Cilicia*. British Archeological Reports, International Series 879. Oxford: BAR Publishing.

BLUMENTHAL, E., 1963, *Die altgriechische Siedlungskolonisation im Mittelmeerraum unter besonderer Berücksichtigung der Südküste Kleinasiens*. Tübinger Geographische Studien 10. Tübingen.

DES COURTILS, J., MORETTI, J.-CH., & PLANET, F. (eds.), 1991, *De Anatolia Antiqua/Eski Anadolu I*. Bibliothèque de l'Insitut français d'études Anatoliennes d'Istanbul XXXII, Paris.

DAGRON, G. & FEISSEL, D., 1987, *Inscriptions de Cilicie*. Travaux et memoires du Centre de recherche d'histoire et civilization de Byzance. Monographies, Paris.

EDWARDS, R., 1987, *The Fortifications of Armenian Cilicia.* Dumbarton Oaks Studies 23. Washington D.C.: Dumbortan Oax Research Library Collection.

ERTEN, E., 2002, 19th Century Travellers and Soli Pompeiopolis. In *Kolokyum. 19 yy'da Mersin ve Akdeniz Dünyası. Mersin Türkiye. 18-20 Nisan, 2002/Mersin, the Mediterranean, and Modernity. Colloquium. Heritage of the Long Nineteenth Century. Mersin, Turkey, April 18-20, 2002.* T.C. Mersin Üniversitesi Yayınları 7/Akdeniz Kent Arş. Mrk. Yayınları 1, Mersin: Şehir Ofset (ISBN 975-6900-10-5) pp. 117-123.

GARSTANG, J., 1953, *Prehistoric Mersin. Yümük Tepe in southern Turkey. The Neilson Expedition in Cilicia.* Oxford: The Clarendon Press.

GOLDMAN, H., 1950, Buildings and Habitation Levels. In *Excavations at Gözlü Kule, Tarsus I: The Hellenistic and Roman Periods,* edited by H. Goldman. Princeton, N. J.: Princeton University Press, pp. 5-28.

GOTTWALD., L., 1941, Burgen und Kirchen in mittleren Kilikien. *Byzantinsche Zeitschrift* 41, pp. 82ff.

HEBERDEY, R. & WILHELM, A., 1896, *Reisen in Kilikien, ausgeführt 1891 und 1892 im Auftrage der kaiserlichen Akademie der Wissenschaften (Widmung seiner Durchlaucht des regierenen Fürsten Johann von und zu Liechtenstein).* Denkschriften der kaiserlichen Akademie der Wissenschaften. Philosophisch-historische Classe. Vierundvierzigster Band, VI. Abhandlung, Vorgelegt in der Sitzung vom 24. April 1895. Vienna, Verlag der Österreichische Akademie der Wissenschaften.

HELLENKEMPER, H. & HILD, F., 1986, *Neue Forschungen in Kilikien.* Tabula Imperii Byzantini 4/Denkschriften der Österreichischen Akademie der Wissenschaften, Philosophisch-Hististorische Klasse, Band 186. Vienna, Verlag der Österreichische Akademie der Wissenschaften.

HILD, F., 1977, *Das byzantinische Straßensystem in Kappadokien.* Tabula Imperii Byzantini 2/Denkschriften der Österreichischen Akademie der Wissenschaften, Philosophisch-Hististorische Klasse, Band 186, Vienna, Vienna, Verlag der Österreichische Akademie der Wissenschaften.

HILD, F., 1991, Die Route der Tabula Peutingeriana (Tab. Peut.) von Iconium über Ad Fines und Tetrapyrgia nach Pompeiopolis in Kilikien. *De Anatolia Antiqua/Eski Anadolu* I, pp. 311-316.

HILD, F., & HELLENKEMPER, H., 1990, *Kilikien und Isaurien.* Tabula Imperii Byzantini 5/Denkschriften der Österreichischen Akademie der Wissenschaften, Philosophisch-Historische Klasse, Band 215. Vienna, Verlag der Österreichische Akademie der Wissenschaften.

HOPWOOD., K., 1991, The Links between the Coastal Cities of western Rough Cilicia and the Interior during the Roman Period. *De Anatolia Antiqua/Eski Anadolu I,* pp. 305-309.

KALKAN, H., 2002, Anchiale in Kilikien. *Epigraphica Anatolica* 34, pp. 160-169.

KÖROĞLU, G., 1997, Ortaçağ'da Yumuktepe. *İçel Sanat Kulübü, Aylık Bülteni* 62 (Eylül), pp. 16-18.

LAFLI, E., 1995a, Kaleköy'deki Kalıntılara Ait Yeni Gözlemler. *İçel Sanat Kulübü, Aylık Bülteni* 41 (Kasım), p. 29.

LAFLI, E., 1995b, Eski Mezitli Köyü'ndeki Kalıntılar, *Yelken. Aylık Kültür-Sanat Dergisi* 4 (Haziran), p. 27.

LAFLI, E., 1995c, Çukurkeşlik (Mersin) Köyü Yakınındaki İki Yapı. *Ankara Üniversitesi, Dil ve Tarih-Coğrafya Fakültesi, Seminerler Dergisi* 3/6-7 (Nisan –Eylül), pp. 37-42.

LAFLI, E., 1999, Studies on the Topography of Pompeiupolis and its Surroundings (Cilicia/Southern Turkey) in Late Antiquity. Results of a Survey. In *Shifting Frontiers in Late Antiquity III: Urban and Rural in Late Antiquity. An Interdisciplinary Conference. Emory University, Atlanta, Georgia, USA, March 11-14. Program & Abstracts,* edited by J. W. Eadie. Atlanta, pp. 25-28.

LAFLI, E., 2001a, Geschichte und Perspektiven der archäologischen Erforschung des eisenzeitlichen Kilikien. In *Akten des IV. internationalen Kongresses für Hethitologie. Würzburg, 4.-8. Oktober 1999, edited by G. Wilhelm.* Kommission für den Alten Orient der Akademie der Wissenschaften und der Literatur, Studien zu den Boğazköy-Texten 45. Wiesbaden: Harrassowitz, pp. 308-325.

LAFLI, E., 2001b, Bemerkungen zur byzantinischen Archäologie vom Rauhen Kilikien (Südtürkei): eine Wohnhöhle in der Nähe von Çukurkeşlik Köy bei Mersin. In *XXe Congrès international des études byzantines. Collège de France-Sorbonne, 19-25 Août 2001, Pré-Actes. III. Communications Libres.* Paris, pp. 299-300.

LAFLI, E., 2001c, Das eisenzeitliche Kilikien: Zur Geschichte und materiellen Kultur einer *hurro-luwischen* Kulturlandschaft im südlichen Kleinasien während der Eisenzeit (*ca.* 1200 bis 600 v. Chr.). *Archäologische Informationen* 24/2, pp. 335-344.

LAFLI, E., 2002a, Güney Anadolu Müzeleri Antik Dönem Seramikleri 2001 Çalışma Raporu – İlk Sonuçlar. *Arkeoloji ve Sanat Dergisi* 24/108 (Mayıs-Haziran), pp. 33-44.

LAFLI, E., 2002b, Zu spätantik-frühbyzantinischen Tonunguentarien aus Kleinasien: Neue Erkenntnisse aus Pisidien und Kilikien (Südtürkei). *Mitteilungen zur spätantiken Archäologie und byzantinischen Kunstgeschichte* 4 (in print).

LAFLI, E., 2004a, Zur Keramik aus Kilikien zwischen *ca.* 12. und 6. Jh. v. Chr. *Hethitica. Bibliothèque des Cahiers de l'Institut de Linguistique de Louvain (BCILL) XVII (2004). L'Anatolie et les îles de la Méditerranée orientale - 3e journées Louis Delaporte et Eugène Cavaignac (Institut catholique de Paris, 17-18 mai 2002). Acta Colloquii edenda curavit René Lebrun* (in print).

LAFLI, E., 2004b, Eine hellenistisch, römisch-kaiserzeitliche und spätantik-frühbyzantinische Nekropole aus Kilikien: Gayrettepe bei Mersin, for 2004 in preparation.

LAFLI, E., 2005, *Mersin II. Results of the Archaeological Field Survey Campaigns of Mersin Region in Cilicia (southern Turkey),* for 2005 in preparation.

LAFLI, E., 2006, 2004 Yılı Mersin İli Merkez İlçesi Arkeolojik Yüzey Araştırmaları Raporu. In *T. C., Kültür Bakanlığı, Anıtlar ve Müzeler Genel Müdürlüğü, 23. Araştırma Sonuçları Toplantısı, Mayıs 2005, Ankara* (Kültür Bakanlığı Yayınları/Anıtlar ve Müzeler Genel Müdürlüğü Yayınları), for 2006 in preparation.

ROTHER, L., 1971, *Die Städte der Çukurova: Adana, Mersin, Tarsus. Ein Beitrag zum Gestalt-, Struktur- und Funktionswandel türkischer Städte.* Tübinger Geographischer Studien 42. Tübingen.

ROTHER, L., 1972, *Gedanken zur Stadtentwicklung in der Çukurova (Türkei).* Beihefte zum Tübinger Atlas des Vorderen Orients, Reihe B, Nr. 3. Wiesbaden.

SAYAR, M. H., 1995, Kilikya'da Epigrafi ve Tarihi Coğrafya Araştırmaları 1993. In *T.C. Kültür Bakanlığı, Anıtlar ve Müzeler Genel Müdürlüğü,* pp. 39-60.

SCHAEFFER, F. X., 1903, *Cilicia.* Petermanns Mitteilungen, Ergänzungsband 30/Ergänzungsheft 141. Gotha.

T.C. Kültür Bakanlığı, Anıtlar ve Müzeler Genel Müdürlüğü, XII. Araştırma Sonuçları Toplantısı, 30 Mayıs-3 Haziran 1994, Ankara. Kültür Bakanlığı Yayınları 1735/Anıtlar ve Müzeler Genel Müdürlüğü Yayınları 95.06.Y.0001/Sempozyum Serisi

43. Ankara: T.C. Kültür Bakanlığı Milli Kütüphane Basımevi 1995.

ÜNLÜ, Y. & GÜRKAN, F. G., 2001, Mersin Gayrettepe Kurtarma Kazısı. In *T. C., Kültür Bakanlığı, Anıtlar ve Müzeler Genel Müdürlüğü, 9. Müze Kurtarma Kazıları Semineri. 27-29 Nisan 1998 Antalya*. Kültür Bakanlığı Yayınları 2193/Anıtlar ve Müzeler Genel Müdürlüğü

Yayınları 76. Ankara: T.C. Kültür Bakanlığı Milli Kütüphane Basımevi, pp. 89-94.

VANN, R. L., 1995, Survey of Ancient Harbors in Turkey: The 1993 Season at Pompeiopolis. In *T.C. Kültür Bakanlığı, Anıtlar ve Müzeler Genel Müdürlüğü*, pp. 529-534.

YAĞCI, R., 2003, Soli/Pompeiopolis 2002 Kazıları. *San Kulüp. İçel Sanat Kulübü Bülteni* 119 (Ocak), pp. 30-34.

www.ingramcontent.com/pod-product-compliance
Lightning Source LLC
Chambersburg PA
CBHW051306270326
41926CB00030B/4747